# A Political Anthropology of Yemen

*Contemporary Issues in the Middle East*
Mehran Kamrava, *Series Editor*

**Select Titles in Contemporary Issues in the Middle East**

*Arabs in Turkish Political Cartoons, 1876–1950:*
*National Self and Non-National Other*
Ilkim Büke Okyar

*Conflict Mediation in the Arab World*
Ibrahim Fraihat and Isak Svensson, eds.

*Kurds in Dark Times: New Perspectives on Violence and Resistance in Turkey*
Ayça Alemdaroglu and Fatma Müge Göçek, eds.

*Life on Drugs in Iran: Between Prison and Rehab*
Nahid Rahimipour Anaraki

*The Muslim Social: Neoliberalism, Charity, and Poverty in Turkey*
Gizem Zencirci

*The Myth of Middle East Exceptionalism: Unfinished Social Movements*
Mojtaba Mahdavi, ed.

*Victims of Commemoration: The Architecture and Violence*
*of Confronting the Past in Turkey*
Eray Çaylı

*War Remains: Ruination and Resistance in Lebanon*
Yasmine Khayyat

For a full list of titles in this series,
visit https://press.syr.edu/supressbook-series
/contemporary-issues-in-the-middle-east/

# A Political Anthropology of Yemen

## Concept and Critique

Edited by
**Ross Porter**

Syracuse University Press

This book will be made open access within three years of publication thanks to Path to Open, a program developed in partnership between JSTOR, the American Council of Learned Societies (ACLS), University of Michigan Press, and The University of North Carolina Press to bring about equitable access and impact for the entire scholarly community, including authors, researchers, libraries, and university presses around the world. Learn more at https://about.jstor.org/path-to-open/

First Edition 2025

25  26  27  28  29  30      6  5  4  3  2  1

For a listing of books published and distributed by Syracuse University Press, visit https://press.syr.edu.

ISBN: 9780815638582 (hardcover)
        9780815638599 (paperback)
        9780815657361 (e-book)

**Library of Congress Cataloging-in-Publication Data**

Names: Porter, Ross (Lecturer) editor
Title: A political anthropology of Yemen : concept and critique / [edited by] Ross Porter.
Description: First edition. | Syracuse, New York : Syracuse University Press, [2025] | Series:
    Contemporary issues in the Middle East | Includes bibliographical references and index. |
Identifiers: LCCN 2024050008 (print) | LCCN 2024050009 (ebook) | ISBN 9780815638599 paperback |
    ISBN 9780815638582 hardback | ISBN 9780815657361 ebook
Subjects: LCSH: Yemen (Republic)—Politics and government | Yemen (Republic)—Social conditions
Classification: LCC DS247.Y48 P65 2025  (print) | LCC DS247.Y48  (ebook) | DDC 953.3—
    dc23/eng/20250325
LC record available at https://lccn.loc.gov/2024050008
LC ebook record available at https://lccn.loc.gov/2024050009

The authorized representative in the EU for product safety
and compliance is Mare Nostrum Group B.V.
Mauritskade 21D, 1091 GC Amsterdam, The Netherlands
gpsr@mare-nostrum.co.uk

# Contents

List of Illustrations     *vii*

Transliteration Note     *ix*


Introduction: *Grounding Anthropological Critique*
Ross Porter     *1*

1. "X"
Steven C. Caton     *16*

2. In/Security: *Rethinking Uncertainty
and Refashioning Piety in a World of Ruins*
Kamilia al-Eriani     *41*

3. Class: *Not in Agrarian Yemen?*
Martha Mundy     *76*

4. Honor: *Beyond Glorious Deeds, an Ethos of Ordinary Insecurity*
Luca Nevola     *105*

5. The State: *Metaphorical and Material*
Susanne Dahlgren     *140*

6. Refugee: *Yemenis Navigating Humanitarianism
and Human Rights in the Afro-Asian Circuit*
Nathalie Peutz and Angie Heo     *168*

7. Friendship: *Ethical Engagements and Dilemmas
in Times of War and Conflict*
Marina de Regt     *211*


List of Contributors     *237*

Index     *241*

# Illustrations

1. A demonstrator stands for agriculture in 1973     *79*
2. Political hope in a 2011 Sanaa protest march     *96*
3. "The Graduation Diploma of 'Ali 'Abdullah Saleh"     *97*

# Transliteration Note

In this volume we follow the transliteration guidelines of the *International Journal of Middle East Studies* and its list of Arabic words that are commonly used in the English language. We merge these guidelines with the ones set by Syracuse University Press, which requires that the only diacritics to be used are *'ayn* and *hamza*. The result is an extremely pared-down transliteration. Words and sentences written in colloquial Arabic are slightly less formulaic in their transliteration, which expresses the different regional pronunciations found throughout Yemen.

# A Political Anthropology of Yemen

# Introduction

*Grounding Anthropological Critique*

Ross Porter

How can anthropologists take differences seriously while being politically engaged? Among the more practical answers to this question, over which much ink has been spilled, is that anthropology has a special capacity to supplement the "anti" with the "alter" in its mode of critique, owing to the role that differences play in its theorizing and comparative undertaking. By transposing possibilities across and within worlds, Ghassan Hage tells us that anthropologists are ideally positioned to show how "we can be other than what we are" (2012, 303). To take differences seriously is thus to take possibilities seriously, and it is on the threshold between the two that Hage suggests a "critical anthropology" becomes a "critical politics."

In this volume, we take a parallel approach to the study of differences and possibilities. Focusing on Yemen, a highly contested national community that has been at war with itself and a plethora of global superpowers for the last decade, that has witnessed multiple revolutions, and where political dissensus is the prevailing norm among the populace, we propose that anthropologists set on being "critical" in their study of this place and time should begin by listening to how critique is being exercised ethnographically. Tuning into the ground below enjoins us to document the concepts through which Yemenis contest their own political forms and who, in doing so, are the primary exponents of an alter-politics. The role of the anthropologist as witness is to write in a manner that sustains these critical contestations and, in so doing, sheds light on the differences and possibilities that matter most to the people whom they study.

In 2019, a dozen social scientists with long-standing ethnographic commitments to Yemen met in response to an impasse.[1] War had been raging throughout the country since 2015 between the Saudi-led coalition and Ansar Allah (commonly known as "Houthis"), who had overthrown the government some months before. Hundreds of thousands of people had been killed, and swaths of the population were severely malnourished, homeless, and on the move. The impasse was that the more intense the conflict was becoming, the more that knowledge of life in the country among social and political scientists was tightening around an interventionist political language. It is the kind of language that is adept at tidying divergent political energies, passions, beliefs, and values into "threats" and "crises," often oblivious to why people might *refuse* to contain their politics within liberal models of democratic consensus building (cf. Mouffe's 1999 critique). This tightening was coupled with the rising difficulty for anthropologists to complement the work of their colleagues in political science, owing to obvious impediments to conducting ethnographic fieldwork, even remotely. Getting to the ground below had become a difficult task, and participant observation had to adapt.

What we thought was necessary for the current period was greater insight into the concepts through which Yemenis, at a range of social positions, live their lives. The aim of this task was to achieve greater parity in the distribution of theoretical voice, especially pertaining to the nature of the political. In pursuit of this aim, what came across clearly in the papers at the meeting and later contributions to this volume was that a more grounded theoretical analysis was to be found not in showing how people differ in relation to dominant patterns of knowledge production in the academic metropole (which can often be more of an intellectual framing than an ethnographically situated conversation), but rather in focusing on how people critically engage with more immediate forms of knowledge production within their own worlds. Certainly, ethnography

1. The contributions in this volume grow out of the presentations given at the 2019 Gulf Conference at the University of Exeter, "Zones of Theory in the Study of Yemen." I thank Claire Beaugrand, Helen Lackner, and Marc Valeri with whom I organized this event.

can be a "revolutionary praxis" (Shah 2017) when it forces us to reflect on the bases of our analytical judgments and the limits of our knowledge. However, where the anthropologist's desire for revelation and surprise becomes excessive is at the point at which it renders secondary the conceptual conflicts (and revelations) that are most meaningful to the people they write about. Confining the study of differences to difference in relation to a notional "us" always carries with it the risk of dislocating critique from the subject.

The approach taken in this volume is one encouraged, in part, by the composition of the book form. Instead of an edited volume in which each chapter presents a different ethnographic snippet from a different area of the globe in relation to a single theoretical premise, here each chapter focuses on a different aspect of a single (highly contested) national community. By narrowing the regional scale, less pressure is put on the editor to inhabit an analytical third voice through which to engage in comparison between the different explorations (cf. Strathern's critique in 1990, 212). We are freer, that is, to remain focused on the social life of concepts as animate densely concentrated conflicts internal to a society (conflicts that also extend to the constitution of "society" itself) and that most occupy its members.

Although all good ethnography deals with concepts—minimally defined as the building blocks of thought through which people order and inform their experiences—their location and genealogy matter when considering the quality of the differences that the ethnographer hopes to unearth. Our task in this volume navigates two positions. On the one hand, we are not looking for or privileging ethnographic concepts that are radically different from, say, the stipulations of the secular Enlightenment, liberal thought, universalist political theory, or whatever else that is often contained within the term "Western." This is simply for the reason that such stipulations are not the direct objects of critique against which the people in these ethnographies articulate their own conceptual ground and assert their differences. On the other hand, we remain cautious of the ease with which ethnography can descend into an extended conversation with the latest theoretical turn in anthropology (or philosophical guru) at the expense of more grounded and particular concepts and comparisons.

In between these two poles, we seek to understand how people in Yemen—tribesmen, farmers, refugees, revolutionaries, state workers, charity workers, the unemployed, and the destitute—critically engage with familiar, often universalist concepts that emanate from locally regnant forms of governmentality. Where people in these discussions exert difference in relation to these concepts is to be found in their day-to-day experiences of them, which sometimes encompass defiance, sometimes passivity, and other times the assertion of counter-concepts. When we refer to "the state," "refugee," or "honor," for instance, we do so therefore as translations of signifiers that oscillate between a range of scales and relations of power. In all cases, however, it is less the final revelation of difference in relation to distant theoretical conventions that is our concern than the continuous and emergent *conflict* through which people claim conceptual ground for themselves.

Although we are primarily concerned with how people contest concepts within their immediate worlds, this is not to say that anthropological theory does not enter the fray. Beyond what the interpreter will always bring to the interpreted in terms of their conceptual horizons and predilections, the discussions in this volume by Mundy and Nevola in particular highlight how place and theory intersect in ways that directly enter the ground of contestation. This intersection is especially likely when ethnographic concepts become what Arjun Appadurai (1988) calls gatekeeping concepts, which are concepts that act like "showcases" for nations and swaths of geography in anthropological comparisons (see discussions by Fardon 1990 and Strathern 1988; cf. Dresch 1992). Such concepts possess force not because they are externally imposed, but because they mark a confluence between a select local reality and a scholarly convention (for example, "caste" for India, "reciprocity" for Melanesia, "segmentarism" for Yemen). In this confluence, writes Appadurai (1988, 40), gatekeeping concepts can form "metonymic prisons for particular places," capturing "internal realities in terms that serve the discursive needs of 'general' theory in the metropolis" (46). Where gatekeeping concepts are of relevance to our project is in the extent to which they function as barriers to accessing divergent, locally meaningful, and plural conceptual contestations. As we will see, however, accessing these contestations is not always an easy task when the silences perpetuated by gatekeeping concepts align with the silences enforced by statist ideologies and within which one's ethnographic informants may be enmeshed (see Mundy's 1995 critique and in this volume).

Documenting critique is the primary component of the political anthropology we propose in this volume, where "critique" at its broadest pertains to the "movement by which the subject gives himself the right to question truth on its effects of power and question power on its discourses of truth" (Foucault 1997, 32). The men and women in these ethnographies who seize the right to dismantle select unities of truth and power do so as an expression of their desubjugation. By desubjugation we do not, however, mean only the negative move through which people assert oppositional agency within relations to power. Anthropologists have rightly noted that a political anthropology whose avowed aim is to show how the dominated resist their domination in purely negative terms can very easily descend into a totalizing commentary on power (Foucault tells us that power is everywhere, after all) at the expense of the concepts around which people positively value and/or organize their lives (for example, Piliavsky and Scheele 2022, 689–91). For a volume that seeks to shed light on the range of concepts around which people articulate their alter-politics, such a move would be devastating. To mitigate this risk, we need to complement an understanding of resistance as opposition with insights into how the dominated positively construct and enact transformations in themselves and their worlds, on their own terms (Ortner 1995). Doing so requires a political anthropology that is at once attuned to the effects of power, the contents of resistance, and the concepts through which other worlds are imagined. It is a political anthropology that supplements critical investigation into the operations of power with ethnographic sensitivity to moral oughts (cf. Robbins 2013).

In much of the now classic ethnographic literature on Yemen, based on fieldwork in the 1970s and '80s, we encounter precisely this combination of negative and positive critique, and it is this tradition that we seek to augment. From this period, we have an invaluable corpus of material regarding nonstate legal, moral, communitarian logics and cultures, modes of exchange, and property relations, all of which shed light on the contested building blocks of politics in the country from the local level (for example, tribes or households?) and the concepts that mediate and sustain hierarchies and in/equalities (for example, honor or economics?) (see Caton 1990; Dresch 1989; Mundy 1995; Weir 2007). We learn from these works about the range of concepts around which political life was once valued and contested in the country, while also sensitive to how a way of life was steadily eroding amid the expanding authoritarianism of the Yemeni state in the rural, agricultural majority of the country.

Thus far we have defined the task of a political anthropology as the ethnographic documentation of critique, and specifically critique that challenges concepts with concepts, where concepts also speak to values. Each chapter in this volume goes about this task in its own way. We hear about members of a charitable organization who assert a pious, Islamic, understanding of "security" as uncertainty, subverting the concept from statist projects to bring certainty to the future; about Yemeni intellectuals who have fought to expound the role of social class in rural life, the contingent grammar for which ("land") has been concealed by a regime that has stood to gain from ideations of an egalitarian society; about tribesmen who defy codifications of "honor" from the incumbent regime in Sanaa and a general theory from elsewhere and who reclaim this concept within an "everyday ethos of insecurity"; about individuals who engage with "the state" not as a transcendent entity imbued with sacrality and omnipotence (the state's own prose), but as a tangible vocabulary of corruption that may be mastered, cynically, by its employees; about people who seek to ascend to the status of "refugee" as a coveted concept of political personhood and legal protection, fleeing a country in which they were only ever "virtual citizens"; and about the critical languages of "friendship" during times of extreme human suffering and what they imply for ethical engagement across worlds.

The people who appear in these discussions express varying degrees of what Hage calls "the ungovernable," defined as "that which becomes immune to the possibility of capture by any existing political assemblage and as such requires a radical rethinking of the very nature of politics itself within it" (2012, 294). In the throes of everyday life within an authoritarian context, ungovernability may pertain to the exercise of critical agency through which people appear compliant yet subtly sow the seeds for world-changing events, or delicately articulate a politics of freedom, individual and/or collective, within the confines of regnant political formations (cf. Graeber 2004, 25–37). In more extreme terms, to write of the ungovernable is to write of those individuals and groups who have been cast out of a political community by a sovereign power, rendered politically illegitimate through speech acts ("national threats," "terrorists"), and subjected to extraordinary levels of extrajudicial violence. To study the ungovernable is to study those persons who *refuse* to have their political forms translated and tidied into government-as-usual. We may also extend this definition to those Yemenis who refuse to have their agonistic political energies contained within the reconciliatory procedures of liberal democracy, where the purification of the political is felt to mark its eviction (see Rancière 1998, 62; cf. Porter 2017, 278; and Boutieri 2021, 70–74).

To study the history of ungovernability in Yemen from the mid-twentieth century to the present day is to study the history of people evading the politics of the center. From the republican and Marxist undercurrents that erupted into the liberationist movements of the 1960s in the two Yemens, to the ongoing independence movement in the South following unification with the North in 1990, to the nationwide revolution in 2011 against the rule of ʿAli ʿAbdullah Saleh (1978–2012), and to the military ascension of Ansar Allah to high office in 2014, this history is one of mass political dissensus. It is also a history of people prefiguring alternatives to (as much as reconstituting) central power, from the revolutionaries who in 2011 sought to ensure that power remain diffused within an imaginary of "the people" (Porter 2017) to the enduring traditions of local self-governance, peace building, and legal arbitration in rural areas where state control withers (Carapico 1998; Challand and Rogers 2020; Yadav 2022). As for the ongoing conflict between Ansar Allah and the Saudi-led coalition, it may also be understood as a conflict over the composition of the political, whereby the moral politics of Ansar Allah (see al-Eriani, this volume) marks an evasion of imperialist realpolitik. This evasion is itself evaded by the more diffuse political grammars simmering below among the populace.

Thinking analytically with the ungovernable brings us to Steven Caton's opening chapter. Caton argues that if we are to theorize productively with the elusive democracy of the "multitude," we must first confront the role that strong sovereign political formations ("the transcendent") in the Arabian Peninsula play in both silencing and reharnessing "immanent" political languages (and possibilities). It is no coincidence, Caton writes, that as imperial sovereignties (the United Arab Emirates) and empires (Saudi Arabia) have found their footing in Yemen, we have become increasingly accustomed to hearing about an inherently lawless Yemeni subject and a "war without end." He writes that the pervasive imagery of tribes in Yemen as feud-addicted entities in constant need of pacification—which no amount of anthropological writing to the contrary has been able to dislodge—has come to form part of the juridical basis for imperial intervention in the country. From tribes he pivots to the revolutionaries of 2011, questioning why the success or failure of these individuals as revolutionaries has been so widely judged according to whether their actions translate into the kind of "transcendent" politics they oppose. Caton's argument is a plea to scholars of Yemen to exercise sensitivity in the translation of concepts, especially when it plays into imperial designs or local tyrannies, or both. This sensitivity requires that we make space in our analyses for the emergent and inherently evasive political languages that *refuse* to be translated into what they are not. "X," the title of Caton's chapter, is an allusion to such languages as presently defy dominant forms of political recognizability.

Working ethnographically within a similar tension between immanence and transcendence, Kamilia al-Eriani brings our attention to a pious, Islamic, conception of "security" as *uncertainty*. She begins by explaining how the current regime in Sanaa views the calamity in Yemen, and specifically its own losses on the battlefield, as being the result of waning piety among the population, something that can be reversed only by strictly policing moral life. Al-Eriani contrasts this epistemic logic with the self-understandings of volunteers within a charitable organization who seek out the poor, destitute, wounded, and mentally ill in the streets of Sanaa, Taiz, and al-Hudayda. Contrary to statist endeavors to "secure" future certainty, we learn from these volunteers that the present humanitarian tragedy can be reversed only by acknowledging the *unknowability* of God's will and, by extension, uncertainty as to the beneficence of one's actions. Drawing on the philosophy of Abu Hamid al-Ghazali, al-Eriani explains how the recognition of future uncertainty is understood as central to the alleviation of human suffering among the faithful. "Security" in this formulation is rooted precisely in this recognition. Such a nonsecular understanding of security, merging the political and spiritual, may be difficult for some readers to digest, but ultimately one that they must if they wish to understand the entanglements of faith and resilience in the harshest of circumstances.

If in the first two chapters Caton and al-Eriani seek an ethically grounded alter-politics, in the third chapter Martha Mundy reminds us of two crucial points to bear in mind in pursuit of this goal. The first is not to overlook the role of the Yemeni state in the production of sociological knowledge of the country, and the second is that anthropologists must do more to think with those Yemeni scholars, past and present, who have challenged dominating forms of knowledge production within the country itself. Failure to address both points risks overlooking the intellectual and political gatekeepers that often hold sway over analytical (including ethnographic) visions of Yemeni society. In her earlier work, Mundy (1995) argued that segmentarist visions of tribal society in the 1980s focusing on male agency, genealogy, and egalitarianism reflected, in part, a statist ideological discourse that sought to obfuscate the economically exploitative practices of a hegemonic class, especially in rural areas wherein reside most of the population. In her chapter, Mundy extends her earlier critique by exploring several intellectual currents that have served to consolidate the hegemony of what she calls a "people as tribes ideology" over the past several decades. Extending the observations of Yemeni philosopher Abu Bakr al-Saqqaf, she argues that the component and ethnographically grounded grammar of class—"land" and "household"—quite suddenly vanished from political and scholarly vocabulary (Yemeni and non-Yemeni) following Saleh's defeat of the National Liberation Front in the late 1970s with the help of the "Islamic Front." She argues that following this defeat there ensued both a rapid increase in the securitization of Yemeni sociology and with it the production of conceptual foci that have actively diverted attention away from what matters most to rural Yemenis: land and property, both of which have historically been as central to the constitution of political personhood as they have been to the distribution of power.

Mundy's long-standing endeavor to counter totalizing visions of Yemeni society (what she earlier referred to as the "Durkheimian tapeworm") through "morphological representations of social practice" (1995, 6) finds renewed expression in Luca Nevola's chapter. Nevola seeks to capture the everyday languages of "honor" (*sharaf*), arguing that there has been a "conceptual mismatch" between honor as it features in everyday parlance and honor as it has featured in much of the (earlier) anthropology of the region as well as in certain codifications of the concept emanating from the incumbent regime. During his fieldwork in a town to the north of Sanaa, Nevola encountered no evidence of an overarching theory of *sharaf,* much less one that is written around heroic deeds of military prowess, weapons, and territory and that is passed down through inheritance. Nevola's "tribesman" does not defend or assert his honor as if it reflected a set of structural principles within an overarching cosmology. Rather, the word "honor" appears in his fieldwork as a floating signifier, without content of its own, that creeps up on the individual as a moral demand in inconsistent, contradictory, and highly variable ways. Nevola brings a heavy dose of ethical realism to honor as something that is won and lost within what he calls an "everyday ethos of insecurity." Shifting from the theoretical codifications of anthropological theory to the Yemeni state, he shows how Ansar Allah's recent attempt to codify a theory of honor within their "Tribal Charter of *Sharaf*" appears distinctly superfluous to lived reality (and potentially tyrannical). The ways in which people have reacted to the charter should stand as a warning to social scientists against the codification "tribal" personhood around limited, morally prescriptive conceptions of honor.

By and large, contributors relate to the Yemeni state, directly or indirectly, as something against which to reclaim more vernacular conceptual languages, especially pertaining to the political. The reason they take this approach is not because they are suggesting that human agency must take the state as its object of critique (none of the chapters are "antistate" ethnographies, per se), but because they recognize that knowledge production in and of Yemen is deeply entangled with this entity. There is a risk, however, that by repeatedly invoking "the state" as if it were a sovereign actor we invest in an illusion, concealing actual political practices and relations among individuals within its apparatus. Phillip Abrams's (1988) call to sociologists in the 1980s to "demystify the state idea" can be read alongside A. R. Radcliffe-Brown's message to anthropologists in the 1940s in which he described the state as a "fiction of philosophers" and the task of the social scientist to instead speak of what lies within: "a collection of individual human beings connected by a complex system of relations" (xxiii). Grounding the state is precisely the task that Susanne Dahlgren sets herself in her chapter, specifically by shedding light on the "languages of stateness" as spoken by individuals who work for the state apparatus.

Dahlgren describes the case of a civil servant in the former People's Democratic Republic of Yemen (South Yemen) who, following unification with the Yemen Arab Republic (North Yemen) in 1990, moved to Sanaa with his family to take up a position in the Ministry of Health. Having worked alongside this man in a Finnish health project during the years preceding and following unification, Dahlgren charts the process through which he actively sought to master the everyday language of this "state" as an outsider. Thinking about the state through its more vernacular working language brings the state down to earth. In this case, grounding the state highlights the significance of nonhuman objects in lubricating the state machinery. It was this employee's privileged access to the elusive (and technically illegal) whiskey store in Sanaa that enabled him to make the state function and get permissions, papers signed, and the health project in which he was involved (with Dahlgren) under way. Thinking about how the state becomes material through its workers and the objects that mediate and constitute their relations serves as a reminder of the need to consider the everyday conceptual grammar of "stateness" for those individuals who work within the corridors of the Yemeni "state" itself. It is also a subtle reminder of how, with cynical agency, people can both invest in and engage critically with such lofty political formations.

Few individuals are so attuned to the interplays of power and categorization as the aspiring refugee. In their chapter, Nathalie Peutz and Angie Heo bring our attention to those thousands of Yemenis who are currently on the move, traversing continents, seeking a more dignified life for themselves. In a desert camp in Djibouti, we hear about Yemenis who seek to preserve their government-recognized status as "refugees" in the face of a "competitive humanitarianism" that seeks to rebrand them as "displaced persons," which entails a loss of humanitarian and legal rights. In the small South Korean island of Jeju, we hear about Yemenis who also aspire for official refugee status as they battle accusations that they are not "real refugees" because they lack recognizable signs of vulnerability. This battle is coupled with the indignity, for many, of being granted a "humanitarian stay," understood as a mere gift of temporary relief. In both cases, we learn how the concept "refugee" translates through everyday critical engagements with power. Moreover, Peutz and Heo suggest that the struggle to become a "refugee" must be understood not as a story of gradual loss of political rights attached to citizenship of the Yemeni state, but as an attempt to inhabit an ascendant, even liberatory political category elsewhere. Among their interlocutors, we hear of individuals for whom the war was an "opportunity" to become a "real refugee," having felt like "virtual refugees" in Yemen owing to emic forms of abjection pertaining to weak genealogy, skin color, gender, and class. Two further lessons follow from Peutz and Heo's ethnographic work in Djibouti and South Korea. The first is to avoid falling back on supposedly emic ideations of social life when tracing how people challenge categorizations from elsewhere. The second is to avoid confining the political imagination to "home," especially when "home" is a place one would flee at the earliest opportunity.

In the final chapter, Marina de Regt thinks through the conflicts that extend directly to the anthropologist during fieldwork, owing to the structural inequalities that overwhelmingly infuse relations between interpreter and interpreted. In charting the trials and tribulations of several of her friendships with Yemeni women over the past few decades—from her work in a development project in Rada' in the early 1990s to her later anthropological fieldwork and more recent WhatsApp conversations during the current war in which old friends have requested (and at times expected) financial assistance—de Regt argues for brutal honesty about the expectations of "friendship" in anthropologists' ethical engagements. What comes to light in de Regt's recollections are not glorified moments of militant intervention by a fieldworker-hero with ready-made moral solutions, categorical imperatives, and frames of reference, but a more tumultuous and conflictual image of an anthropologist who must imperfectly navigate moral demands without always clear knowledge of how to act well. Thinking through the terms of friendship brings to light a contested politics of life across worlds—full of love, danger, and guilt—in which it is the anthropologist, as "friend," who finds herself in the daunting position of subject. For de Regt, engaging ethically with the ground below demands a form of listening and writing that implicates the anthropologist far beyond the customary nod to intersubjectivity.

As a collection, these explorations push for a political anthropology sensitive to how people contest and reorientate concepts within their own worlds, where concepts speak to both differences and possibilities. This task requires that we document critique in a way that supplements the "anti" with the "alter," for it is in the alter that we find the concepts and values around which people transform themselves and their worlds. Going forward, this volume is a plea to anthropologists of Yemen to remain firm in their commitment to perspectival inquiry, where doing so means not withdrawal into apolitical relativism, but working to document (and publicize) the conceptual contestations that matter most to Yemenis, especially at a time when most people in the country are struggling desperately to build better lives for themselves. In this endeavor, the contributions to this volume are suggestive rather than conclusive.

## References

Abrams, Phillips. 1988. "Notes on the Difficulty of Studying the State." *Journal of Historical Sociology* 1, no. 1: 58–89.

Appadurai, Arjun. 1988. "Introduction: Place and Voice in Anthropological Theory." *Cultural Anthropology* 3, no. 1: 16–20.

Boutieri, Charis. 2021. "The Democratic Grotesque: Distortion, Liminality, and Dissensus in Post-revolutionary Tunisia." *Cambridge Journal of Anthropology* 39, no. 2: 59–77.

Carapico, Sheila. 1998. *Civil Society in Yemen: The Political Economy of Activism in Arabia*. Cambridge: Cambridge Univ. Press.

Caton, Steven C. 1990. *"Peaks of Yemen I Summon": Poetry as Cultural Practice in a North Yemeni Tribe*. Berkeley: Univ. of California Press.

Challand, Benoît, and Joshua Rogers. 2020. "The Political Economy of Local Governance in Yemen: Past and Present." *Contemporary Arab Affairs* 13, no. 4: 45–69.

Dresch, Paul. 1989. *Tribes, Government, and History in Yemen*. Oxford: Oxford Univ. Press.

———. 1992. "Ethnography and General Theory; or, People versus Humankind." *Journal of the Anthropological Society of Oxford* 23, no. 1: 17–36.

Fardon, Richard, ed. 1990. *Localizing Strategies: Regional Traditions of Ethnographic Writing*. Edinburgh: Scottish Academic Press.

Foucault, Michel. 1997. *The Politics of Truth*. Edited by S. Lotringer. Translated by L. Hochroth. Los Angeles: Semiotext(e).

Graeber, David. 2004. *Fragments of an Anarchist Anthropology*. Chicago: Prickly Paradigm Press.

Hage, Ghassan. 2012. "Critical Anthropological Thought and the Radical Political Imaginary Today." *Critique of Anthropology* 32, no. 3: 285–308.

Mouffe, Chantal. 1999. "Deliberative Democracy or Agonistic Pluralism?" *Social Research* 66, no. 3: 745–58.

Mundy, Martha. 1995. *Domestic Government: Kinship, Community, and Polity in North Yemen*. London: I. B. Taurus.

Ortner, Sherry B. 1995. "Resistance and the Problem of Ethnographic Refusal." *Comparative Studies in Society and History* 37, no. 1: 173–93.

Piliavsky, Anastasia, and Judith Scheele. 2022. "Towards a Critical Ethnography of Political Concepts." *HAU: Journal of Ethnographic Theory* 12, no. 3: 686–700.

Porter, Ross. 2017. "Freedom, Power, and the Crisis of Politics in Revolutionary Yemen." *Middle East Critique* 26, no. 3: 265–81.

Radcliffe-Brown, Alfred R. 1940. Preface to *African Political Systems*, edited by Meyer Fortes and E. E. Evans-Pritchard. London: Oxford Univ. Press.

Rancière, Jacques. 1998. *Disagreement: Politics and Philosophy*. Minneapolis: Univ. of Minnesota Press.

Robbins, Joel. 2013. "Beyond the Suffering Subject: Toward an Anthropology of the Good." *Journal of the Royal Anthropological Institute* 19, no. 3: 447–62.

Shah, Alpa. 2017. "Ethnography? Participant Observation, a Potentially Revolutionary Praxis." *HAU: Journal of Ethnographic Theory* 7, no. 1: 45–59.

Strathern, Marilyn. 1988. "Concrete Topographies." *Cultural Anthropology* 3, no. 1: 88–96.

———. 1990. "Negative Strategies in Melanesia." In *Localizing Strategies: Regional Traditions of Ethnographic Writing*, edited by Richard Fardon, 204–16. Edinburgh: Scottish Academic Press.

Weir, Shelagh. 2007. *A Tribal Order: Politics and Law in the Mountains of Yemen*. Austin: Univ. of Texas Press.

Yadav, Stacey Philbrick. 2022. *Yemen in the Shadow of Transition: Pursuing Justice amid War*. London: Hurst.

# 1

X

Steven C. Caton

Let me first talk about the image that appears as the title of my talk.[1]

Unlike a language sound, it is meant to be seen, not heard. And unlike language, it isn't meaningful in a referential sense. To put it in semiotic terms, following Peirce, it is pure *qualia*.

Yet it would be absurd to assume that such an image doesn't have representational meanings that can be interpreted in a conventional sense. There are many of them, too many in fact.

X-marks-the-spot, whether it be treasure on a pirate's map or a house in which a victim of the Black Plague died or the crosshairs on a television screen during a drone attack.

X, as in to expunge or annihilate.

X, as in former, past (such as ex-husband).

X, as in alias.

X, as in extra (or X-Men, presumably because they have enhanced powers).

X, as in x-factor, an unknown element that is decisive.

It can also mean death, as in the skull and crossbones.

Or X, as in forbidden or X-rated.

X, as in crossing or crossroads.

Change the size of the arms slightly, and you get the cross, a Christian symbol. Change them slightly again, and you get Excalibur,

1. This paper was delivered as the keynote address at the conference "Zones of Theory in the Study of Yemen," held at the University of Exeter on July 1, 2019.

the sword of King Arthur, the mythical symbol of English sovereignty.

And, of course, there is Malcolm X.

I could go on, but thankfully won't. Like many of you, I've had nightmares about Yemen these last several years, and when not nightmares, then many sleepless nights. When I came across this image, it seemed to capture the disturbances of my dreams and my in-between state of agonized dreaming and fearful wakefulness.

In thinking about the several topics I will discuss in this chapter, this image has been helpful to me. I'm not going to be so literal as to suggest which of its representations corresponds to which topic; I leave that to the reader's imagination. The topics have to do with my sense of the complex situation Yemen is facing at the moment, which we only partially and perhaps only superficially understand—a giant $X$, if you will. The number I've chosen is hardly exhaustive, but I would argue is crucial. The topics are logically interconnected and not just a list, and I think of their interconnection as a Constellation.[2] No one topic is sufficient for coming to grips with the situation but only in dialectical relationship to all the others can we get a sense—albeit an always incomplete sense—of the "bigger picture."

## Imperialism and Empire

I argue that what we are witnessing in Yemen today is the action of national imperialisms on the part of Saudi Arabia and the United Arab Emirates (UAE) (Caton 2020). This linking of imperialism to these particular states may seem incongruous, if we think of imperialism, at least historically in the period after 1400, as associated with nations like Britain, France, Holland, Spain or Portugal, and Turkey, and in the twentieth century with Germany, Japan, and of course the United States; in other words mainly a phenomenon of European nation-states. Relatively recently, however,

---

2. "Constellation" is a theoretical term I take from Adorno (1994, 71, 162–66, 370, 407). Adorno saw parallels between the concept of Constellation and what Max Weber called "ideal types." Adorno apparently also drew inspiration from the methodology of Benjamin (1999).

non-European empires have begun to be compared with European variet-
ies, casting into doubt the assumption that the European case can be taken
as representative of imperialism tout court, and the question is posed of
understanding how imperialisms develop in the context of local histories
and particular politico-economic and cultural dynamics.[3]

Welcome though the comparative perspective may be, it is noteworthy that empires are still spoken of as mainly in the past, with perhaps an ethnographic glance at the way their residual effects linger on in
the present moment. But what about imperial formations other than the
US one, which may indeed have had their origins in the past, but are still
very active today? For example, see Russia's moves into Crimea and now
Ukraine or China's military occupation of islands in the South China Sea
over which the Philippines and Vietnam have claimed sovereignty. Are
these moves not also imperial formations? And what about the actions
of Saudi Arabia and the UAE in Yemen today? Are they merely doing the
bidding of other hegemonic superpowers such as the United States; or are
they, as I would argue, agents of imperial formations *in their own right*;
and if so, what are the historical and other factors that have produced
their formations?

As this chapter is supposed to delineate "zones of theory," let me propose one of them to be imperialism, which is to be understood, to be sure,
as a historical phenomenon but also as reemergent today, striking at the
very heart of Yemen's existence and threatening also the sovereignty of
far more powerful Gulf states such as Qatar. In theoretical terms, what do
we mean by imperialism? And how might we use a theory or theories of
imperialism to understand, critique, and possibly challenge its formations
in the Arabian Peninsula today?

To grapple with these questions, we have to come to grips with the
famous and influential theoretical text by Hardt and Negri called *Empire*
(2000), which draws a distinction between older forms of national imperialism, already theorized by such thinkers as Marx, Lenin, and Rosa

---

3. See Stoler, McGranahan, and Perdue (2007) who make this point about comparison.

Luxemburg, to name just a few of the Marxists who have conceptualized it, and what they call "empire" in the late twentieth century and that they associate with three trends:

a new kind of epistemology and aesthetic called postmodernism;

a globalization and monopolization of capital and financial flows on a scale never seen before, especially in the seeming porosity of national borders to such flows;

which in turn have been made possible by new information technologies and what they call newly networked publics accessible through computers and social media.[4]

Unlike earlier national imperialisms, as theorized by earlier Marxists, this one is not located in any given territory, much less that of a nation-state, but is to be found in large-scale transnational corporations and transnational institutions such as the International Monetary Fund and the World Bank. Hardt and Negri want to examine the "juridical" basis (others might call it ideology) by which these huge transnational entities legitimate their "governance of the world" (33–35).

Hardt and Negri's aim is to historicize this complex formation of empire in what they call the "crisis of modernity," which they trace back to the beginning of the European Renaissance. They define this crisis as a dialectic between what they call "immanence" (or the finding of the political will to govern from *within* the "populace" or the "multitude"), an immanence that has, more often than not, led to conflict and even civil war and for that reason has called out its dialectical opposite, or what they call "transcendence," usually in the form of the strong sovereign or state. Indeed, at the very heart of this book is a prolonged discussion of sovereignty, which may well be its most interesting and most enduring legacy. According to their argument, the synthesis of sovereignty and global capital leads to a transformation of power from the "multitude," as seen on a

4. This list is a summary or distillation of their concept, gleaned from different sections of Hardt and Negri's book *Empire*, and especially xiv–xv, 29.

sliding scale from the individual to the nation-state, to a transcendence in the form of empire, as described earlier.[5]

Rather than choose between these theories of imperialism, let us treat them as Weberian ideal types that we can call on *together* to explain what is happening in places like Yemen today. That is, one ideal type, national imperialism, may be better suited to explain Saudi Arabia's imperial formation, while Empire may be better suited to explain the UAE's imperial formation.[6] The justifications given by Saudi Arabia and the UAE for their intervention in Yemen (and I hasten to add that not all citizens of these countries are in favor of this war) are based on the claims that they are defending a democratically elected president from being ousted from power (God help us should we have to rely on autocracies such as these to defend democratic principles) and that they are responding to Iranian intervention in the Yemeni civil war on the grounds that it threatens the sovereignty of countries in the Gulf (I am reminded here of America's Monroe Doctrine that claimed it was legitimate for the United States to confront any European power that dared to intervene in the power dynamics of the Americas). I take these justifications as mere window-dressing for brutal acts of aggression against a country they wish to dominate, and whose territory they want to exploit for one reason or another, whether to put an oil pipeline from Saudi Arabia through Yemen to the Arabian Gulf in order to circumvent the current route through the Strait of Hormuz, which is constantly being threatened by Iran; or to have access to water resources in the Hadhramawt and to the Port of Aden, one of the largest "natural" ports in the world and a real prize for the container-shipping industry that is dominated in the Middle East by Dubai; or more distantly the Yemeni island of Socotra that is being eyed as a luxury ecocultural tourist destination. Isa Blumi in his recent book *Destroying Yemen* (2018) is perhaps the first to rigorously analyze this imperial formation, but he still views Saudi Arabia and the UAE largely as "agents" of an imperialism from afar,

5. Hardt and Negri's book has been severely criticized, especially by Marxist Brazilian thinker and critic Atilio A. Boron (2005). More generous to Hardt and Negri, but in their criticisms no less pointed, are the contributors in Passavant and Dean (2004).

6. I defend this argument in greater detail in Caton (2020).

rather than asking the question of whether what we are seeing today is a "distance-near" imperialism, one with historical roots in Saudi Arabia's hegemonic drive to control the entire Arabian Peninsula, an imperialism that has been ongoing since the eighteenth century. The other imperialism, which Hardt and Negri call Empire, has to do with the UAE's position as a hub in global flows of finance, labor, and commodities, in which Yemen is seen as a margin or frontier not only whose resources must be exploited but whose troublesome democracy of the multitude must also be "transcended."

As the earliest theorists of imperialism understood only too well, with imperialism come conquest and war. Saudi Arabia and the UAE have been eager consumers of state-of-the-art fighter planes and other weaponry that they have bought from the United States and its European allies in order to propagate a ferocious war in Yemen but also to test their preparedness for the war they see themselves having to fight eventually with Iran by turning Yemen into a proving and training ground (an "experiment," as I believe Martha Mundy [2018] once called it) for their newly purchased military hardware and their relatively unseasoned air forces. In other words, it is a military intervention that by no means is merely a defense against some supposed aggressor like Iran but the building of an army or armies (as in a coalition) intended for imperial intervention and expansion, and not just in Yemen but in other hot spots in the region. A war machine.

**War and Politics**

And this point gets us to the next zone of theory, war, which as we can see is linked to empire and imperialism. Hardt and Negri have claimed, "Every imperial war is a civil war, a police action. . . . In fact, the separation of tasks between the external and the internal arms of power (between the army and the police, between the CIA and the FBI) is increasingly vague and indeterminate" (Hardt and Negri 2000, 189).

Anthropologists who have studied war in Yemen have linked it less to the actions of a national army, which arguably has never been very large or impressive in any case, than to the actions of armed tribes clashing over their boundaries, over resources such as land or water, or over questions of

honor, and occasionally also over disagreements with the state. It is striking that in both the imamate or Kingdom of Yemen and the Republic that
succeeded it, Yemen's governments relied principally on tribal militias to
bolster their armed forces in the event of war. Further, the Republic waged
a civil war twice, once at the time of its founding in 1962 (which lasted
until roughly 1970) and again in 1994, and in each instance tribal militias
formed the backbone of the national armed forces.

However, that warfare was more or less part of tribal society is a tricky
thing to aver. The orientalist conception of tribes as "feud-addicted" and
driven to "self-help" through the threat or actual use of physical force is
a conceit at least as old as Hobbes's idea of man in the "state of nature"
expressed in his *Leviathan*, published in 1651. Within academic anthropology it was given theoretical formulation in the functionalist model of
the segmentary lineage system by Evans-Pritchard (1940), Ernest Gellner
(1969), and Emrys Peters (1990), to name just a few. A generation of anthropologists working in Yemen have countered these conceptions, not
by claiming that war doesn't occur in tribal society, but by showing that
what is meant by war requires a lot more cultural interpretation and analytical nuance than a simple idea of the threat or actual exercise of force
and the resort to "self-help" that the functionalist model implies. Further,
the moral imperative to resolve differences peacefully—even at the most
agonistic level of one person challenging another's honor over, say, non-
payment of debt—runs very deep, as does the collective responsibility to
adjudicate it. The exercise of force is a tactic of last resort, not the preferred
means to resolve differences. And, finally, rather than there not being laws
to refer to in the adjudication of differences, the reverse is true: there are
too many—tribal or customary, religious or shari'a, and civil—all of which
are consulted and meticulously interpreted by legal experts (see Dresch
1989; Mundy 1995; Adra 1982; Weir 2007; Caton 2005). Of course, it has
been pointed out again and again that the Yemeni state encouraged and
directly abetted violence among tribal peoples as a way of dividing them
and weakening them, an age-old tactic of divide and rule, which made it
more and more difficult for the tribal system to respond to this violence
through mediation and litigation. But the state was not successful across
the board in this tactic of "war of all against all," nor could it have been if

in Change Square during the Yemeni Arab Spring many tribal delegations laid down their weapons to pursue a peaceful confrontation and dialogue with the regime (Porter 2015).

To repeat, a whole generation of anthropologists working in Yemen has been at pains to document this more nuanced view of warfare, yet their efforts seem to have made no difference at all in dislodging the orientalist conception of tribes that informs public opinion, and, worse, policy makers. Tribes are still seen as "lawless" or without "a rule of law" (meaning, of course, without Western state law), and this claim has in turn served as a juridical basis for imperial intervention in the Arabian Peninsula. It was invoked in the late eighteenth and early nineteenth centuries when it was the "lawless [Qasimi] pirates" in the Arabian Gulf who threatened British maritime trade and the British installed puppet regimes to "maintain the peace," regimes that are in power to this day. In Yemen, it was the British again who established "peace" in southern Arabia in order to secure the hinterland of the Port of Aden, the gateway of commercial traffic between India and the Mediterranean. Occasionally, they did so brutally by aerial bombardment of Yemeni villages in Hadhramawt (Smith 2002, 10). And in Saudi Arabia it was the Americans through the ARAMCO oil company who helped the country modernize in a way that stabilized the Saudi regime, a regime that would otherwise have had little legitimacy to govern other than through its alliance with the Wahhabi 'ulama.[7] In an important sense, then, the imperialist interventions of Saudi Arabia and the UAE in Yemen are part of a longer history of European and American colonialism in the region (not to speak of much earlier Ottoman imperialism), and armed violence was then, as it still is today, both the pretext and the means for imperial intervention and control.

But today's wars on the Arabian Peninsula are not being waged by European powers, as in the past, though it may be their arms and assistance that are making these wars possible; they are being waged by Arab Peninsula states. That being the case, does it make sense to ask, "Is warfare

7. The pathbreaking political economic analysis of ARAMCO is Vitalis (2006). Jones (2010) shows how ARAMCO pushed for and directed Saudi Arabian development, which, in turn, was an ideological justification for the Saudi elite to rule the country.

in Yemen today different in nature than any of the imperial wars we have seen in the past?" As Mundy has pointed out, not only are the Saudi-led coalition forces testing their abilities to use their newly purchased US military hardware on targets in Yemen, but they are also precision-targeting infrastructures essential for water provisioning and food production and seriously undermining peoples' livelihoods to the point that their very existence is in the balance (Sowers 2018). Public health services have been so badly damaged that their ability to provide basic health care, let alone combat the outbreak of cholera and other diseases, has been severely hampered. To be sure, the other side in this conflict, the Houthis, who are opposing the Saudi/UAE-backed al-Hadi government and receiving Iranian military assistance to do so, are not exactly blameless in the toll this war has exacted on Yemeni lives and livelihood. For example, Doctors Without Borders has complained that corruption within Houthi-administered territory has made delivery of urgently needed health care on the ground extremely difficult, and at times impossible (Beaumont 2019). Yet human rights organizations monitoring the war concur that the preponderant damage and loss to life have been caused by coalition forces (Human Rights Watch 2018). In other words, not only has warfare been waged inside the country on an unprecedented scale, but its promulgation has been *tactically* connected to other destructive effects to the civilian population (famine, epidemics, homelessness, and dispossession), to the point where one has to ask whether the intent is to combat an enemy or destroy a country and its people; in short, it is a form of ethnocide through killing and attrition.[8] We should add to this tragedy the destruction of Yemen's historical cultural heritage, as recorded by archaeologist Lamya Khalidi (2017) and her Yemeni colleagues. Yemen harbors some of the most significant archaeological sites to be found in the Middle East dating at least as far back as the Bronze Age (and even much earlier). They include the Great Dam in Marib (considered one of the engineering marvels of the ancient world); the nearby monumental temple of the Queen of Sheba, who is

---

8. This tactic seems to be used in conflicts more generally in the Middle East, including Israel, Palestine, Syria, and more recently Libya. See Sowers, Weinthal, and Zawahri (2017).

believed to have ruled over the vast and powerful Sabaean Kingdom that grew rich in the incense trade with the Mediterranean world; monumental buildings at other sites associated with the Sabaeans and with the later Himyarite Kingdom; and elsewhere. Museums have been built to house and curate these priceless collections, but both the sites themselves and the museums have been targeted by Saudi air strikes (Khalidi 2017).

Another aspect to this terrible situation is that it seems to be "a war without end," as a number of journalists, including Dexter Filkins (2008), have characterized the wars in Afghanistan and Iraq. One explanation might be that too many parties profit not only from its continuation but also its intensification, among them both the arms dealers like the United States and the protagonists who buy them. But a war without end also plays into a certain politics that I will theorize next. Perhaps here the works of Michel Foucault on biopower, of Giorgio Agamben on sovereignty, and of Achille Mbembe on necropolitics might be illuminating.

Foucault argued in his 1975–76 lectures at the Collège de France titled *Il faut défendre la société* that a new form of power—other than the state as sovereign lord, or of power as punishment and discipline—arose in seventeenth-century Europe in the form of the art of managing and controlling *populations*, which he eventually called biopower (Foucault 2003). For example, the idea arose that states should compile statistics on the spread of diseases in populations, not only in order to combat epidemics and other public health threats but also to better manage or control the populations under their charge at other times as well. Another example would be to stockpile food and water in the case of famine or drought and to track how delivery of basic food and water to populations might save the most number of lives, tactics that at the same time are techniques of population management.

In these cases, Foucault was talking of knowledge about disease and nourishment as a means to *sustain* the life of populations while also exercising the state's power over them. But in fact, power defines itself in relation to a population (or, more broadly, a biological field) by deciding who can be helped in those situations, *as well as those who must die*. Not everyone can be saved or helped, so the question arises, who will be helped, and who not? Foucault uses the term *racisme* to label such decision-making powers. As he puts it, "[Racism is] the condition for the acceptability of putting to death" (229). What is radical about Foucault's argument is that the "right to kill," which is inscribed in the techniques of biopower, is *inherent to modern state power*; far from being the exception, they are the rule. Whether it be the Reign of Terror in the French Revolution, the Stalin gulag, the Nazi death camps, or American slavery: an "Othering" of the subject (what Foucault calls *racisme*) makes acceptable a politics of death. Just what the stereotypes are that "otherize" Yemenis—men, women, and children—such that they can be targeted for death, regardless of their role in the war, is something we need to look into, though I am unable to provide concrete examples.

Another way of theorizing sovereignty under the sign of death is offered by Agamben (2005). Agamben argues that violence is integral to sovereignty, which makes it at heart contradictory: the sovereign is supposed to rule by law in order that violence may be contained or even eradicated, yet the law can be exercised by the sovereign only through violent means. Whereas Foucault connects a politics of death with the advent of biopower in the modern era, Agamben goes back to the ancient world. He contends that the Greeks understood this paradox or contradiction of sovereignty most profoundly and that it was the Romans who ritualized the paradox in the form of *Homo sacer*, or the person who can be killed for no other reason than that the sovereign orders it. In our own times I have argued (Caton 2006) that the detainees in the prison of Abu Ghraib abused by American soldiers during the Iraqi occupation are *Homo sacer*; in other words, they illustrate the idea of exception to the rule of law exercised by sovereignty in order to perform the sovereignty of US imperialism in Iraq. More recent is the example of the murder of Jamal Khashoggi that a recent UN report alleges was planned and ordered by the Saudi Arabian state; he was *Homo sacer*, the man who can be killed because sovereignty qua sovereignty has the power to exercise the exception to the rule that all citizens should be protected under the law. This violence exercised by sovereignty on the human body—be it detainees in a prison or a critic of a regime—is "bare life" (a term Agamben derives from Walter Benjamin [1986] in his essay "Critique of Violence"), which in the most extreme case led to the Nazi extermination camps. Examples closer to our own era are the ethnocide in Rwanda and Bosnia, the long wars of attrition against Palestinians, the war of self-preservation waged by the Syrian regime, and now we can add the coalition war against Yemen. As Mundy again has pointed out, the food embargo on Yemen, combined with a strategic destruction of its essential infrastructures, is causing Yemen to starve (Mundy 2018).

Foucault and Agamben allow us to think about sovereignty as not just instrumentalized for human existence—albeit to ultimately control it—but its opposite, destruction not only of singular human bodies but of entire populations. To my knowledge, the leading theorist on this question today is Achille Mbembe (2019) and his concept of "necropolitics," or politics as the work of death. For Mbembe, colonialism and occupation are closely connected to necropolitics. They are concerned with dividing populations into those who must be occupied and those who are not, creating borders or boundaries between such populations, and creating hierarchies between them that are often justified in racialized terms, which in turn legitimize resource extraction and labor exploitation, and of course killing. If for Foucault a politics of death was crucial for understanding modern biopower and for Agamben it was crucial for understanding sovereignty (though I have suggested in my analysis of Abu Ghraib that Agamben is useful for understanding the sovereignty of empire), the utility of Mbembe's formulation of necropolitics is that it *explicitly* brings us back to war and imperialism, the two zones of theory of immediate concern to us. In other words, war and imperialism are ontologically connected—the one cannot be studied without the other—and thus are part of the constellation of zones I trace in this chapter. But just as today's imperialism has taken a different form and been pursued by different agents than in the past, so too do today's imperial wars assume tactics of death, material and environmental destruction, obliteration of cultural heritage, and long-term duration (possibly without end) on a scale we have not seen before.

## From Migrants to Refugees

And among the casualties of wars, of course, are refugees, fleeing violence and extreme deprivation in search of safety, shelter, and sustenance, which they sometimes find within their own countries, but in extreme circumstances such exist as in Yemen today, more often by crossing national borders and seas to countries that will take them in and grant them asylum, if such countries can be found. Should they be lucky enough to escape and arrive "elsewhere" with their lives intact, they are usually placed in refugee camps until it is determined whether they will stay and make a life for themselves in that country, often with the assistance of humanitarian relief organizations, or move on to another destination in another country or return to their home countries, if and when it is safe to do so. For many refugees, their status as refugees remains permanent, and they are stuck in a political limbo for the rest of their lives, citizens displaced from their own countries but never becoming citizens of another, and therefore having rights only as refugees. Or as Hannah Arendt (1973 [1948]) asserted in *The Origins of Totalitarianism*, arguably the first political theoretical text to draw attention to the peculiar status of refugees as stateless citizens, they have only "the right to have rights" as granted by the charter of the United Nations.[9] With economic opportunities greatly diminished, refugees lead lives of material deprivation and of psychological desperation. Of course, not all—sadly, perhaps not even most—people can find a safe haven because they lack the financial means to leave their war-torn situations and become refugees. It is saying a lot about how bad things really are when refugees are the lucky ones because they can get out of the hell on earth in which the less fortunate ones are left behind.

The figure of the "migrant" is an old one in Yemeni studies, one well researched from the 1970s until the present.[10] But these diasporic persons

9. In other words, the category of refugee is a category of rights, to which some people actually aspire, having lacked any such rights in the situations they come from. See also the argument of Peutz and Heo in this volume.

10. The literature on Yemeni migration is large. One of the earliest—if not the earliest—to work on Yemen migration was anthropologist Jon C. Swanson who published a series of articles on the subject in the 1970s through the mid-1980s (see Swanson 1979a, 1979b). That early research was focused on migration to Saudi Arabia and the Gulf States from the 1960s until 1990 when Yemeni males worked in the booming construction industry and sent remittances back to their communities to spur local development. See Fergany (1982) and Stevenson (1983). It also looked at diasporic Yemeni communities, particularly in the United States and Britain. See Swanson (1986) and Halliday (1992).

were, for the most part, in search of better livelihoods that they found more often than not in the United Kingdom and the United States rather than fleeing war-torn conditions (with the exception, of course, of the Yemeni civil war from 1962 to 1970). Their remittance payments were a bulwark of the Yemeni national economy, and before economic development was centralized under the aegis of the national government, the Local Development Associations were responsible for the building of roads, schools, and clinics, paid for largely through Yemeni remittance payments of Yemeni migrants. What has emerged in the present period is another diasporic figure, the "refugee," and on a scale that is both staggering and alarming. Unlike the figure of the migrant, the refugee is specifically linked to humanitarian crises of warfare, environmental disaster, and pandemics (Peutz 2019).

It is important to note that before the collapse of the 'Ali 'Abdullah Saleh regime in 2013, Yemen was in fact a country that took in asylum-seeking refugees from other countries in the Global South, for the most part the Horn of Africa, and in significant numbers (Peutz 2019). Thus, a refugee crisis, if this overused term is at all helpful in describing the situation, already existed inside the country before the current war/civil war produced an even greater catastrophe (see Cabot 2019).

**Barriers, Boundaries, Borders**

Imperialism, war, and refugees get us to the border, the fourth zone in our theoretical constellation. Imperialism is about expanding the borders of one's territorial control, usually at the expense of the borders of other political entities, which in the modern era are usually other nations. War is about aggression against another political entity *across* one's own border, except in the case of civil war. Biopolitics and sovereignty, subthemes of our zone of theory about empire and imperialism, are also about racism,

---

In the 1990s until the present, the focus shifted to Yemeni migration across the Indian Ocean, which has much deeper historical roots. See especially Boxberger (2002) and Ho (2003). The third wave of scholarship is on Yemeni migration across the Red Sea to the Horn of Africa. See de Regt (2014).

and seeking refuge may not only be about fleeing life-threatening catastrophes but also about genocidal practices by crossing over a border to another country.

Before we ask the theoretical question of how to think about borders, let us note that barriers, boundaries, and borders are interesting analytical corollaries (they are logically related to each other). Barriers can be man-made (as in a blockade) as well as natural. There were geographical barriers long before there were geopolitical borders, as in the extensive seas that surround the peninsula (the Red Sea, the Arabian Sea, and the Arabian Gulf), though barrier is perhaps a misnomer for bodies of water that for millennia *connected* Arabia through maritime traffic to other civilizational centers in Africa, the Mediterranean world, Central Asia, and South Asia and facilitated the movement of trade goods and people (and arguably was the bridge for the migration of *Homo erectus* from Africa into Arabia and the landmasses of Europe and Asia beyond). Or consider the great interior desert of Arabia, the Rubʿ al-Khali, the largest contiguous sand desert in the world. It virtually transects the peninsula into two halves, northern and central Arabia above it, southern Arabia below it, and was impassable for most of the year except by nomadic Bedouin— until, that is, the construction of highways and the introduction of cars and trucks to pass over them. And then there are the mountains of Oman and Yemen. Not only has their rugged terrain been a hindrance to others such as imperial powers that have tried to traverse them, let alone to control the peoples who settled in them, but they at the same time have been a bridge, as it were, for the exchange of goods and people from the maritime coast into the desert interior and back again. So these environmental zones—maritime, desert, and mountain—were corridors or bridges as much as they were natural barriers.

As for boundaries, one way to think of them empirically is in relation to tribes. The *hadd* of a tribe is often translated as its boundary, though perhaps a better way to think of it is as a tribe's territorial *limit*, or the extent of land that it can cultivate or on which its herds can graze and so forth. In geometrical terms, a limit is the radius of the circle, or the farthest one can go in a straight line from the *center*, and is thus egocentric. A boundary is more than egocentric; it demarcates an inside *and* an outside and is concerned with the *difference* between one entity and another rather than the extent of an entity's control or sovereignty regardless of what stretches beyond it. A limit becomes a political boundary when another entity can potentially lay claim to or encroach upon another entity's limit. A boundary presupposes a self/other distinction, which a limit does not, or not necessarily.

From barriers, limits, and boundaries, we get to *borders*, as in what separates the modern nation-states of the Arabian Peninsula. The question of limits and boundaries is an ancient one in the Arabian Peninsula, going back who knows how many thousands of years, whereas the question of borders is recent, and especially so in Yemen. There was not much of a border, either in a legal sense or in a material-infrastructural sense, between the nation-states of Saudi Arabia and Yemen until quite recently, the year 2000 in fact, when the border was delimited by international treaty. I can remember driving north on the highway from Saʿdah in the late 1970s and hardly noticing that a national *border* had been crossed. Now, of course, it is a different matter altogether. Because of the war between Saudi Arabia and Yemen, the border has become heavily securitized and militarized, to appear more like a wall or physical *barrier* than a border per se. Yemenis accustomed in the past to moving freely back and forth between Yemen and Saudi Arabia are now blocked from doing so. In short, it has become more like the barriers Israel has set up to contain Palestinians or more like the kind of wall President Trump wishes he could erect between the United States and Mexico, to stem the flow of migrants from Central America. These borders as barriers contribute to the mentality that a nation is under siege from "alien" others that seek to radically undermine its safety and sovereignty. Again, we are dealing with a kind of ethnic othering and racism that are the possibility for the modern state's biopower to determine who gets in and who doesn't.

Oman and Yemen agreed to their common border in 1992, and there the situation, until fairly recently, has been different from the Saudi-Yemeni barrier, because Oman pursued a different tactic of working with local Jabali tribesmen to help police the border rather than using high-tech surveillance equipment and physical constraints to both monitor and control the flow of goods and people. Arguably, the same tactic was deployed by the Yemeni state until only quite recently in northern and eastern Yemen, using armed tribesmen on tribal lands adjacent to or straddling national boundaries to defend these spaces from encroachment by a foreign power. However, since the intervention of the Saudi-led coalition in Yemen in 2015, Oman has started to build a security wall that, by the time it is finished, will extend several hundred kilometers from north to south in Dhofar Province (which abuts Yemen). The official reason for this wall is to better control the flow of munitions, drugs (mostly qat), and possible terrorists coming into Oman from Yemen. Soldiers from Muscat have been called in to patrol the barrier and Jabali tribesmen to man the checkpoints. But it should be noted that a fair number of Yemenis who have lived in Salalah (capital of Dhofar Province) go regularly back and forth between both countries for family and other reasons; while security has tightened, it would appear that Oman is still letting this traffic through. In other words, the border is still porous. A hospital has been set up near Salalah to treat Yemeni victims of the war, though it is uncertain whether these refugees are granted asylum within the country or returned after being treated. The point is that there is more of a *borderland* on the Oman-Yemen border than there is on the Saudi-Yemen border, that is, a "third space," one might call it, for people who can live near the border because they have economic and social ties in both countries that require them to cross the border on a regular basis.

I submit that borders and borderlands are one of the most fascinating new sites to be studied ethnographically on the Arabian Peninsula, and in Yemen in particular, though I would urge this study for reasons beyond sovereignty and security concerns. Borders and borderlands are in-between or liminal spaces, at one and the same time encouraging mobility but also slowing it down or disrupting it, and they have people who work and live in them. These individuals are not only the security personnel who man the checkpoints and the military who patrol the areas (who often come from those areas and thus know the terrain), but also citizens who make a living, illegal or otherwise, by bringing goods from one side to the other and back again, and who maintain kinship ties with relatives who live on the other side of the border.

The difficulty seems to be coming up with a theory of the border that is germane to the Arabian Peninsula. Nearly all analytical work on borders has been done on the US-Mexican border, which makes it US-focused and concerned mainly with borders between the Global North and South. Somewhat similar is the work done on refugees attempting to cross the Mediterranean from North Africa into Italy and Greece or from Tangiers into Spain or from Syria into European Union countries and eventually into Germany. But we now have crossings at borders between countries in the Global South that are as massive in scale as, say, the US-Mexican border, such as the border between Pakistan and India or between Bangladesh and India, and there is every reason to believe that, despite an internationalization of the security industry, the security and infrastructural features of these borders, let alone the borderlands along them, will not be the same in each case and thus will require different analytical lenses. Yemenis crossing between Yemen and Oman or between Yemen and the Horn of Africa are part of a Global South border phenomenon that we are only just beginning to work on, and the findings will contribute to our understanding of one of the most vexing issues of our time: the fraught nature of borders connected both to national sovereignty as well as to imperialism and occupation.

**Revolution**

I would like to end this chapter on a more hopeful note, with a zone of theory I call revolution. In a way we are back to Empire, except its dialectical opposite, the resistance on the part of the "masses" against the forces of global capital and totalitarianisms that oppress not just common laborers but to some degree all of us. A "totalistic system," however defined, is what conjures up a sweeping resistance, such as revolution. Revolution is what Hardt and Negri would call an immanent political force, that is, coming from within the "multitude" rather than from some superordinate power such as a sovereign. It is a politics of life rather than a politics of death, though heaven knows many revolutions ended up that way (the Reign of Terror, the gulag, and so forth), and some would argue *need* to end up that way, if they are to be "successful."

During the "Arab Spring" Yemen was the only country in the Arabian Peninsula, along with Bahrain to some extent, that had a sustained uprising against its regime and, unlike any other, succeeded in toppling it. The other moments of dissent (it would be too much to call them uprisings) were all swiftly and often brutally crushed, showing the true colors of these autocratic regimes and, in the case of Saudi Arabia and its actions in Bahrain, their imperial reach and ferocity.

After a long hiatus in the social sciences (Barrington Moore, Theda Skocpol), the comparative study of revolution seems to be making a comeback, spurred in part by the uprisings of the Arab Spring and also by the Occupy Wall Street movement. Yet a theoretical challenge has emerged in trying to understand how these movements can be called "revolutionary" when they don't seem to correspond to the way political scientists and historians have classically defined revolutions. Like the problem of defining an "event" in historical and anthropological analysis, a revolution is "really" a revolution, according to this view, only if a structural or systemic transformation has taken place; otherwise, it has "failed" and wasn't a revolution "after all." In short, this language is to define revolution teleologically, in terms of its outcome rather than what it is in media res. But if a person is in a moment or event that is being called "revolutionary" and feels that it fits with their own subjective experience at the time, doesn't it also count for something in the analysis? This reasoning would be to answer the question "What is a revolution?" from a phenomenological point of view, or would be called Verstehen in Weberian interpretive sociology, that is, to understand the event or action from the subjective view of the actors.

It is interesting that the Yemen Arab Spring might have looked more revolutionary in the classical understanding of revolution had various forces not worked against it. I refer to the National Dialogue Conference, a truly innovative political process in which the myriad parties and "stakeholders" were supposed to come together to envision a future nation, one that looked more and more like a federation of semiautonomous states, before the talks collapsed with the civil war. Although federation is not exactly unique on the peninsula (the UAE is a federation, after all, as is the Gulf Council), it would have been something Yemen had not seen before.

But the hegemonic national drive of the Houthis combined with the imperial interventions of Saudi Arabia and the UAE nixed that experiment. In other words, it is not too far-fetched to say that the Yemeni revolution was hijacked by forces inimical to the idea of a pluralistic and democratic nation. Yet to aver as much is to revert back to an earlier way of thinking about revolution as necessarily leading to structural change, and it is precisely this necessity that needs to be challenged in order to understand revolutionary moments, both in the past and today.

Then there is the question of revolutionary leadership, the usual paradigm of revolutionary analysis requiring there to be a cadre of leaders with a clear ideological vision of what the goals of political action are to be and clear tactics of how to achieve them. But what was noteworthy in the movements of both the Arab Spring and Occupy Wall Street is that such hierarchical leadership, let alone a guiding ideology, was deeply distrusted and therefore eschewed. Submit to leaders, and the power of the "people" or of the "multitudes" will be lost. Insofar as these revolutions failed to realize transformative change, they were criticized as lacking the "necessary" organization or leadership to carry through their revolutionary goals. And in some ways that analysis is true, except it does not follow that the only workable or potentially successful organization is the one typified by previous revolutions such as the Russian one or even the Iranian one; the real question is whether an alternative form of organizing revolution exists but has not yet been found, one immanent in the revolutionary moment itself.

How, then, might one rethink what it means to be revolutionary when the central conditions of possibility for revolution as posited by classical theory—structural change and a discernible leadership—are absent? This question is the challenge Ross Porter (2015) poses for himself in his extraordinary ethnography of revolutionary life in Yemen. He puts forward the idea of "being change" or the notion (at heart a dialectical one, or so I would say) of agents in revolutionary action becoming conscious of what held them back from being democratic or self-sovereign in the past and how they need to think about the present in order to create something new and desired in the future. In other words, seeing the present moment as a sense of rupture with the past, at the same time as it is a sense of becoming into the future. He borrows from philosopher Henri Bergson the idea of duration to capture this sort of "being change," an enduring of revolutionary creativity and capacity into the (indefinite) future. There is certainly more to be said about this concept of revolution (not least that others in other disciplines such as history are also struggling to rethink the notion of revolution as well), but I want to highlight the fact that it engages one of the more interesting theoretical moments in contemporary anthropology, that of temporality.

Not only do I think this idea is a more interesting way of thinking about revolution than the question of "real" structural change, but I also think it is more productive. The regimes in the region quashed these revolutions, giving everyone the impression that the revolution is "over," and securing for themselves another term in office. But if we rethink the temporality of revolution, then it has not been quashed but endures as a future anticipation of present-day ideas and practices. That the regimes in the region suspect as much and are terrified of it is manifest in the brutal ways in which they have clamped down on criticism and dissent in the media sphere, let alone acts of resistance in ordinary public spaces. They suspect that they will not have the last word in the matter after all.

## Conclusion

I have presented a number of topics that I argue are of key theoretical interest to us who work on Yemen today. They are: empire and imperialism, war, refugees, borders, and revolution. I see these topics not as forming an itemized list but rather as a constellation of interconnected topics. Empire and imperialism entail war (or what is sometimes called "police action") and borders, since it is to spread their influence across borders that imperialism and Empire are inclined. War in turn entails victims of war (and efforts of humanitarian assistance), including refugees, and refugees seek asylum across borders. Empire and imperialism also spark revolutions.

How to think about any one of these topics in relation to the Arabian Peninsula, and to Yemen in particular, is not self-evident. As I have suggested, it goes against the grain of conventional theoretical thinking to argue that contemporary non-European and non-American states engage in imperial formations, but once one takes seriously this possibility, the question arises as to whether they are engaging in national imperial formations or what Hardt and Negri have called Empire. With regard to Yemen, I have argued that Saudi Arabia fits the model more of national imperialism, whereas the UAE fits the model of Empire. Understanding war from the perspective of imperialism and Empire is no less challenging. War seems to be one of bare life and attrition, of ethnocide and endless destruction of the enemy's life-supporting infrastructure, not to mention the destruction of cultural heritage with which an enemy nation identifies, which is one reason that the figure of the refugee takes on such urgency in the contemporary period, and especially so in Yemen today. Because borders as national boundaries are relatively recent in Yemen yet have taken on great significance in such a short period of time, they need to be examined, just as the borders are between the United States and Mexico, or the border between India and Bangladesh, or China and Myanmar. The interesting question is whether a notion of the border emerges in Yemen (and by extension the Arabian Peninsula) that is different from these other cases, with the possibility of rethinking the border as a theoretical concept in general. And finally, revolution may be at once the most difficult and significant topic to theorize. It has been suggested that a more traditional notion of revolution, one that looks for lasting structural change made possible by a strongly centralized leadership, may have to be rethought for countries like Yemen and their Arab Spring. Revolution may have to be rethought more as the *duration* of what Porter calls "being change" than of actual structural change, which counterrevolutionary forces in the Arabian Peninsula today have quashed. It would be a revolutionary politics of maintaining the duration of such aspirations in an enduring struggle, until such time that the ancien régime may be overthrown and a new order created.

The question that I have not adequately addressed in this theoretical chapter is the empirical and ethnographic one: How do we study imperialism and Empire, war, borders, refugees, and revolution on the ground? In a sense, this work has already begun and is reflected in many of the chapters in this volume. As this work gains momentum, what we have known as "Yemeni studies" may not look like what we have known it to be in the past. Even when this "endless war" is finally "over," I doubt that we can go back to the status quo ante and simply take up the threads of research that were dropped as a result of this terrible conflict. Our zones of theory are not the result of a mere change in intellectual fashion but are the result of the dire realities Yemen is facing today—so dire, in fact, that the Yemen of the past, to a significant extent, no longer exists. It is one of the great tragedies of our time, but one we have to face head-on.

## References

Adorno, Theodor. 1994. *Negative Dialectics*. New York: Continuum.

Adra, Najwa. 1982. "Qabyalah: The Tribal Concept in the Central Highlands of Yemen." PhD diss., Temple Univ.

Agamben, Giorgio. 2005. *Homo Sacer: Sovereign Power and Bare Life and State of Exception*. Translated by Kevin Atteli. Chicago: Univ. of Chicago Press.

Arendt, Hannah. 1973 [1948]. *The Origins of Totalitarianism*. New York and London: Harvest Books.

Beaumont, Peter. 2019. "Yemen: Houthi Rebels' Food Aid Theft Only Tip of Iceberg, Officials Say." *Guardian*, Jan. 2, 2019. https://www.theguardian.com /global-development/2019/jan/02/aid-officials-aware-for-months-of-widespread-food-aid-theft-in-yemen.

Benjamin, Walter. 1986. "Critique of Violence." In *Reflections: Essays, Aphorisms, Autobiographical Writing*, edited by Peter Demetz, 277–300. New York: Schocken Books.

———. 1999. *The Arcades Project*. Translated by Howard Eiland and Kevin McLaughlin. Cambridge, MA: Belknap Press of Harvard Univ.

Blumi, Isa. 2018. *Destroying Yemen: What Chaos in Yemen Tells Us about the World*. Berkeley: Univ. of California Press.

Boron, Atilio A. 2005. *Empire & Imperialism: A Critical Reading of Michael Hardt and Antonio Negri*. London and New York: Zed Books.

Boxberger, Linda. 2002. *On the Edge of Empire: Hadhramawt, Emigration and the Indian Ocean, 1880s–1930s*. Albany: State Univ. of New York Press.

Cabot, Heath. 2019. "The Business of Anthropology and the European Refugee Regime." *American Ethnologist* 46, no. 3: 261–75.

Caton, Steven C. 2005. *Yemen Chronicle: An Anthropology of War and Mediation*. New York: Hill & Wang.

———. 2006. "Coetzee, Agamben and the Passion of Abu Ghraib." *American Anthropologist* 108, no. 1: 114–23.

———. 2020. "The New Old Imperialism in the Arabian Peninsula." *History of the Present* 10, no. 1: 101–15.

de Regt, Marina. 2014. "Close Ties: Gender, Labor, and Migration between Yemen and the Horn of Africa." In *Why Yemen Matters: A Society in Transition*, edited by Helen Lackner, 287–303. London: Saqi Books.

Dresch, Paul. 1989. *Tribes, Government, and History in Yemen*. Oxford: Clarendon Press.

Evans-Pritchard, E. E. 1940. *The Nuer*. Oxford: Clarendon Press.

Fergany, Nader. 1982. "Impact of Emigration in National Development in the Arab Gulf Region: The Case of the Yemen Arab Republic." *International Migration Review* 16: 761.

Filkins, Dexter. 2008. *The Forever War: Dispatches from the War on Terror*. New York: Vintage.

Foucault, Michel. 2003. *"Society Must Be Defended": Lectures at the Collège de France, 1975–1976*. Translated by David Macey. New York: Picador.

Gellner, Ernest. 1969. *Saints of the Atlas*. London: Weidenfeld and Nicolson.

Halliday, Fred. 1992. *Arabs in Exile: Yemeni Migrants in Urban Britain*. London: Taurus.

Hardt, Michael, and Antonio Negri. 2000. *Empire*. Cambridge, MA: Harvard Univ. Press.

Ho, Engseng. 2003. *Graves of Tarim: Genealogy and Mobility across the Indian Ocean*. Berkeley: Univ. of California Press.

Human Rights Watch. 2018. "Yemen: Events of 2018." https://www.hrw.org/world-report/2019/country-chapters/yemen.

Jones, Toby Craig. 2010. *Desert Kingdom: How Oil and Water Forged Modern Saudi Arabia*. Cambridge, MA: Harvard Univ. Press.

Khalidi, Lamya. 2017. "The Destruction of Yemen and Its Cultural Heritage." Special issue, *International Journal of Middle East Studies* 49, no. 4: 735–38.

Mbembe, Achille. 2019. *Necropolitics*. Durham, NC: Duke Univ. Press.

Mundy, Martha. 1995. *Domestic Government: Kinship, Community and Polity in North Yemen*. London and New York: I. B. Tauris.

———. 2018. *Strategies of the Coalition in the Yemen War: Aerial Bombardment and Food War*. Somerville, MA: World Peace Foundation of Tufts Univ.

Passavant, Paul A., and Jodi Dean, eds. 2004. *Empire's New Clothes: Reading Hardt and Negri*. New York and London: Routledge.

Peters, Emrys L. 1990. *The Bedouin of Cyrenaica: Studies in Personal and Corporate Power*. Edited by Jack Goody and Emanuel Marx. Cambridge: Cambridge Univ. Press.

Peutz, Nathalie. 2019. "'The Fault of Our Grandfathers': Yemen's Third-Generation Migrants Seeking Refuge from Displacement." *International Journal of Middle East Studies* 31, no. 3: 357–76.

Porter, Ross. 2015. "'Being Change' in Change Square: An Ethnography of Revolutionary Life in Yemen." PhD diss., Univ. of Cambridge.

Smith, G. Rex. 2002. "Ingrams Peace, Hadramawt, 1937–40: Some Contemporary Documents." *Journal of the Royal Asiatic Society* 12, no. 1: 1–30.

Sowers, Jeannie L. 2018. "The Saudi Coalition's Food War on Yemen: An Interview with Martha Mundy." *Middle East Report* 289: 8–11.

Sowers, Jeannie L., Erika Weinthal, and Neda Zawahri. 2017. "Targeting Environmental Infrastructures, International Law, and Civilians in the New Middle Eastern Wars." *Security Dialogue* 48, no. 5: 410–30.

Stevenson, Thomas B. 1983. "Yemeni Workers Come Home: Reabsorbing One Million Migrants." *Middle East Report* 181: 15–20.

Stoler, Anne L., Carole McGranahan, and Peter C. Perdue, eds. 2007. *Imperial Formations*. Santa Fe: School for Advanced Research.

Swanson, Jon C. 1979a. *Emigration and Economic Development: The Case of the Yemen Arab Republic*. Boulder, CO: Westview Press.

———. 1979b. "Some Consequence of Emigration for Rural Economic Development in the Yemen Arab Republic." *Middle East Journal* 33, no. 1: 34–47.

———. 1986. "Sojourners and Settlers: Yemenis in America." *MERIP* 139: 5–21.

Vitalis, Robert. 2006. *America's Kingdom: Mythmaking on the Saudi Oil Frontier*. Stanford, CA: Stanford Univ. Press.

Weir, Shelagh. 2007. *A Tribal Order: Politics and Law in the Mountains of Yemen*. Austin: Univ. of Texas Press.

# 2

# In/Security

*Rethinking Uncertainty and Refashioning*
*Piety in a World of Ruins*

Kamilia al-Eriani

Yaman Jadid—New Yemen—is a Facebook charitable group. Many of the photographs Yaman Jadid posts capture various images of social and economic impoverishment many Yemenis have come to experience since March 2015. Extreme poverty, illness, and starvation are only some of the daily insecurities the posts bring to followers' attention. Captions and descriptions attached to photographs often deploy Islamic ethics and encourage followers to tend to the urgent needs of those individuals who suffer secretly, unable to make ends meet or afford immediate medical care. Many of the posts are a plea to encourage all followers to check in on their neighbors, relatives, and friends whose economic and social circumstances have been suddenly altered by the war and are likely to be ashamed of asking for help. Other images and posts capture practical aspects of the charity work done by the group that tended to some of these insecurities, providing food, medication, blankets, and other everyday necessities. Neither the donor's nor the donee's identity is disclosed in these posts or photographs. As I followed this Facebook page over the years, I came to ask: Can acts of everyday benevolence and charity mobilized by groups like Yaman Jadid reveal something about an alternative understanding of (in)security to that of the modern state?

Yemen as a people and a state has long been haunted by the phantom of (in)security. It is common to hear ordinary Yemenis, particularly in the

North, complain about an absence of *amn* (security) and *istiqrar* (stability). When Yemenis grumble thus, it is also common to hear them lament: *ma 'ad fish amn; ad-dunia gad hi kharba* (the world is no longer secure; it has turned into a ruin). The country's long-standing anxieties and fears that have animated such a sense of insecurity articulate themselves through declaring that there is no state—*ma 'ad fish dawla*—and Yemeni politicians are corrupt and deceitful and can confer neither security nor stability on Yemen and Yemenis. Nevertheless, people consistently conclude with the reassuring declaration that God is their protector—*Allah al-Hafiz*—and make a *du'a* (prayer) that Allah may grant the country security, *Allah yahfaz al-Yaman*.

Over the *longue durée*, foreign policies of the Kingdom of Saudi Arabia (KSA) and United States have relentlessly staged anxieties about Yemen's security problem or crises that then were adopted by Yemeni elites in power. As Buzan, Wæver, and de Wilde (1998, 204) pertinently argue, a security problem as a performative speech act is "a quality actors inject into issues by securitizing them, which means to stage them on the political arena" and have them internalized and accepted by international actors to devise a defensive solution. Indeed, the Yemeni state has relied on a security culture of angst to extend its own power. Since the birth of the Republic in 1962, similar anxieties had been deployed to justify regional and international interventions throughout the country, permitted under the pretext of securing the "weak" Yemeni state, and by implication securing KSA and US regional interests.

Amid this long-standing obsession over Yemen's security, little do security experts and analysts, who inform much of the KSA-US foreign policy,[1] express curiosity about how Yemenis themselves fathom the muddled fragments that make up their fractured world. The invitation by the Hadi government[2] to the KSA coalition for military intervention in

---

1. The enduring epistemologies articulated by such dominant forms of security analysis have entrenched hegemonic approaches in studying Yemen and its society (Blumi 2019).

2. The transitional government of Hadi was installed by the Gulf Cooperation Council Initiative by way of appeasing the revolutionary youth into abandoning their protest camps and, ultimately, ending the 2011 Youth Revolution and its demands for change.

Yemen in 2015 exacerbated the general skepticism about Yemeni politicians' capacity to secure Yemen. By contrast, in the imaginaries of ordinary Yemenis, *amn wa iman*—security and faith—are intertwined, and security is not something that can be sought through corrupt politics. It is this understanding of security that I want to reflect upon in this chapter. In doing so, I wish to explore how Yemenis have tried not only to make sense of the war but also to stitch together a world turned into ruins.

Since the advent of the war, I have had animated conversations with my family and friends in Yemen over these themes as they inform their daily existence. We would acutely follow trending conversations on social media in the country, and my sisters and friends added me to numerous online groups on WhatsApp and Facebook, consisting of kin and people with shared interests in Yemeni politics and everyday affairs. In the early days of the war, when communication was disrupted and access to news was limited, these groups provided spaces of reflection to make sense of the present. One such post I encountered during those days captured what I saw as the prevailing quotidian understanding of insecurity: "It's common knowledge that 'whatever calamity befalls upon you, it is due to what your hands have earned' (Qur'an 42, 3). In other words, God does not change a people unless they change what is in their souls. Let us reflect on our misdeeds and make a promise to *islah* [self-reform]. Let us promise God that we will do the *salaa* [prayer] on time, not inflict any harm or injustice, and pay heed to our neighbors and care for the afflicted."

The individual who posted this verse sought to interpret Yemeni daily affairs as overly preoccupied with worldly, selfish, and individualistic desires at the expense of matters of the soul. The post invoked fear by implying that the unfolding war was a sign of God's estrangement from Yemenis owing to their waning piety. Simultaneously, it exhorted hope in averting further calamity by calling upon the faithful to commit to self-reform. In many ways, the post captures the vision embedded in the work done by Yaman Jadid, with which the chapter opened. Such posts, I will suggest, unveil a novel meaning of (in)security to which securitizing rhetoric suffused with anxiety has blinded scholars. It is a notion of (in)security that aims at pursuing and practicing self-critique, questions unethical modes of being, and aspires for certainty in an alternative mode of being and acting as a precondition to mend one's broken world.

This chapter offers a preliminary reading of everyday good deeds as an alternative mode of inhabiting (in)security informed by Islamic tradition. Specifically, it considers how fears over *amn wa istiqrar* (the absence of a state that can ensure the well-being of its citizens) are accompanied by a conviction that security can be granted only by God, that God's security may be granted only by attending to the self, and that ethical self-reformation demands attending to the broader community's everyday insecurities. By examining the activities of Yaman Jadid, this chapter attends to those forms of temporal subjectivity through which ordinary Yemenis seek to retain some form of moral order in their lives (cf. Haanstad 2009). Specifically, it acknowledges the long-standing *uncertainty* of the status of one's deeds in this life and the next, which encourages ongoing ethical self-cultivation and reform. Self-cultivation is a mode of self-critique as well as a critique of normative understandings of security within political science that continues to induce violence on Yemen and Yemenis. I will briefly distinguish between two approaches to (in)security and the different, contradictory, epistemologies that underpin each to demonstrate how "(in)security can be simultaneously enacted within and across multiple temporal logics" (Holbraad and Pedersen 2013, 2).

The first approach is the Hobbesian, secular notion of security that is pivotal to modern politics (a term I will justify throughout this chapter). Hobbesian understanding situates security in a linear progression, starting with a state of divine interventions fraught with uncertainties and insecurities and moving to a form of secular time that projects the responsibility of security, present and future, onto the state. Since security in this conception hinges on and concerns itself with a future wherein potential threats and hopes reside (Samimian-Darash 2013; Stockdale 2015), central to this mode of security is the desire and ambition to make the unseen seen and the uncertain *certain* and intelligible. Its epistemic and temporal logic produces a present haunted by anxieties attached to a future that is yet to arrive. It prompts political actors to devise preemptive defensive solutions to ward off future threats. In the context of Yemen, this understanding has played out most pervasively in the rhetoric of needing to resolve what is evidently rendered a security crisis and secure the power of the "weak state" as a prerequisite for a future where political progress, economic modernity, security, and stability are ensured.

The second approach to (in)security is informed by the Ghazalian tradition, which calls for individual self-cultivation by directing the faithful's gaze inward. This tradition serves as a reminder that one's own security—a notion that hooks the here and now with the future in both this life and the next—is permanently uncertain and contingent. With this open-ended comprehension of security, agitating the self toward self-reform is necessarily an ongoing process, as piety inevitably progresses and regresses exposed to "heterogenous knowledge" (Moosa 2005), multiple subjectivities and different zones of temporality simultaneously coursing through and over the self (Connolly 2011). It is this open-ended uncertainty that endows the self with a multitude of intents and desires that are often contradictory, thereby making one perennially vulnerable to unethical seductions. The soul, as such, is in an ongoing struggle between hopes to realize a virtuous mode of being and the forces that oppose these attempts. A notion of security rooted in the Ghazalian tradition is based on teaching ways to live by the ethical truth that regards ethical self-cultivation as a prerequisite for a virtuous community to thrive, to "secure" the present fractured world, as well as one's fate in the hereafter. Unlike a Hobbesian notion of security that revolves around a totalizing temporal notion of security and certainty indexed to securing the modern secular state, the Ghazalian tradition, I argue, finds *certainty* and perhaps security in acknowledging the irreducible *uncertainty* of the present and the future.

In what follows, I hope to show that there are clear merits in contrasting Thomas Hobbes and Abu Hamid al-Ghazali. Both wrote about fear and hope to theorize their respective conceptions of order, and both engage with the relationship between human subjectivity, agency, and temporality. Furthermore, their thoughts continue to travel across time and space as a universalized ideal (Hobbesian) and as part of a lived discursive tradition (Ghazalian).

**Yaman Jadid**

During the 2011 Yemen Youth Revolution, I came across Mohammad's Facebook page, Yaman Jadid.[3] In my inability to return to Yemen yet seeking to observe the events through their eyes, I followed many revolutionaries on social media, and Mohammad was one of them. Mohammad was one of many young Yemenis who took to the streets in 2011, hoping to bring about change through political action. Yet by 2014 he was disillusioned by politics, announcing to his followers on the page that he no longer believed that change or a New Yemen could materialize through such means. A recent turn of political events, which I introduce below, had rendered positive change through political parties and institutions impossible. This disillusionment directed him toward everyday simple acts of kindness, which he believed could potentially bring about mundane yet genuine change in the lives of individuals who are suffering and living in destitution as a result of political turmoil. To him, the true route toward progress and change is the route of God.

In Yemen today, political insecurity is compounded by severe economic and social insecurities.[4] The country is one of the poorest in the region and, since 2015, has become one of the worst humanitarian crises in the world. The enduring war has suspended the already weak economy, leading to unprecedented unemployment and loss of livelihood, and millions now suffer from deteriorating living conditions (*United Nations News* 2019). While Yemenis are seized by fear of a violent death from above, in the form of an air strike, from below the constant specter of economic insecurity and uncertainty is something with which they grapple daily without respite. Posts on Yaman Jadid tend directly to these economic insecurities but speak back to political insecurities and corruption that created prevalent economic inequalities.

---

3. To protect the privacy of the group, the Facebook account is anonymized, and the URLs to the group's posts on Facebook are not provided.

4. In a recent report, the United Nations declared that more than 233,000 Yemenis have been killed and injured since the beginning of the war from direct and indirect causes (*United Nations News* 2020).

In 2014, when Mohammad renamed his page to Yaman Jadid, he was convinced that creating a New Yemen by attending to the immediate needs of the community was the right path to pursue. As the war broke out and quickly became protracted, the group's initiatives expanded and branched out to meet new community challenges. By early 2022, the page had more than eighty-nine hundred followers with an ever-growing team of volunteers in Sanaa, Taiz, and al-Hudayda. Mohammad told me that volunteers were mostly family members, friends, and colleagues and that many previously unknown followers of the page also became active members.[5]

In recent years, beneficence—*ihsan*—initiatives online as well as offline have become a familiar phenomenon in Yemen. Some predate the war, while many others emerged during. Many founders of these initiatives concede that solidarity with the poor and displaced was a result of their disillusionment with politicians and the rampant partisanship that exploited them during the 2011 revolution.[6] They denounce the political elite who continue to enjoy a wealthy life, while ordinary Yemenis are left prey to poverty, violence, and political corruption.

Mohammad and his team implement a range of beneficent campaigns. Either the group is approached by the penurious, or, as is often the case, they visit different localities in the three governorates, detecting spaces and places inhabited by people gripped by destitution and illness, from orphans to the displaced. The team visits hospitals to identify persons who have been abandoned in its corridors because they could not afford medical treatment. They visit orphanages and the homeless to offer food, blankets, and medicines. They survey schools at the start of each academic year to identify children whose clothes and shoes are worn out and who do not have school bags, uniforms, and stationery. Through its posts on

5. In a private conversation via Facebook Messenger, Jan. 15, 2021.

6. This form of Islamic solidarity, I contend, should not be confused with "neoliberal" Islamic charity, which has become the focus of a particular strand of anthropological inquiry in recent years (see Atia 2013). While neoliberal Islamic charity is seen as a form of governmentality that allows the modern state to exercise even greater power, the form of solidarity I discuss here will draw attention to a radically different epistemic logic that challenges a modern secular perception of security.

Facebook, the Yaman Jadid team encourages donations and alms giving to help them carry out their campaigns. They rely on in-kind and personal labor and monetary donations from Yemenis living in the country as well as from migrants in the Gulf and beyond.

What is remarkable about the rhetoric with which Yaman Jadid encourages these acts is its ability to utilize balanced referents to both fear and hope that approximates the very insecurities of the afflicted to those of the benevolent. The posts constantly caution the group's members that benevolent subjectivities and intentions are always in flux, rendering the realization of a virtuous mode of being and perfect state of piety forever uncertain. Mohammad delivers this warning by invoking the multiple knowledges, temporalities, and even multiple selves induced with contradictory intents and desires between which the soul vacillates. Mohammad is aware that to live in Yemen today is to live war's epistemic rationality that fractures families and communities along irreconcilable political, ideological, and economic incentives; personal calculations; and objectives. In the midst of this rationality can also be found an Islamic discursive tradition, its authoritative ethical knowledge providing to some the means to resist this war rationality. Such opposing forms of rationalities generate multiple subjectivities/selves between which the soul (the higher self) infinitely oscillates. As we will see, actualizing Yaman Jadid in practice hinges on a Ghazalian notion of therapy of the soul. Its aim is to bring the soul into a state of balance, understood as a higher level of spiritual development, through the cultivation of rectitude, perseverance, sincerity, and a desire for intimacy with God. Invoking fear and hope in a way that links one's own pious insecurity to the community's everyday insecurities can be therapeutic in achieving this balance. As Mohammad puts it, "Caring for members of our community is an Islamic duty. More important, helping the weak is a virtuous act that brings forth God's pleasure, which is necessary to sustain and ascertain God's bounty, be it wealth, health, or security."[7] Mohammad alludes to a (in)security refashioned through faith and Islamic tradition, but one that is also not foreign to the (in)security

---

7. In a private conversation via Facebook Messenger, Jan. 15, 2021.

lexicon that historically existed in Yemen and still exists today at the level of a human subject that toils through the multiplicity of human conditions and seeks refuge in the transcendent power of the divine realm.

## (In)security: Two Epistemologies

The Hobbesian modern secular theory that indexes security to modern state institutions and its legal apparatus is contemporary to the political culture of North Yemen. I focus on the North for two reasons. First, it did not experience direct European colonialism, leading many observers to conclude that Yemen prior to the 1962 Republican Revolution was immune to secular modernity and trapped in Middle Ages–like conditions. As a result, scholars frequently dismiss that aspects of modern sovereignty existed in the imamate's domain of government. Second, the first republican state and the second (after the 1990 unification of North and South Yemen) were overwhelmingly perceived by scholars as dominated by northern tribal Islamists, at least until 9/11 when Saleh's regime systematically marginalized them. Such perceptions overlooked how northern elites had cultivated certain secular subjectivities around a lexicon of progress and security within which "religion" was firmly hinged onto the worldly sovereignty of the modern state.

Although this secular notion of security might be formally traced to the first republic of 1962 and the transformation of its legal apparatus, certain features of it may be observed in the Mutawakkilite Kingdom of prerepublican North Yemen (Messick 1992; Willis 2012). John Willis argues that the "economy of moral and political power" that underpinned the imamate had "dual genealogies" (107). The first was predicated upon the self-projected Islamic ideals of Imam Yahya Hamid al-Din (1918–48), which were enunciated through his concerns about spatial security and *fawda* (chaos) geared toward cultivating ethical subjectivities among believers, that is, fighting injustice by words and deeds and the proper application of shariʿa. The second genealogy drew upon the modern secular Tanzimat state program introduced by the Ottomans.

To cede power after the Ottomans, Imam Yahya relied on rallying his self-projected Islamic ideals against the secular Tanzimat state program. Yet his style of governance was deployed "in the service of an old notion of sovereignty that equated [a modern understanding of] obedience to the state with moral rectitude" (Willis 2012, 107). It borrowed heavily from the Tanzimat program to lay the foundation of the Mutawakkilite Kingdom (107–8). In other words, Imam Yahya's rule was an alliance of modern secular state power from the Tanzimat, integrated with Islamic learnings that sought to construct a moral geography—a domain of shari'a, inhabited by morally upright subjects who abide by the tenants and practice of Islam (117–18). Moral subjects were constituted by a political vision that imagined the morality of subjects and the morality of the social order to be "coterminous" with the morality of the state (118; Haykel 2003). However, it is also these "dual genealogies" that would make the imamate's ethical ideals susceptible to the seductive power of the modern state.

Nonetheless, as Brinkley Messick argues, pre-1962 North Yemen possessed the historical conditions in which shari'a as a "total" discourse consisting of "rules suffused with premodern ethical and moral concerns" thrived and governed *ibadat* (daily worships) and *mu'amalat* (interactions) (Messick 2018, 40).[8] The reformist work of jurist Muhammad al-Shawkani (1759–1835) that reconciled Zaydi-Shi'i and Sunni Shafi'i,[9] the two main doctrines in North Yemen, was significant in laying the foundation of what Messick (1992) calls "shari'a society" that extended beyond the imam's control (cf. Haykel 2003).[10] Al-Shawkani, who was Ghazalian in his approach to Islamic revivalism (Moussa 2012), operated from within the imamate structure and liberated the enterprise of *ijtihad* from the persona of the imam to the jurist. In doing so, he disentangled Islamic truth from political power (Haykel 2003, 84). Authoritative texts issued

8. Messick argues against Wael Hallaq's claims that a full articulation of a premodern shari'a community "could not exist except at the level of the abstract and theoretical" (Hallaq 2009, 369).

9. On the doctrinal differences between Zaydi-Shi'i and Sunni Shafi'i, see Haykel (2003).

10. In the imam's domain of security, he mobilized his soldiers to discipline those individuals who disobeyed him. Yet there were also those domains of shari'a as a "total discourse" that thrived in everyday life.

by judges and muftis that described the polity during the imamate were much broader in reach than the state ruled by the imam. Private shari'a scholars who acted as interpreting muftis represented an important segment of textual authority that contributed to regional and local potency outside the control of the imamate state (Messick 1992, 253), creating spaces in which the interaction between the two powers—the modern state and shari'a—was quelled.

It was not until September 1962, when the republican state in the North was born, bringing an end to Zaydi imamate rule, that the gradual emergence of a secular modern state power came into full force through the imposition of a distinctive temporal regime. Here, secular power did not amount to a political doctrine of secularism, as had occurred in the South. Neither did it operate through a separation between the sacred and the profane. Rather, and to draw from Asad (2003), secular power homogenizes time into a proper history, wherein the secular power does its work through the cultivation of a set of sensibilities, concepts, and practices, producing a form of subjectivity and modern institutional arrangement bound by a certain conception of time. Asad situates modern secular power at the heart of modern state sovereign power that discursively defines, reshapes, and governs religious life and gives it a natural quality. He argues that it is very difficult to grasp the secular, as one is always compelled to approach it through its shadow, religion (16). In Yemen, the secular power of the modern Republic operated through a persistent regulation of religion to resolve political questions of state identity, security, and progress toward modernity. Religion, as such, became a tool in the maintenance of the secular sovereignty of the Republic and in attaining post-imamate reform. Religion co-opted by state power is a secularized religion that prioritizes modern state interests at the expense of the well-being of the community. Intellectuals who led the 1962 revolution, such as Mohammad al-Zubayri, Ahmad Nu'man, and 'Abdulrahman al-Iryani, were students of the al-Shawkani school but imbued with Egyptian Sunni revivalist Rashid Rida's liberal Islamic notions of progress. In their political imagination, they had hoped to form a republic as a vessel through which Yemen could be alleviated of its "backwardness" and "poverty" as sustained under the imamate. To this end, they sought to apply al-Shawkani's methods to the new legal apparatus to secure an ethical order, which they envisioned would be integral to the Republic (Haykel 1993, 62).

In the years following the 1962 revolution, the republicans were fraught by challenges, starting with Gamal Abdel Nasser's arrival, at the invitation of the republicans, to help install and protect the Republic. Not only was Nasser's secular constitution for Yemen what rendered the Yemeni revolutionary intellectuals' vision questionable, but the arrival of his troops in Yemen was also coupled with an opening of the country to a specific form of security-progress rhetoric (liberal and communist), redolent of the Cold War period in the region, and that subjected religion to suspicion.

For the Yemeni republicans, moving Yemen out of its state of "backwardness" and toward a progressive and prosperous modern polity was slowly but firmly ascribed to the visibility of a strong state with a robust security apparatus. Investing hope for a secure modern existence intertwined with a powerful state apparatus is a European secular project that, at its roots, is profoundly influenced by Hobbesian philosophical projections of the legitimate modern sovereign state in seventeenth-century Europe. Although European in origin, its universalization as the foundation for the modern state, wrapped up with modernist conceptions of human progress, allowed its travel across time and space with striking resilience. Religion and spirituality, for Hobbes, induce a superstitious fear that makes men unfit for civil obedience (1971 [1651], 14). Indeed, Hobbes refers to indigenous peoples as a referent for the God-given "natural liberty" he equated with the state of nature (Agathangelou and Killian 2016). To Hobbes, the cyclical time (Hom et al. 2016, 5) of the disordered state of nature should give way to a new linear time and political order in which a Leviathan is firmly in control of the political present and future. He believed that a state of nature that relies on God's will and reason without tangible material patterns is shot through with contingency, open-ended possibilities, and risks (Bain 2017, 287). He resolved this issue by introducing the all-encompassing earthly sovereignty, the Leviathan, to whom individuals submit their natural freedom in exchange for security (287–88). He insisted that earthly sovereignty was the only solution to natural freedom espoused by the state of nature and its temporal contingencies. In other words, Hobbes's philosophy leverages the temporal regime of the Leviathan as imposing its political temporality on its subjects and, in the process, desubjecting them from multiplicities and contingencies of spiritual and religious temporalities (Agathangelou and Killian 2016, 7). State secular power, above all, manifests in a hope born of fear of future uncertainties and the kind of uncanny contingencies that would keep the soul and body in disarray (Hobbes 1971 [1651]). The Cold War era marked the postcolonial moment in the Global South that universalized Hobbesian secular sovereignty (Buzan 2017, 227)[11] and its epistemic foundation of security that indexes progress, security, and a knowable and determined future to the modern state and its homogeneous linear time.[12] It is because of such hope in a political and temporal notion of progress and security invested in the modern state, alongside fear of open-ended possibilities evocative of the "state of nature," that nationalists, including Islamists, are typically so committed to capturing state power. The possibilities of progress toward a secure, unified, and prosperous national community hinges on a single totalizing hope: the state.

The formation of the post-imamate Yemen Arab Republic (YAR) was embedded in an international and universalizing context (Halliday 1997, 36), born during the Cold War when Yemen's state security intersected with the security interests of the United States (and KSA), on the one hand, and the USSR (via Egypt), on the other.[13] This context gave way to a new culture suffused with anxiety that discursively attached the novice Republic's security and progress to the security of KSA and US regional

11. See also Schmitt's *Nomos of the Earth* (2007) on the universalization of European sovereignty that is no longer limited to countries that were part of the Westphalian system.

12. That is not to say that the trajectory and history of the formation of the post-imamate Republican Yemeni state was similar to its Western and Arab counterparts, even though it continued to conform to the objective goal of the modern state, which is state security at the expense of justice and equality (al-Eriani 2023).

13. The royalists, loyal to the deposed Imam Ahmad, were supported by KSA, while the republicans were supported by Egypt.

interests. Throughout its modern history, the Yemeni state has consistently been rendered "weak" and in "crisis" through the KSA's and United States' political lexicon of security: threatened by Nasser, threatened by the Left and communism in South Yemen and the USSR, threatened by "Islamic terrorism" after 9/11, and most recently threatened by Iran.

Since the modern republican state is also a secular temporal regime that perceives a continuum from tradition/religion toward a modern notion of progress and security, anxieties about the weak Yemeni state have also been attributed to an absence of modernity. This presumed absence has pervasively informed various foreign policies, which frequently found in Yemen's "tribal-religious" social structures key causes behind Yemen's lagging and inability to join the march toward modernity and, by implication, security. To these anguish narrators of Yemen, it seemed as if the new ruling elites in the 1960s and beyond had failed to break away or "desubject" themselves from the heterogeneous multiplicities of religious and tribal temporalities, permanently dragging the weak Yemeni state into premodernity, chaos, and even a "state of nature." Representing the Yemeni state as permanently in a state of regress rather than progress rests on a certain understanding of the relationship between time, temporality, and politics in international relations (IR).[14]

Nonetheless, the new Yemeni elite would adopt the new secular temporality by allowing this culture of anxiety and suspicion about the future of the Yemeni state to seep into their practices and orient their interventions, permitted both from within and without, in the name of state progress and security. Such anxieties would go on to generate what Hussein Ali Agrama (2012) calls "a problem space of secularism," within which evocative questions about the relationship between religion, politics, progress, and security of Yemen would be raised simultaneously to devise political

---

14. Time at work in IR analyses is seen as universal, assuming that the past, present, and future are settled entities (Little 2022, 6). It is through such representation of time that analysts produce an enduring hierarchy sustained through a secular perception of time and temporality that (un)wittingly centers European knowledge, experiences, histories, and interests (cf. Abourahme 2016; Acharya 2014; Ahmad 2021; Agathangelou and Killian 2016; Hutchings 2007, 2008; Hom et al. 2016).

responses. One instance that can explicate this contention is when Nassir withdrew from Yemen in 1967. The new republic was thereafter declared a liberal Islamic republic as agreed with KSA and assuaged US anxiety that the state may slip to the Left or, at its extreme, communism. Young republican officers led by 'Abd al-Raqib 'Abd al-Wahhab who largely represented the Left remained subject to the suspicious gaze of traditionalist elites, consisting of tribalists and Islamists, particularly Prime Minister Hassan al-'Amri. The republican elites believed that the Left intended to seize total power and alter the "liberal-Islamic-tribal identity" of the new republic. As intentions do not always have a material presence yet carry multiple contingencies to which secular temporal power cannot remain indifferent, the traditionalists remained apprehensive and uncertain about whether the Left would strike. This anxiety justified a series of brutal crackdowns on the Left under the pretext of securing the Islamic identity of the Republic. The first of them was the 1969 corrective movement, during which young officers led by 'Abd al-Wahhab were circled and slaughtered by al-'Amri's men, later followed by conflict in the years 1979–83 in the central regions after the Left formed the National Democratic Front with support from the communist regime in South Yemen (al-Eriani 2016). The 1994 war between North and South was no different. After 9/11, the problem of religion was no longer about how to maintain the Yemeni state's "Islamic identity" by way of securing its power; rather, it shifted to the question of how to *contain* religion, epitomized by political Islam (namely, al-Islah Party, al-Qai'da in the Arabian Peninsula, and recently Ansar Allah, which many people see as a proxy of Shi'i Iran). All of these pivotal historic moments, in their own ways, have given life to a secular temporality in Yemen imbued with uninterrupted anxieties about the relationship between politics and religion in governance.

As for integrating al-Shawkani's open methodology of shari'a as envisioned by the first generation of republican intellectuals, the project never fully materialized (Haykel 1993). The 1962 republican state gave rise to a new articulation of shari'a through the centralized apparatus of the modern republican legislations. As Messick illustrates, the new republican legislations drew on Western civil codes, including civil, commercial, and criminal, as well as *fiqh*. However, these legislations gave way to "a new legal space [that] privileged enclosure of fixed and orderly rules," curtailing the "open argument that characterized the *fiqh* as well as the pre-republican North Yemen" polity (Messick 1992, 69–70). The modern legal codes were fixed to relegate any contingencies that would come along through open-ended codes, which leverage open ranges and multiplicities of temporal experience, knowledge, and intents.

Islamic legal subjectivity places intent in the realm of inwardness and as something never fully ascertainable (Messick 2001, 151, 178), an understanding of which Yaman Jadid is also well aware. By contrast, the modern secular state and its legislative system place demands on its subjects by seeking certainty in intent by privileging material patterns of public presentation at the level of the self and its temporal experience. This epistemic sensibility inevitably trickles down into Islamic rhetoric through the authority of the modern legal system, despite its inherent contradiction to the tradition. A close look at the rise of Ansar Allah and their leader, 'Abd al-Malik al-Houthi, is telling.[15] Al-Houthi's brother Hussein initially emerged as a Zaydi revivalist in the 1980s against the central government's economic and political discrimination as well as the Salafi intrusion in Sa'dah, the heartland of Zaydism. Since capturing state power in September 2014, Ansar Allah have deployed the state's legislative system they inherited from the previous government to determine and establish a *certain* moral order in the name of security. While their rhetoric may not differ from that of the imamate, their capacity to mobilize the modern legal system makes the moral order they claim to establish even more incongruous.

In one of 'Abd al-Malik al-Houthi's online lectures (al-Houthi 2019c), he warns of two dangers to which Islam in Yemen is subjected: *tahrif* (distortion) and *inhiraf* (perversion).[16] He begins his lecture by stressing the nature of faith and piety as being at the heart of Yemeni identity by drawing on the oft-cited Prophetic Hadith: "Yemenis are the most gentle and soft-hearted people." Al-Houthi then proclaims, "Piety and spirituality

15. For an elaboration on this discussion of al-Houthi, see al-Eriani (2021).

16. The lecture was delivered on the occasion of Friday of Rajab, celebrated annually as the day Yemenis entered Islam voluntarily in 6 AH (628 CE).

are what authenticate such an identity and can be cultivated only by resolutely keeping to Islamic rituals and attending prayers and religious learning circles in mosques." He continues with a warning: "But this identity
is threatened by the *takfiri* forces, supported by the US and Saudi Wahhabism that seek to distort Islam and separate Yemenis from their authentic faithful identity." Perversion is related to infiltration and imitation of
Western practices, including gender mixing in public venues, hairstyles,
codes of dress, and listening to music. Because of these two imminent
dangers (perversion and distortion), Ansar Allah have declared that the
current struggle against imperialism and its regional proxies is broader
than the physical and material conflict on the battlefield (al-Eriani 2021).
For Ansar Allah, it appears to have been important for them to define
the infiltration of both a distorted Islamic doctrine and the infiltration
of Western culture into Yemeni society as a "soft war" (al-Houthi 2021).
Accordingly, the battlefield extends to Yemeni society itself at the level of
faith and, as we shall see, the human soul.

Ansar Allah also issued decrees and legislation aiming to impose restrictions on established public mores according to their interpretation
of Qur'anic teachings. These restrictions attempt to target many aspects
of Yemeni public life and social gatherings, such as enforcing gender segregation in universities, private schools, conferences and training events,
public transportation, parks, restaurants, and cafés (Alaraby 2020). In the
universities, Ansar Allah deploy their agents to police student behavior,
and on occasion, when male and female students are deemed noncom-
pliant with accepted moral demeanor, they are subjected to disciplinary
measures (*Irfaasawtak* 2020). 'Abd al-Malik al-Houthi maintained that
such practices and activities flouting moral decency veer away from an
ideal faithful identity—*al-huwiyya al-imaniyya* (al-Houthi 2019a). More
interesting is his claim that the visibility of these practices in public space
is evidence of an absence of piety—a sign of *fuqdan*, a decaying social
and moral order. As a result, Yemenis need to be protected and immu-
nized—*muhassan* (al-Houthi 2019b). It is for these reasons, in al-Houthi's
interpretation, that the war rages on and their victory against the KSA-US
coalition has not yet been achieved. The seemingly absent public performance of piety makes the strength of the population's piety uncertain,

which in turn renders uncertain their victory on the battlefield. In an endeavor to increase the certainty with which Yemen's future victory and security can be determined, Ansar Allah insists that public moral conduct must be regulated, specifically by ensuring that piety be given absolute material visibility.

Ansar Allah have also assumed the right to surveil one of the most private domains of society—women's bodies. Yemeni society at large still perceives women's daily activities in public as a domain that should not be accessible to an outsider's gaze, including that of state policing. Households are intensely private spaces and are largely considered women's quarters.[17] Ansar Allah's desire to govern so many aspects of Yemeni daily religious life has even expanded to include social niches that have traditionally and Islamically been defined as *hurmat*, a *fiqh*-based concept that grants certain spaces the status of sanctuaries and prohibits public incursion into them (al-Eriani 2021). Ansar Allah formed an all-female armed force, called al-Zaynabiyat,[18] in order to lawfully access these spaces. The Zaynabiyat have been trained to conduct raids into homes and make arrests to suppress women protesters and detractors, also surveilling females in weddings, private gatherings, and workplaces. They especially target female activists or female relatives of male activists, usually those who have been accused of espionage.[19]

Ansar Allah deploy religion through the modern secular state apparatus to determine grounded religious truth in empirical and material evidence (al-Eriani 2021). In doing so, what they achieve is a successful reproduction of the secular epistemic rationality and desire to make subjects' religious sensibility and intents visible and, by implication, calculable

17. Except for some males' quarters where guests are hosted. Those are relatively isolated from women's quarters.

18. Named after Sayyida Zaynab, the daughter of Ali ibn Abi Talib. They take Zaynab as a role model for her chastity, morality, patience, responsibility, and everything she embodied.

19. During Saleh's reign, secret police composed of females were also used but mostly to spy on elite families—and within women's domains—that had direct political connections and mainly to collect political information covertly.

and docile (Mahmood 2009, 853). Secular rationality achieves its objective through the "pervasive techniques of surveillance and the administrative regulations . . . [that flow] from an external order with a view to dictating the very processes of the body's activities." The techniques applied on the self by the self no longer seek the "renunciation of the material world" but become a performance that satisfies the modern secular state's demands for material certainty (Hallaq 2013, 75).

To the suspicious and fearful Ansar Allah, acquiring certainty about a future military victory is to proclaim themselves the primary authority in protecting and restoring an authentic faithful identity. When public order is at stake, the state's suspicious gaze is directed toward the invisible interiority of its subjects, demanding the visibility of an otherwise invisible interiority so as to deem it known and definite. However, as we shall see, their claims in this regard are challenged as they operate through and with the invasive desires of the modern secular state. In the following section, I sketch a different epistemic rationality that Yaman Jadid invokes in addressing the multiplicity of human experiences that oscillate the soul between inwardness and outwardness, intentions and desires. This oscillation draws our attention to how Yaman Jadid theorizes an epistemic logic of hope and fear aimed at bringing the soul (and, by extension, the community) into a state of equilibrium through which order and security can be restored.

## Uncertainty: Toward Virtuous (In)Security

This section delves into the epistemology of fear and hope embedded in Islamic tradition deployed by the faithful to fathom calamity, insecurity, and crises and that underpins Yaman Jadid's community actions. In particular, it examines this group's enduring reflections on the multiple knowledges and temporal subjectivities they inhabit, along with the uncertainties these entail. Although Yaman Jadid does not iterate its actions in explicitly political terms, they nevertheless indirectly speak to the political as their work toils through the wreckage it has unleashed on both the soul and the community. Cultivating fear and hope as a means to cure and refashion the soul is upheld, in their work, as a precondition for securing a peaceful and healthy community of the faithful.

This epistemology takes its cue from the practical philosophy of Abu Hamid al-Ghazali (d. 505 AH/1111 CE). In *Kitab al-Khawf wa-l-Raja'* (The Book of Fear and Hope), al-Ghazali focuses on hope and fear as techniques of self-discipline—*riada*—to secure *najat* (salvation). One of the key ideas that informs al-Ghazali's techniques of the self is a rejection of linear, progressive, time. To him, everything rests not on the law of nature as a guiding continuum but on an inexhaustible divine sovereignty and grace that renders anything possible and contingent (Moosa 2005, 31). Accordingly, one can be certain about neither the present nor the future, this life or the next. The beginning of time is when God created the universe, and then there is the end of time, or the day of judgment when deeds, virtues, and vices bear witness for or against the faithful. Between the beginning and end of time there is the discursive tradition and temporality. Within this temporality, the faithful must, in an unwithering fashion, acknowledge the multiple human conditions and desires that vacillate the soul in different directions, rendering the future and life in the hereafter fraught with open-ended possibility. Al-Ghazali elaborates on this temporal openness by drawing on the following hadith:

> Let a man do the works of the People of the Garden for fifty years, so that only a span remains between him and the Garden (and, in a variant, only the time between two milkings of a she-camel), then the Book will predestinate and seal him with the work of the People of the Fire. And the interval between two milkings of a she-camel does not allow the possibility of an action with the members. It is no more than the duration of a fleeting impulse which penetrates the heart at death and decrees the Seal of evil, and how can one be secure from that? (al-Ghazali 1965, 48)

Al-Ghazali here highlights the mystery of predestination (seal) that resides beyond the subject's knowledge, leaving the possibility of facing a sudden reversal of the heart impressing on a man's life and the seal of evil wide open. For al-Ghazali, teleological certainty prompts the faithful to cultivate self-elation, and eventually a fantasized sense of *amn* (security) that amounts to arrogance (al-Ghazali 2005, 1498). By contrast, a notion of the soul as something caught in the *uncertain* temporal flow of the events of everyday existence and the cosmic meaning one ascribes to them offers the therapeutic means for the soul and the community to restore a state of equilibrium (Moosa 2005, 72). Fear and hope allow the faithful to negotiate, to grapple and struggle with multiple knowledges and the divergent and overlapping subjectivities they inhabit to secure *najat* (29).

In his observations of the violence that ravaged seventeenth-century Europe, Hobbes directed his gaze outward in search of a materialist solution for achieving social order within a modern notion of time. By contrast, for al-Ghazali social order, or equilibrium, is an ongoing and open-ended endeavor that starts from within—through curing the soul (*'ilaj al-ruh*). For him, metaphysical and material worlds cannot be separated when thinking about a healthy polity, for the governance of the *polis* and the governance of the self exist in a dialogical relation. Indeed, when al-Ghazali discussed politics, he utilized the same metaphors as when he discussed the ethics of the self (Moosa 2005, 214–15). Hobbesian notions of security, by contrast, take the promotion of fear of the "war of all against all" as a pretext to justify subjects' submission to the terror of the state as its starting point. Al-Ghazali, by contrast, critiqued a politics of fear as promulgated by religious authorities that employ an excess of fear that may throw the soul into despair rather than bringing it back into balance. Using the metaphor of a physician, al-Ghazali recommends the deployment of a therapy of fear *and* hope that, when performed skilfully without excesses, can restore the soul's healthy state (2005, 1498).

Indeed, al-Ghazali did promote fear but of a different and higher form: fear of God based on knowledge of God as an articulation of ethical truth. He espoused fear defined as *recognizing the limit of one's knowledge of God's will* (1504). Such aptitudes for fear and hope are repeatedly observed in Yaman Jadid posts that seek to encourage self-cultivation (or reform) among their followers, volunteers, and contributors to the extent that ethical acts become habitual (cf. Asad 1993; Hirschkind 2006; Mahmood 2005). Repetitive acts of self-cultivation are juxtaposed with, and shaped by, an awareness of the multiple and contradictory desires and moral frameworks that inevitably mediate Muslims' lives (Schielke 2010; Laidlaw 2014;

Lempert 2013).[20] Consider the following post on Yaman Jadid: "God's grace brings upon us discipline when we worship God for the sake of worldly desires. God will deprive you of the world until sincerity (*ikhlas*) returns to your heart and you acquire the habit of worshiping him, the most Merciful. It is only then that he will give from his inexhaustible bounties" (Yaman Jadid, November 24, 2019). The post seeks not only to employ a therapy of fear of God's discipline when sincere intent is absent, but also instills hope for the bounties granted by him when sincerity returns to the heart. The post is also a reflection on the heterogenous temporalities and experiences that induce different motivations, desires, and intentions. For al-Ghazali, to fear in the service of a higher state of piety is to ensure "sincerity, which is the tearing of one away, outwardly and inwardly, from what is other than God" (al-Ghazali 2005, 32). This quote may be read as a call to persistently discipline the soul by reflecting on what William Connolly calls different tiers of temporality and their disparate force fields (2011, 9) that pull and push the soul in opposite directions, which makes the unfolding possibility of being swayed from the virtuous path too likely. These different tiers of temporality and forces can be recognized only through incessant self-reflection in the hope that the potentiality of the soul is realized through the tradition (Asad 2018).

Mohammad, the founder of Yaman Jadid, openly acknowledges that his conscience can be pulled and pushed in opposite directions. Echoing al-Ghazali, he finds the solution to this conundrum, as one who "traverses the multiplicity of human life" (1965, xviii), is to make claims and cultivate perseverance through Islamic teachings. In my exchanges with Mohammad via the online chat program Messenger, he pointed out that "perseverance in acts of beneficence draws one closer to God the Merciful. Being close is to be favored by God in that he will induce in me an ongoing desire for acts of beneficence and therefore to continue to be favored by God."[21] Such

20. While I agree with these anthropological insights that draw attention to the multiplicity of moral forces and codes that constitute the human condition, I am skeptical about their focus on agency seen as a creative resistance to "religion" (cf. Fadil and Fernando 2015).

21. Private conversation via Facebook Messenger, Jan. 15, 2021.

a realization necessarily assumes the centrality of self-cultivation based on training and learning to orient the self toward God. According to al-Ghazali, "Such expectation as his [the faithful] is hope in its essence, commendable in itself, and giving him an incentive for perseverance and endurance, in accordance with the means of faith, in perfecting the means of pardon until death" (1965, 4). For al-Ghazali, hope is a companion to fear, not its antithesis.

Beneficent acts performed by Yaman Jadid encourage others to habitually live out this epistemic rationale, not in solitude but through an active engagement with the insecurities of others that the war and corrupt politics have brought to the community at large. Mohammad observed, "The war has left the community severely vulnerable, and we try to identify and respond to new needs as they emerge every day." He continues, "We know that sincere acts of beneficence—*ihsan*—which seek the pleasure of God have the power of creating positive effects and changes in the world. Once we tend to those positive changes, we can cultivate a taste for closeness to God, and can potentially sustain an appetite for virtuous deeds (*a'mal saliha*)."[22] Mohammad's sense of hope is one that is therapeutic to the soul and community, which according to al-Ghazali must be "tasted" to be known. This truth is not accessible in words or thoughts but "expressible only in action" and specifically an action informed by knowledge of God (Ormsby 2007, 13). Mohammad and his team aspire to cultivate a unique form of selfhood that is oriented toward God and his creatures (al-Ghazali 2005; Asad 2018) and that can be attained only through abiding reflection on and resistance to the opposing forces that generate the possibility of alienation between community members.

Most of Yaman Jadid's posts start by sharing the cheerful news of the team's recent accomplishments in helping individuals who have been most afflicted by the war, highlighting the joy elicited among orphans, the homeless, and the destitute. The tone always abruptly shifts to a plea in the second part of the post:

> Brothers and sisters, however, we are still far from helping everyone in desperate need of assistance. Winter is still here and there are hundreds

22. Private conversation with Mohammad via Facebook Messenger.

who suffer from destitution. There are also the homeless, orphans, and families that refrain from asking for charity. Many of them live in tents, shops, under stairs or in the ruins of Sanaa's suburbs. They have nothing to protect themselves from the stings of cold. I beg of you to check in on your neighbors who suffer silently. Sift through your neighborhood and find those displaced, the needy, the orphans, the homeless in your neighborhood. Organized initiatives like Yaman Jadid have their own limits. We cannot reach those who suffer quietly because they refrain from asking. Remember that helping the needy averts calamity and illnesses. (Yaman Jadid, March 4, 2021)

This post establishes to the group's followers that past acts of beneficence should not induce a fantasized sense of self-elation as if one has achieved a desired end goal and can thus rest on their laurels. Rather, these posts are to be read as calls to exercise doubt pertaining to the sufficiency of one's virtuous deeds. The group's posts incite the *habitual pursuit of perseverance* in acts of beneficence. I asked Mohammad how he and his team managed to maintain their efforts over the years. As a human being, in Mohammad's rendition, the vitality of one's interests in certain practices inevitably wanes and perhaps disappears over time. He recognizes the multiplicity of human temporal experiences, some of which can become sidelined or displaced altogether and acknowledges a struggle to maintain momentum. Mohammad asserts, "But in continuing to do what we do, we are not considering our efforts as doing the community a favor. Personally, I'm always in desperate need to put my wealth and labor at the service of the afflicted on a daily basis. By helping others, I'm actually helping myself." When I asked him why he is in desperate need to do this, he asserted, "We try to help the afflicted members of our community in the hope that God will not only avert catastrophe, but also *suʿ al-khatima*, the seal of evil (hell)."[23] Mohammad refers indirectly to the indefinite possibilities that might bring about the seal of evil that, to draw on al-Ghazali, no matter how long one is dedicated to rectitude, the possibility of death descending at a time when one is perusing only worldly affairs and intentions could

23. Private conversation.

predestine one to hell. Mohammad also approximates the worldly insecurities of the indigents and his duties to attend to them with his own sense of pious (in)security that springs from life's contingencies. The purpose is to elicit a habitual state of self-cultivation. For *al-khatima*, the faithful's end, whether in paradise or in hell, is not predestined by God's decree but perceived as "potentialities in the dialectics of human intentional action and God's will" (Nevola 2018, 306). It is only through the habitual cultivation of perseverance that the possibility of *su' al-khatima* is averted.

The repetitive practices that Mohammad and his posts on Yaman Jadid evoke seek to measure the extent to which they have taken root as dispositions (cf. Mahmood 2005, 164). The constant reminders that characterize the posts locate every act of beneficence in the realm of the *uncertain*. It is this ever-present indefinite uncertainty that spurs the group on in the disciplining of their desires and the cultivation of perseverance. The possibility of *su' al-khatima* is one they cannot evade unless they cultivate an aptitude for perseverance since, according to Mohammad, *su' al-khatima* is attributed to a lack of a sustained perseverance. Such uncertainty brings forth "eschatological themes of death, judgment, and suffering that had always been central to shaping the ethical sensibilities or virtues that underlay correct conduct—such as . . . fear of God" (Hirschkind 2006, 37). The frequent emphasis on uncertainty in shaping one's *khatima*, despite one's past deeds, ascribes ongoing self-cultivation as a necessity to secure *najat*. Crucially, acknowledging the ultimate unknowability of one's moment of death means that every deed can potentially be the final one, which serves as a caution and a reminder of human vulnerability.

Furthermore, and as Mohammad asserted above, ethical self-cultivation and perseverance in beneficent deeds—sharing one's wealth with persons living in destitution—is pivotal for anyone hoping for closeness to God (al-Ghazali 1965, 10).[24] As Paul Dresch observes, Muslims

---

24. In Islamic tradition, there are two forms of alms giving. *Zakat* is one of the five pillars of Islam and is an obligatory annual payment. *Sadaqa* is a voluntary gesture made with the intention of helping others as an act of beneficence and is encouraged throughout the year. Yaman Jadid and similar groups receive donations in these two forms.

believe that "wealth in goods and children, as it were, comes vertically from God . . . not from horizontal transactions and interdependence among persons" (Dresch 1998, 1:114). This vertical notion of wealth also connotes *fitna*, a test of one's perseverance, because wealth is seductive and may come to be worshiped as if a god, giving an illusory sense of certainty and security that may impair the soul from sustained acts of Islamic virtue (Noor 2012). Subsequently, perseverance wanes as affairs of material wealth preoccupy and entrap the soul in unbalanced worldly desires at the expense of what is needed in the beyond, which might lead to a seal of evil. As al-Ghazali asserts, drawing on the Qur'an, giving with sincerity to others part of what God has given to you, either in secret or openly, articulates "hope in a merchandize that will not pass away" (1965, 8). Yaman Jadid frequently posts reminders on its page that alms giving is precisely a "hope in a merchandize that will not pass away" (December 4, 2018) and has the power to avert *su' al-khatima*. The group implicitly acknowledges the economic reality of war where many have lost their income and live off savings and in which providing for their children is a priority that may instigate fear of destitution and thus induce subjective desires to withhold *sadaqa*. The posts remind us that *sadaqa* should not elicit a fear of exhausting one's own limited wealth or capacity to provide for one's own family. God adores the earnest benevolent and will bless them from his inexhaustible bounty (Yaman Jadid, March 10, 2019).

When the war erupted in 2015, it was taken by many as a divine sign—a calamity that had befallen upon Yemenis as a result of being seduced by worldly individualistic and selfish desires at the expense of the matters of the soul. Such an understanding alluded to an absence of mercy in the heart and soul that can be restored through the therapy of fear. Indeed, when I converse with family and friends in Yemen, they often attribute the ruthlessness that they experience in their everyday lives by lamenting *"ma 'ad fish fi qlub an-nas rahma, ma 'ad fish khawf men Allah"* (mercy and compassion ceased to exist in people's hearts, and so did fear of God). To them, to be compassionate and merciful, one must be fearful of God. Posts on Yaman Jadid frequently display the suffering and pain of the afflicted in a spectacular fashion so as to "enliven the audience's sense of pious fear" (cf. Hirschkind 2006, 37). Posts seek to "enliven" in a number of ways. One post asserts, "Remember, God will hold us accountable for those who died because they could not afford to pay for food, medications, or blankets that could protect them from the sharp stings of winter" (October 17, 2018). Another post reads, "There is a virus called hunger that has been killing hundreds of Yemeni children for too long, but no one talks about it because it doesn't kill the rich. Helping the starved through *zakat* and *sadaqa* will grant us God's mercy. Only God has the power to dislodge calamity and pandemics. Have mercy on one another, so God may grace us with his Mercy (*tarahamu yarhamakum Allah*)" (April 2, 2020). The group attributes the everyday insecurities endured by the destitute to those people who hold a fantasized confidence that God's bounty (wealth, health, and safety) is always secured and sustained, and therefore withhold *sadaqa*.

To highlight accountability before God for what God has given is also to acknowledge, as Yemenis do, that wealth and safety are from God alone. If they are not used wisely and virtuously, there is always the possibility of becoming alienated from God with the result that he can reverse individuals' circumstances from one of wealth to destitution. Thus, a will to sustain some sort of security hinges on one's own capacity to cultivate the will to constantly tend to the insecurities and needs of others. Any sense of security that operates on a different logic is deceptive. The illustration of pain and suffering of fellow Muslims incessantly captured through images and posts on Yaman Jadid is meant to put demands on the contributors and followers to recognize how the soul oscillates between multiple desires and subjectivities, that is, between *a'mal saliha* (virtuous deeds) and *maslaha* (worldly bargain). In several posts, images are used to display daily wage laborers toiling through current economic troubles: "Day laborers are deserving of your compassion. Their labor is their only capital through which they preserve dignity. They work hard, they cannot afford to get sick because they must provide for their children. Support them in a dignified way. Don't bargain or display dexterity with them. Give them more than their wage. Pay them more than the market price and make it a merchandize with God. Cooperate in righteousness and piety. Let us have mercy on one other. May the Merciful have mercy on us all" (December 4, 2018).

Ethical subjectivity garnered by Yaman Jadid seeks to construct a unique subjective self-comprehension liberated from the shackles of ego-istic individualism that defines both the possibilities and the limitations to ethical self-realization. Living an individualistic existence assumes the other—in this case the afflicted, who require *sadaqa*—as being either un-deserving or a source of material impoverishment and future insolvency. To give individualism the upper hand, the unreflexive sense of self—*al-nafs al-ammara bi-l-su'* (or ego)—permits the self-ego to become sovereign over human conduct, commanding selfish acts, withholding support, and viewing the other merely as a hurdle toward securing one's own worldly interests. On the other hand, a reflexive self gazes inward to identify the limitation of such a worldly perspective and views the other as a threat to the soul's ethical integrity. The reflexive self that agitates itself to restore balance to the soul, and cultivate ethical purification, sees in the suffering of the other an ethical truth—the possibility of arriving at true knowledge (*ma'rifa*) of God's nature or attributes through spiritual combat toward self-authentication embodying God's attributes, a state wherein the soul cultivates a higher level of spiritual development (al-Ghazali 1965, 37). In other words, dispelling the ego-self, transcending earthly desires and re-placing them with virtuous habits attributed to God (such as mercy, grace, compassion, generosity, aid, and protection), signals the embodiment of an ethical truth through which the soul is cured and a healthy community secured.

Yaman Jadid's posts also point to what alms giving and broader acts of beneficence mean in the Islamic tradition and how it informs a complex understanding of (in)security (emotional and physical). A recent post, for instance, reiterates the importance of minding and restoring the dignity of those individuals who are in need but refrain from asking by helping them secretly (January 24, 2021). Begging and asking for help is seen by many in Yemen as *'ayb*, an undignified and dishonoring act, especially if they can use their labor to secure daily sustenance.[25] Posts documenting

---

25. *'Ayb* has an Islamic connotation pertaining to a lack of *t'affuf* (temperance). Re-straining oneself from begging is a virtuous quality that the Prophet Mohammad encour-aged in his followers to maintain dignity and honor.

the beneficent acts of the Yaman Jadid group always hide or alter the faces of the beneficiaries in their photos so that their identity is protected and dignity preserved. The posts remind us that many of the afflicted are new to their conditions, having lost their livelihoods solely because of the war, and are now struggling to make ends meet.

Donor names on Yaman Jadid are also never revealed. This omission is not only an act of dignified care but also alludes to an ethic of *ihsan* that is reflexive and seeks to secure an equal relationship between the financially abled self and the other living in destitution. It thereby lays bare a unique relationship between the virtuous self and the other that is not reduced to *alterity*. The self in this equation is *indifferent* and *oblivious* to the other's economic difference. On the surface, encounters with otherness might appear to align with Emmanuel Levinas's ethics, whose condition is the recognition of the face[26] of the different/other. However, as Atchrati (2006) avers, the face of the other is inadequate to fathoming ethics in Islam in which it is the face of Allah that imbues every act of beneficence. In Islamic tradition, Atchrati states: "A consciousness that has access to itself through the concept of the other impinges on the purity of faith, the will to submission and the fitness of mind that is called to bear witness to Allah. . . . Alterity is theologically incommensurate with the systemic inclusiveness and plenitude of *wajh Allah* [the face of Allah] which spans at all states of life: 'and wherever you turn your face . . .' Yet this originary plenitude in which the Islamic ethics finds its source is not an outward directionality, but an inward intentionality" (2006, 501). Approximating others' (in)securities to one's own is therefore to be understood as both a quest for self-authentication and a quest to arrive at true knowledge—gnosis of God's attributes. It is this ethical truth pursued through a therapy of fear and hope that may allow the self to perform *true* acts of beneficence. It is this truth that will ultimately bring the soul closer to God, bring forth God's pleasure and his enduring blessings, and bring both the soul and the community into a state of equilibrium, heralding an ethical order.

---

26. Levinas uses the face to refer to the living presence of another person, commanding ethical and responsible sociality.

## Against the Tyranny of Certainty

While modernist theories of security travel across time and space, in most instances the analyst never leaves home, at least not epistemologically. Theories may become universal tools in the service of comparative politics while, in the process, undermining differences that are concealed within hegemonic traveling signifiers, such as that of (in)security. This chapter has sought to demonstrate how theory and analysis of (in)security as governed by secular time have resolutely informed KSA and US foreign policies in Yemen, as well as that of Ansar Allah and the "legitimate" government. They have justified violent interventions and atrocities in the name of ascribing Yemen a future that is known and certain. This dominant mode of theorization persistently blinds scholars to the multiplicity of human conditions and different temporalities that people in Yemen experience and navigate in their attempt to retain a semblance of order in their lives. This chapter has explored a fundamentally different epistemic terrain: the temporal subjectivities of (in)security that analysts in "security studies" rarely have access to because of their refusal to leave their epistemic home and dwell on the epistemic worlds of others, as well as their investment in a totalizing notion of security vested in the sovereignty of the modern secular state and its conception of time.

The alternative terrain I have outlined is one that vests sovereignty not in the political entity that is the state, but in the interdependent community of the faithful. Beneficent groups such as Yaman Jadid, along with other such initiatives currently working throughout the country, should be understood as an inhabitation of the ethical practices that sustain them, and specifically their calls for self-cultivation and reform in the face of a future that is not and cannot be accessible, known, or certain. Their projects endeavor to respond to the severe absence of material security and stability in Yemen—*amn wa istiqrar*—by pursuing an ethical notion of security that lends a meaningful way of being in the *uncertain* realm of the divine—in *Allah al-Hafiz*. These embodied practices, while attendant to the immediate insecurities of the afflicted, are also constituted in ethical terms through the very presence of vulnerabilities, future insecurities, and uncertainties in this life and the hereafter. Vulnerability here pertains to the sheer instability of human desires, intentions, and motivations that are often pushed and pulled in different and opposing directions, imbuing a change of heart, threatening a potential bad end, and rendering the beneficence of one's actions always *uncertain*. Embracing uncertainty as a means to secure unwithering self-cultivation stands in stark opposition with notions of *amn wa istiqrar* peddled by political analysts, policy makers, and politicians, who see uncertainty as little more than a threat to security. An ethos of self-cultivation among the members of Yaman Jadid, by contrast, unveils the manner in which ethical acts oriented toward one's own *uncertain* end simultaneously attend to the broader community's insecurities and needs. In this terrain, the spiritual interdependence of the self and the community of the faithful is upheld as a prerequisite for the fashioning of a unique understanding of divine security, extended into an uncertain future.

## References

Abourahme, Nasser. 2016. "The Productive Ambivalences of Post-revolutionary Time: Discourse, Aesthetics, and the Political Subject of the Palestinian Present." In *Time, Temporality and Violence in International Relations*, edited by Anna M. Agathangelou and Kyle D. Killian, 129–56. New York: Routledge.

Acharya, Amitav. 2014. *Rethinking Power, Institutions and Ideas in World Politics: Whose IR?* New York: Routledge.

Agathangelou, Anna M., and Kyle D. Killian, eds. 2016. *Time, Temporality and Violence in International Relations: (De)fatalizing the Present, Forging Radical Alternatives*. New York: Routledge.

Agrama, Hussein A. 2012. *Questioning Secularism: Islam, Sovereignty, and the Rule of Law in Modern Egypt*. Chicago: Univ. of Chicago Press.

Ahmad, Irfan. 2021. "The Time of Epistemic Domination." *ReOrient* 7, no. 1: 72–95.

Alaraby. 2020. "Mamnuʿat al-Huthiyyin: Hurras al-Fadila." August 29, 2020. https://www.alaraby.co.uk/ممنوعات-الحوثيين-22%حراس-فضيلة-يخنقون22%-سكان-صنعاء.

Asad, Talal. 1993. *Genealogy of Religion: Discipline and Reasons of Power in Christianity and Islam*. Baltimore: Johns Hopkins Univ. Press.

———. 2003. *Formations of the Secular: Christianity, Islam, Modernity*. Stanford, CA: Stanford Univ. Press.

———. 2018. *Secular Translations: Nation-State, Modern Self, and Calculative Reason*. New York: Columbia Univ. Press.

Atchrati, Ahmad. 2006. "Deconstruction, Ethics and Islam." *Arabica* 53, no. 4: 472–510.

Atia, Mona. 2013. *Building a House in Heaven: Pious Neoliberalism and Islamic Charity in Egypt*. Minneapolis: Univ. of Minnesota Press.

Bain, William. 2017. "International Anarchy and Political Theology: Rethinking the Legacy of Thomas Hobbes." *Journal of International Relations and Development* 22, no. 2: 278–99.

Blumi, Isa. 2019. "Speaking above Yemen: A Reading Beyond the Tyranny of Experts." *Global Intellectual History* 6, no. 6: 990–1014.

Buzan, Barry. 2017. "Universal Sovereignty." In *The Globalization of International Society*, edited by Tim Dunne and Christian Reus-Smit, 227–47. Oxford: Oxford Univ. Press.

Buzan, Barry, Wæver Ole, and Jaap de Wilde. 1998. *Security: A New Framework for Analysis*. Boulder, CO: Lynne Rienner.

Connolly, William E. 2011. *A World of Becoming*. Durham: Duke Univ. Press.

Dresch, Paul. 1998. "Mutual Deception: Totality, Exchange, and Islam in the Middle East." In *Marcel Mauss: A Centenary Tribute*, edited by Wendy James and Nick J. Allen, 1:111–33. New York: Berghahn Books.

Al-Eriani, Kamilia. 2016. "The Apprehensive Republic: De-democratising the 2011 Yemeni Uprising." PhD diss., Univ. of Melbourne.

———. 2020. "Mourning the Death of a State to Enliven It: Notes on the 'Weak' Yemeni State." *International Journal of Cultural Studies* 23, no. 2: 227–44.

———. 2021. "The (In)visibility of Piety: Reorienting Piety in North Yemen." *Jadaliyya*, May 11, 2021. https://www.jadaliyya.com/Details/42714/The-Ḥouthīs-and-the-InVisibility-of-Piety-Reorienting-Piety-in-North-Yemen.

———. 2023. "Claiming Democratic Bodies, Ethics, and Equality." *Comparative Studies of South Asia, Africa and The Middle East* 43, no. 1: 94–109.

Fadil, Nadia, and Mayanthi L. Fernando. 2015. "Rediscovering the 'Everyday' Muslim: Notes on an Anthropological Divide." *HAU: Journal of Ethnographic Theory* 5, no. 2: 59–88.

Al-Ghazali, Abu Hamid. 1965. *Book of Fear and Hope*. Translated by William McKane. Leiden: Brill.

———. 2005. *Fi al-Khawf wa-l-Raja'*. Beirut: Dar Ibn Hazm.

Haanstad, Eric J. 2009. "Violence and Temporal Subjectivity." *Anthropology and Humanism* 34, no. 1: 71–82.

Hallaq, Wael B. 2009. *Shari'a: Theory, Practice, and Transformations.* Cambridge: Cambridge Univ. Press.

———. 2013. *The Impossible State: Islam, Politics, and Modernity's Moral Predicament.* New York: Columbia Univ. Press.

Halliday, Fred. 1997. "The Formation of Yemeni Nationalism: Initial Reflections." In *Rethinking Nationalism in the Arab Middle East,* edited by James Jankowski and Israel Gershoni, 26–41. New York: Columbia Univ. Press.

Haykel, Bernard. 1993. "Al-Shawkani and the Jurisprudential Unity of Yemen." *Revue des Monde Musulmans et de la Méditerranée* 67: 53–65.

———. 2003. *Revival and Reform in Islam: The Legacy of Muhammad al-Shawkani.* Cambridge: Cambridge Univ. Press.

Hirschkind, Charles. 2006. *The Ethical Soundscape: Cassette Sermons and Islamic Counterpublics.* New York: Columbia Univ. Press.

Hobbes, Thomas. 1971 [1651]. *Leviathan.* London: Penguin Classics.

Holbraad, Martin, and Morten Axel Pedersen, eds. 2013. *Times of Security: Ethnographies of Fear, Protest and the Future.* Oxon: Routledge.

Hom, Andrew, Christopher Mcintosh, Alasdair Mackay, and Liam Stockdale. 2016. *Time, Temporality and Global Politics.* Edinburgh: Edinburgh Univ. Press.

Al-Houthi, 'Abd al-Malik. 2019a. "Muhadarat al-Sayyid 'Abd al-Malik Badr al-Din al-Huthi bi-'unwān 'al-Iman Yaman.'" *Thagafaqurania.* http://www.thagafaqurania.com/archives/36105.

———. 2019b. "Nas Kalimat Qa'id al-Thawra khilal Tadshin Barnamaj al-Huwiyya al-Imaniyya al-Yamaniyya bi-l-Jami' al-Kabir bi-Sana'a'." *Saba Net,* Dec. 19, 2019. https://www.saba.ye/ar/news3082178.htm.

———. 2019c. "Al-Sayyid al-Qa'id: Al-Tahrif wa al-Inhraf." *Ansarollah,* Mar. 8, 2019. https://www.ansarollah.com/archives/231721. http://www.thagafaqurania.com/archives/36105.

———. 2021. "Nas Kalimat Qa'id al-Thawra." *Itha'at Sana'a'.* http://www.sanaaradio.net/detail.aspx?newsid=33833.

Hutchings, Kimberly. 2007. "Happy Anniversary! Time and Critique in International Relations Theory." *Review of International Studies* 33, no. 1: 71–89.

———. 2008. *Time and World Politics: Thinking the Present.* Manchester: Manchester Univ. Press.

*Irfaasawtak.* 2020. "La-Asas Dini fi Tahrim al-Huthiyin li-l-Ikhtilat." *Irfaasawtak,* Feb. 20, 2020. https://www.irfaasawtak.com/rights-and-liberties/2020/02/20 باحثة-يمنية-لا-أساس-ديني-في-تحريم-الحوثيين-للاختلاط/.

Laidlaw, James. 2014. *The Subject of Virtue: An Anthropology of Ethics and Freedom*. Cambridge: Cambridge Univ. Press.

Lempert, Michael. 2013. "No Ordinary Ethics." *Anthropological Theory* 13, no. 4: 370–93.

Little, Adrian. 2022. *Temporal Politics: Contested Pasts, Uncertain Futures*. Edinburgh: Edinburgh Univ. Press.

Mahmood, Saba. 2005. *Politics of Piety: The Islamic Revival and the Feminist Subject*. Princeton, NJ: Princeton Univ. Press.

———. 2009. "Religious Reason and Secular Affect: An Incommensurable Divide?" *Critical Inquiry* 35, no. 4: 836–62.

Messick, Brinkley. 1992. *The Calligraphic State: Textual Domination and History in a Muslim Society*. Berkeley: Univ. of California Press.

———. 2001. "Indexing the Self: Intent and Expression in Islamic Legal Acts." *Islamic Law and Society* 8, no. 2: 151–78.

———. 2018. *Shariʿa Scripts: A Historical Anthropology*. New York: Columbia Univ. Press.

Moosa, Ebrahim. 2005. *Ghazali and the Poetics of Imagination*. Chapel Hill: Univ. of North Carolina Press.

Moussa, Mohammad. 2012. "A Discourse Analysis of Muhammad al-Ghazali's Thought: Between Tradition and Renewal." PhD diss., Univ. of Exeter.

Nevola, Luca. 2018. "Destiny in Hindsight: Impotentiality and Intentional Action in Contemporary Yemen." *HAU: Journal of Ethnographic Theory* 8, nos. 1–2: 300–313.

Noor, Farish A. 2012. *Islam on the Move: The Tablighi Jamaʿat in Southeast Asia*. Amsterdam: Amsterdam Univ. Press.

Ormsby, Eric. 2007. *Ghazali: The Revival of Islam*. London: Oneworld.

Samimian-Darash, Limor. 2013. "Governing Future Potential Biothreats: Toward an Anthropology of Uncertainty." *Current Anthropology* 54, no. 1: 1–22.

Schielke, Samuli. 2010. "Second Thoughts about the Anthropology of Islam; or, How to Make Sense of Grand Schemes in Everyday Life." *ZMO Working Papers* 2. Berlin: Zentrum Moderner Orient.

Schmitt, Carl. 2007. *Nomos of the Earth: In the International Law of the Jus Publicum Europeaum*. Translated by G. L. Ulmen. New York: Telos.

Stockdale, Liam. 2015. *Taming an Uncertain Future: Temporality, Sovereignty, and the Politics of Anticipatory Governance*. Lanham, MD: Rowman & Littlefield International.

*United Nations News.* 2019. "Humanitarian Crisis in Yemen Remains the Worst in the World, Warns UN." *United Nations News,* Feb. 14, 2019. https://news .un.org/en/story/2019/02/1032811.

———. 2020. "Yemen War Dead at 233,000." *United Nations News,* Dec. 1, 2020. https://news.un.org/en/story/2020/12/1078972.

Willis, John. 2012. *Unmaking North and South: Cartographies of the Yemeni Past, 1857–1934.* New York: Columbia Univ. Press.

# 3

## Class

*Not in Agrarian Yemen?*

Martha Mundy

for 'Abdo
'Abdo 'Ali 'Othman, d. December 21, 2020

This short chapter grows out of my presentation at Exeter University, titled "Missing Words: Agrarian Change and Class Formation." The two
themes, and the words "land" and "household," were present in Arabic,
French, and English writing of the 1970s and into the mid-1980s. Their
subsequent rarity prompted me to pose questions concerning change in
the production of sociological knowledge about Yemen over the years.
Why did such problematics, central to sociologies of the Global South,
disappear in Yemen?[1] In this chapter, I sketch an answer that jolts imperfectly between conceptual, institutional, and sociopolitical history. After
a note situating my own research in rural Yemen, it unfolds through a
short sketch of the development of Yemen's research capacity in the 1970s,
analysis of the fledgling research on agrarian relations by both foreign
and Yemeni scholars in the 1970s and early 1980s, the politics of the basic
terms for agrarian sociology in the case of Yemen, the growth in capacity
for Yemeni university research in the 1980s and early 1990s in the context
of a deepening security state, research in the shadow of neoliberalism and

---

1. There are three major English-language journals devoted to work on such topics:
*Agrarian South*, the *Journal of Peasant Studies*, and the *Journal of Agrarian Change*. The
issues have been central to political economy since the time of Lenin.

the international development complex from the 1990s, and, last, contestation of the marginalization of rural life and its sociology in the midst of social uprising and international war since 2011.

## A Personal Note on Research

In the Exeter meeting, I spoke not as an expert in contemporary Yemen but as an academic with an intermittent yet long engagement with the country. I spent four years in the Yemen Arab Republic (YAR) as a visitor and then a research student in the 1970s (1971, 1972, 1973–77, 1979–80),[2] and in the 1980s returned regularly from Jordan where I taught at Yarmouk University. In 1994, Ra'ufa Hasan invited me to participate in a meeting in Sanaa on land registration. What I learned then in the run-up to the attack on the South directed by President 'Ali 'Abdullah Saleh led me not to return. It was an invitation of 'Abdo 'Ali 'Othman in 2008 that brought me back to attend the first conference of Yemeni sociologists held at Sanaa University.[3] The enthusiasm of the female students of sociology was palpable, and so in 2011 and 2012 I explored whether I could undertake research on the agrarian changes brought about by the introduction of engineered structures, with backing from the World Bank, Kuwait Fund, the European Union, and other agencies in major wadis of Tihama. For those readers not familiar with Yemen, the Tihama denotes the coastal plain on the Red Sea, the major zone of agricultural production in the country. During the winter of 1973–74, with Huriya al-Mu'ayyid, I had participated in field surveys in Wadi Mawr,[4] and in 1979–80, on the basis of research with

2. Mundy 1995 is based on my doctoral work (1973–82). Unfortunately, I do not know the South: the only time I was in Aden was a few days in 1971. My observations here concern the North of the country, the former Yemen Arab Republic.

3. The first and, so far as I know, the only such conference was made possible by both the president of Sanaa University, Khalid Tamim, and the minister of the interior, Rashad al-'Alimi (discussed later), being sociologists. A summary of the conference is available at https://yemen-nic.info/conferences/activ_details.php?ID=16244. As I was not asked to give a paper, I paid my flight from Beirut but enjoyed the university's hospitality while at the conference.

4. Huriya 'Abbas al-Mu'ayyid was a friend and fighter for women. She was a founder of literacy classes for women in Sanaa and of the Women's Union of the YAR. She is honored

agricultural extension officers from the Tihama Development Authority, I wrote a report on Wadi Rimaʿ (Mundy 1980). This report complemented earlier work on Rimaʿ that had argued against the introduction of engineered structures for reasons of ecology and social equity (Makin 1977; Pratt 1977; Williams 1977).

Field research in 2011 proved impossible given the securitization of access by nonnationals to the countryside, and so, together with agronomist colleagues, I wrote two survey papers on agrarian change since the 1970s (Mundy, al-Hakimi, and Pelat 2014; Mundy and Pelat 2015). When reviewing academic writing on Yemen after 1990 for those papers, I found fundamental terms of social analysis—land and household, agrarian change, and class formation—strikingly absent (cf. Ajl 2020).

Thereafter, it proved increasingly difficult to pursue research inside Yemen. The coalition war launched in 2015 required a response from an academic who holds both UK and US passports (Mundy 2015, 2018, 2021). As someone who has lived and worked in *bilad as-sham* since 1982, the war on *bilad al-yaman* revealed once again the force of US-led economic and military imperialism and the domestic contradictions inherent in the social models, visions of Islam, and financial power of the major oil-producing states of the Arabian Peninsula.

**Complex Questions, the Place of Yemen**

The world is one, but from where one looks upon it matters.[5] North Yemen of the 1970s (the Yemen Arab Republic) was a country never colonized, with extant traditions (Shafiʿi and Zaydi) of Islamic scholarship, an agrarian economy of the Global South, and one of two republics, the other the People's Democratic Republic of Yemen (PDRY), in a peninsula of

---

today by an association (Muʾassasat al-Raʾida Huriya ʿAbbas al-Muʾayyid) headed by her daughter, Bushra al-Samawi, Huriya's only child with whom she was pregnant during our joint work in Wadi Mawr. The report on that work was Mitchell, Escher, and Mundy 1978.

5. Yemen could offer "border thinking" to put Latin America to shame, were it not such a theater for international war (1962–68, 1994, 2015–21, 2023–24). On "border thinking," see Delgado and Romero (2000).

1. A participant in the 1973 national-day celebrations in the town of Ibb calling for support for agriculture. "Agricultural development is one of the essential components of a national economy; so let there be manifold increase in production." Credit: M. Mundy.

monarchies. The land of Yemen looks east to South and Southeast Asia, west to East Africa and the Sudan, and north to the Hijaz, Egypt, Greater Syria, and Iraq. From Yemen, one could see the world with intellectual distance and plurality.

In the early 1970s, the Yemen Arab Republic was home to a strikingly rural and agrarian society: 85 percent of the population resided in small villages; the country produced 85 percent of the grain it consumed. Although the proportion of government investment in agriculture was low in the 1970s (8 percent),[6] that proportion was higher than the 2 percent or less allocated in the first decade of the current century. Farmers were keen to have their sector central in state planning (see figure 1). The PDRY

6. Golovkaya (1994, 231) states that under PM Hassan Makki in 1974 the share of agriculture in the state budget was 17 percent.

in South Yemen, with much less agricultural endowment than the YAR, made land reform and crop choice central to its program.[7]

Yemeni thinkers posed fundamental questions: What kind of an agrarian society was Yemen?[8] How could, or should, it be changed for the better? Foreign researchers also asked the first question, the second properly the responsibility of Yemenis, those individuals whose lives were subject to the policies adopted. An answer to such questions requires a vocabulary of analysis ("concepts") and recording of regularities ("facts," statistical and cartographic) beyond individual observation. Two institutions are central in the production of such knowledge: the university and the state statistical services. Reproduction of analysts is the responsibility of the first. The process is slow: a generation to make a scholar and another to build an institution training advanced students. (Universities may include research centers or these may be separate institutions.) State production of statistical knowledge ("facts") has been integral to both sociology and socioeconomic planning, providing essential tools for time sequences tracking change.

Both the states of Yemen established national institutions for social and technical knowledge production in the 1970s. Sanaa and Aden Universities were founded in 1970 after the years of strife in the 1960s. Following the overthrow of the imamate in September 1962, war had followed as the British, Saudis, Jordanians, and Israelis backed the royalists against the republicans, who were supported until late 1967 by the Egyptians. The South fought for independence from the British, achieved in November 1967. In the North, the royalists backed by mercenaries laid siege to Sanaa in November 1967. For seventy days, popular resistance and army units led by younger officers defended the city and preserved the republican form, but the attack ended in a settlement whereby all the other Yemeni "concerned parties," save the family of the imam, entered the political frame (al-Jawi 1975; al-'Uqqab 2011, chap. 5).

7. See Lackner (1985, 170–88). Compare for ethnographic testimony to the impact of such reform and its annulment after 1990 in Seif (2003, 134, 139, 145–52, 154–57).

8. 'Abdullah Ahmad Nu'man completed a doctoral dissertation at Budapest in 1975 titled "Al-Numuw al-Iqtisadi fi al-Yaman wa-bi-Shakl Khass fi al-Qita' al-Zira'i."

The year 1970 was likewise the time when the YAR joined the International Monetary Fund and received the first delegations from the World Bank and the United Nations Development Programme. In the South, the People's Republic of Southern Yemen became, from 1969, the People's Democratic Republic of Yemen. The Yemeni Centre of Studies and Research was established in Sanaa in 1972 and the Yemeni Centre for Cultural Research in Aden in 1974.[9] The Sanaa center offered affiliation to foreign doctoral students and researchers and preceded the founding of foreign research centers, the American Institute of Yemeni Studies in 1978 and the French Center for Yemeni Studies in 1982.[10] The Central Planning Organisation, pivotal in the development of national statistics in the YAR, began work in 1973.[11] The YAR conducted a first population census in 1975 and a first agricultural census in 1979.

The terms and institutions of knowledge production—words and worlds—do not grow spontaneously. Two levels of exchange are critical: Who are the allies or parties in the social and political body with whom researchers can align, and how do national institutions, and the language in which they produce, relate to the same outside?

### Research and Political Economy in the 1970s to Mid-1980s

In both South and North, researchers examined the structure of social differentiation. Most field studies concerned towns. Early and distinguished was Abdullah Bujra's 1971 study of Tarim in the Hadramawt, *The Politics of Stratification: A Study of Political Change in a South Arabian*

9. In 1990, the latter was merged with the former and its budget severely curtailed as lamented to date. See https://www.alomanaa.net/news19080.html and http://old.adengd .net/news/153713/#.XQd1-bxKhm8.

10. During my research in the 1970s, I was affiliated first with the Department of Antiquities and Museums and then the Yemeni Centre of Studies and Research. When contacted, I responded opposing the establishment of the American Institute of Yemeni Studies in 1978. As I saw it, the priority was to strengthen the Yemeni institutions and not to create foreign centers, as I felt that in the long term they were not going to help committed research in Yemen.

11. See the intertwined history of aid and state institutions in Carapico (2007).

*Town*.[12] In 1977, Tomas Gerholm published a study on Manakhah in the North: *Market, Mosque and Mafraj: Social Inequality in a Yemeni Town*.[13] Yemeni writers in the North wrote of status hierarchies as part of a critique of tradition and political society under the imamate—for example, Qa'id al-Sharjabi's 1986 *Al-Shara'ih al-Ijtima'iyya al-Taqlidiyya fi al-Mujtama' al-Yamani*. Some gave a list of status categories with little evidentiary basis or discussion of their relation to class, but later Tha'ira Sha'lan sought to relate the two concepts in her 1993 dissertation "L'interférence entre les concepts de classe et de catégorie sociale dans la société Yéménite." Two subsequent ethnographies also dealt with social inequality, one with its performance by women, again in a town (Zabid), and the other similarly exceptional for field research in Tihama, not the highlands (Meneley 1996; Walters 1987).[14] In the most important agricultural area of Yemen, neither documented rural society.

Among foreign researchers, Richard Tutwiler alone in his 1987 dissertation attempted a unified analysis of class and agrarian change. The results were mixed—strong on depiction of changing economic strategies of small landholders consequent to migrant-labor remittances, but hampered by a simplex three-stage model of economic history in North Yemen—from an egalitarian tribal order prior to the Ottomans, to a tributary mode of production under the imamate, to capitalism under the Republic. Continuity of links to global capitalism, notably through Aden, and the contradictions that generated epochal change are lost in a long work otherwise exceptional in its attention to rural economic transformation. These points are brought home by philosopher and political analyst Abu Bakr al-Saqqaf in *al-Jumhuriyya Bayn al-Saltana wa-l-Qabila fi al-Yaman al-Shamali* (1988 [2020]).[15] Al-Saqqaf stresses the defensive

---

12. Abdullah Bujra was a distinguished Kenyan intellectual, a cofounder of CODESRIA.

13. See the critique of Gerholm's nonconflictual depiction of hierarchy in Seif (2003, 19, 62, 69–73, 331–32).

14. See the critique of the static sociology of Meneley in Seif (2003, 69–70, 72, 90–97, 332).

15. The text, a series of essays, first appeared under the pseudonym of Muhammad 'Abd al-Salam. It has been republished under the author's name as Sanaa, n.p., 2020. The

subjection of the kingdom to both merchant capital in Aden and Saudi hegemony. By contrast, Tutwiler characterizes the kingdom as a tributary economy based on extraction from household subsistence agriculture and stresses integration into capitalism as following the 1962 republican revolution.

The 1970s saw considerable documentation of agrarian practice: anthropologists Daniel Varisco (1982), Geneviève Bédoucha (1987), and Richard Tutwiler with political scientist Sheila Carapico (1981). Numerous geographers published field research in German, the doyen of such work being Horst Kopp (1981).[16] Yet little of the work in German appears to have been integrated by researchers writing in English (the language of international organizations) or Arabic (the language of Yemeni institutions).

The 1970s were likewise years when development agencies, under less constraint to deliver "results" in their projects than in subsequent decades, documented agrarian practice.[17] So, too, there was work on women's roles in agriculture.[18] Foreign researchers were able to access most zones of the country thanks to the open-door policy and rudimentary security state of the YAR in the 1970s.

The 1970s and 1980s witnessed the mass migration of Yemeni rural male labor to form the working class in Saudi Arabia and, to a lesser extent, elsewhere in the Gulf.[19] Together with subsidized wheat imports,

---

pagination is marginally different in the two versions, as are some paragraph breaks. My page references here are to the earlier edition. Both versions are available on the internet. From a very different perspective, the recent work of Blumi (2018) similarly emphasizes the economic autarky of the kingdom. The reading of al-Saqqaf remains the most convincing.

16. See volumes in the series *Jemen-Studien* (published by Reichert, Wiesbaden) the first volume of which appeared in 1982 and continued into the 1990s and the series Erlanger Geographische Arbeiten. There was also valuable field research by Swiss geography research students writing in German (Egli 1978; Escher 1975).

17. See the bibliography in Tutwiler (1990).

18. See the 2013 revision of Adra's 1983 report for the Food and Agricultural Organization giving an overview of research on women's participation in agriculture.

19. The nature and impact of this emigration was the subject of work by Swagman (1988) and al-Qasir (1987).

these processes devalued rural rain-fed grain production and stimulated shifts to the major commercial crop, qat.[20] The open-door policy hastened rapid integration into international commerce; the government, moreover, imposed virtually no control or taxes on the flows of remittances (al-Saqqaf 2020 [1988], 117). Hence, the financial means of the central government remained limited, and self-help local development associations (LDAs) effected much of the rural infrastructural change. Such associations had begun during the war years of the 1960s, but it was from 1973 that a national organization, the Confederation of Yemeni Development Associations, was established. Its elected head was a young military officer, Ibrahim al-Hamdi, who was to seize power as head of the Supreme Military Council in a coup ousting the civilian government of Qadi 'Abd al-Rahman al-Iryani in 1974. Sanaa University sociologists 'Abdo 'Ali 'Othman and Hamud al-'Awdi cooperated in a study on the LDAs for the Central Planning Organisation, an example of coordination between state planning and university researchers ('Othman and 'Awdi 1982). The character of cooperative organization in the PDRY was also a subject examined in Arabic (Nu'man 1987). Foreign researchers also wrote about the LDAs (Carapico 1985).[21]

Kiren Chaudhry has argued that the mass departure of rural farming men deprived Ibrahim al-Hamdi of allies for progressive politics in the countryside and led to the absence of representation of their interests in the construction of the modern state in the Yemen Arab Republic (1997, 127, 135–36). The exclusion did not occur as mechanically as Chaudhry implies. The demonstrator in figure 1 expressed a call that, as we will see,

20. Beyond the work of Tutwiler (1987), see the essay (and review of literature in English) on qat of Elie (2013).

21. Carapico notes: "Agricultural cooperatives, still in their infancy during the first five-year plan, nonetheless represented a possible solution to the dilemma of private sector underinvestment in agriculture. In view of the government's incapacity to tax rural incomes, the mobilization of resources through informal and semiformal channels was impressive. . . . Cooperative investments in roads and utilities facilitated the penetration of capitalism into the periphery and the emergence of a rural and semiurban bourgeoisie" (1985, 228).

political actors took to heart. Yet in the longer term, for a fledgling sociology in the YAR, the mass departure of rural male labor would deprive Yemeni researchers of a vital class alliance for engaged social research.

**The Politics of the Basic Terms for an Agrarian Sociology**

Abu Bakr al-Saqqaf has observed that well before the 1970s, the word "land" was absent from the political vocabulary of the intellectual founders of the Republic, the Free Yemeni Movement (Douglas 1987), notably al-Zubayri (al-Saqqaf 2020 [1988], 65). Nasserite Egypt served as a political model for the army officers of the September 1962 revolution: a one-party secular state hostile to multiparty politics that worked to erase social hierarchies under the banner of social cooperation without mention of class conflict. Yet there was one great absence in the Yemeni officers' borrowing of a Nasserite model for the Republic—a program for amelioration of the conditions of the rural population, agricultural production, and land tenure. Al-Saqqaf explains it in terms of the conjunction of social classes and groups (*tabaqat wa-fi'at*) from which republican leadership was drawn: traders, major landowners, religious leaders, and shaykhs from the northern tribes (*tujjar, iqta', mu'assasat al-qabila*). As noted, the YAR adopted an open-door economic policy in the 1970s, wherein traders had a free hand, landlord and religious leaderships were not delegitimized, and the major shaykhs were repeatedly able—after al-Hamdi's attempt to curtail their political hegemony—to dominate the growing military and security forces and to enjoy independent relations with Saudi Arabia. It is relevant that from 1967 the PDRY took a very different political path, enacting land reform and planning of agricultural production. Landowners and major shaykhs of the YAR could see in the PDRY what they did not want.

North Yemen was not Egypt, where the peasantry faced historical landlordism linked to imperially controlled export markets. In the mountain areas of Yemen, farming households owned most of the land. That said, Tihama and parts of lower Yemen knew (and still know today) true landlordism. As al-Saqqaf notes, aside from leaders of the major landowning families who held political offices in the republican state, the Tihama has had but a token presence in the political order (85). Given the varied components of the political economy of the YAR, and the late and halting development of the state statistical survey—which to date has not included land registration—a coherent analysis of the whole of rural society was not, and is not today, an easy matter. These issues were tackled by 'Abdullah Nu'man in his 1989 study on the 1983 agricultural census.

As al-Saqqaf notes (37–38), in the later writings of al-Zubayri, there is a slippage or equivalence between the word *sha'b* (people) and *qabila* (tribe) when writing of the rural North. The words invoke different worlds, the first a unified people of the Republic and the second the structured and differentiated components of a less unified polity. Historically, in the mountain areas of the North of the country, the term *qabila* denotes the geographically delimited area of a local political unit in which residence, access to landownership, joint responsibility for security (including "protected persons"), and traditions of dispute settlement were proper to the members of the *qabila*. At its most ideological, the term summons a popular conceptual nexus that stresses male agency, genealogy, and egalitarianism and is silent about property. Beyond such local formations is what al-Saqqaf terms the "tribal institution," that is, the integration of leaders with private means of violence and their followers in the military (and then security services) of the state, at the same time as the leaders act as recognized gatekeepers to the areas that they "represent." In the case of the YAR, moreover, over decades their allegiance to the national interest in Yemen has been tempered by the flow of direct payments from Saudi Arabia. For both the first and the second aspects of the *qabila*, knowledge of rural society passes through *ma'rifat al-rijal* (knowledge of men as the agents in history).[22] A sociology of Yemen through the lens of the *qabila* renders difficult the depiction of agrarian structure and its transformation in terms of both "concept" and "fact," obviating the painstaking procedures for rural sociology that start from land, on the one hand, and households, on the other.[23]

---

22. A recent anthropological study with *ma'rifat al-rijal* at the core of the analysis is Brandt (2017).

23. Compare my earlier discussion of these issues in Mundy (1995, 7–9). See also Elie (2003). Brandt (2021) illustrates what a sociology of Yemen in terms of tribe produces.

In monarchies such as the Hashemite Kingdom of Jordan and Saudi Arabia, an ideology of the people as tribes can inform with limited contradiction the structures of self-mobilization and of communication with political authority. Such coherence is evidently more difficult in a republic. Yet it is not only formal republicanism that makes it more difficult in Yemen; it is also the country's internal social complexity and the differentiation of its rural areas. Tihama and large areas of lower Yemen, the most populated areas of the country, are historically zones of peasantries where major traders, landowners, and tax collectors enjoy evident class power. Hence, maintaining an ideology in republican YAR of the people as tribes appears to have required both the integration of northern tribal leadership in the modern repressive agencies of the state and the gradual bolstering of "the tribal institution" by the religious doctrine of a populist, patriarchal stamp.[24] From the earliest days of the Republic, Saudi Arabia was a founder and supporter of proselytizing movements of the Muslim Brotherhood, the fruits of which blossomed from the 1980s, as explained later.

**Speaking of Land**

The presidency of Ibrahim al-Hamdi on the Supreme Military Council (following a military coup on June 13, 1974) marked something of a hiatus in the consolidation of these principles. Al-Hamdi sought to curtail the dominance of major shaykhs in the structures of rule (see Golovkaya 1994, 262–69, 292–98; al-Sayyad 2013, 95; and Nu'man 1989, 202–14). His program entailed support for smaller farmers against the major shaykhs in areas where they were landlords (Golovkaya 1994, 269) and dialogue with the leaders of the left and progressive nationalist parties, which had led the 1967 resistance but had become marginalized in the settlement following

24. See the short overview by Weir (1997). The promotion of such conservative Islam became a mass phenomenon in the 1980s but was present from the earliest days of the Republic. Huriya al-Mu'ayyid recounted how her elder brother was head of the then Saudi-funded association al-Amr bi-l-Ma'ruf wa-l-Nahiy 'an al-Munkar in Sanaa and had offered her a thousand riyals a month (the salary of a government employee at the time) if she would wear the face veil. She did not accept.

the Siege of Sanaa (al-Jawi 1975). These parties developed a common plat-
form in the years following 1973 to form the National Democratic Front in
1976. The Front's policies included land reform through a ceiling on land-
holdings and redistribution to smaller holders and landless cultivators,
and support (including price support for local grain produce) for small
and medium farmers, agricultural cooperatives, animal production, and
fishing communities (Golovkaya 1994, 281). Although al-Hamdi never
granted the Front official recognition, his exchanges with its leaders and
with the PDRY were anathema to Saudi Arabia, its clients, and international backers. Al-Hamdi was assassinated (October 11, 1977) just before a
first trip to Aden. His military deputy Ahmad al-Ghashmi, brother of the
shaykh of Hamdan abutting Sanaa to the northwest, assumed power;[25] al-
Ghashmi was in turn assassinated (June 24, 1978) by a bomb allegedly carried by an envoy from Aden. Immediately following al-Ghashmi's death,
Qadi 'Abd al-Karim al-'Arashi, head of the legislative council (Majlis al-
Sha'b al-Ta'sisi), sought to have civilian rule reestablished, but 'Ali 'Abdullah Saleh, a member of the military council who hailed from a minor tribe
just to the southeast of Sanaa became, with Saudi backing, head of the
Supreme Military Council (July 17, 1978).

Following the killing of al-Hamdi, components of the National Democratic Front took up arms and supported peasant opposition to landlords
and major shaykhs throughout middle Yemen.[26] The early years of Saleh's
rule encountered considerable opposition from army officers,[27] Ba'thists,
and an internally strengthened and restructured National Front (Golovkaya 1994, 313–19).[28] With some support from Libya and the PDRY, the
Front met with sufficient success to prompt Saleh—never an ideologue—
to negotiate with its leaders. In February–March 1979, a military border

---

25. On al-Ghashmi between the National Democratic Front and the major shaykhs,
see Golovkaya (1994, 300–309).

26. On the Jabha Wataniyya Dimukratiyya, see al-Sayyad (2013, 93–100) and https://
ar.wikipedia.org/wiki/%D8%AD%D8%B1%D8%A8_%D8%A7%D9%84%D8%AC%D8%
A8%D9%87%D8%A9.

27. The thirteenth of June *jabha* (Golovkaya 1994, 312–17).

28. See Carapico (1985, 203). See also al-'Ariqi (2020).

conflict between the YAR and the PDRY led to an agreement negotiated by Kuwait. It specified that Saleh should improve relations with the Front. In January 1980, Saleh met with Front leaders who presented conditions before they would lay down arms and participate in future elections. Notable among their demands was the adoption of a program of land reform.

The accommodation of Saleh with the Front and his exchanges with the PDRY alarmed the Saudi regime. Alongside the policy of cutting support to the central government and increasing support for selected northern shaykhs, Saudi Arabia began to escalate its backing of Islamic movements, notably the Muslim Brotherhood. It was the ideological and military support of the "Islamic Front" that finally helped Saleh to defeat the National Democratic Front throughout middle and lower Yemen (Rada' to Rayma, Wusab, Hujariyya, Ba'dan, Damt, al-Bayda) by June 1982.[29] With the Front's defeat, the word "land" vanished once again from the national political vocabulary.

## Knowledge Production in the Yemen Arab Republic, Early 1980s to 1990s

The model for the University of Sanaa was in good part that of Egyptian higher education (al-Saqqaf 2020 [1988], 132). It emphasized the central role of the public university as teaching and technical training in Arabic. Most colleagues in sociology/anthropology at Sanaa University received their doctorates from Egyptian universities, especially 'Ain Shams. Historically, the major school of Egyptian sociology was Durkheimian, and social anthropology was little present outside the University of Alexandria.[30] Unlike the discipline of philosophy, so far as I know, none of those students in sociology in Sanaa had studied in the USSR or Eastern universities. Some were to have doctoral training in the United States, including 'Abdo 'Ali 'Othman, to the memory of whom this chapter is dedicated. That said, the number of staff in the 1970s and early 1980s was small, and

---

29. On this period and the role of the Muslim Brotherhood and Islamic Front, see Golovkaya (1994, 342–47).

30. On sociology, see Roussillon (1999); on anthropology, see Shami (1989).

interaction between those students in sociology, philosophy, and geography was common inside and outside the university.

The intense political debates within Yemen structured the questions motivating Yemeni colleagues and framed the conditions of their work. As noted previously, the Muslim Brotherhood entered an alliance with the Saleh regime in the early 1980s. The movement established hundreds of teaching institutes across the country but did not restrict its ideological investment to them (see Golovkaya 1994, 342–43; al-Saqqaf 2020 [1988], 135, 140).[31] In 1980 a first denunciation of a text of the sociologist Hamud al-'Awdi was made public; it led in January 1985 to a formal *hisba* case (legal claim of apostasy) lodged with the public prosecutor in Sanaa. A court in Sanaa issued a death sentence.[32] This outcome forced al-'Awdi to flee to Aden from where he returned only in the early 1990s after unification of the YAR and PDRY. In philosophy, Abu Bakr al-Saqqaf was repeatedly the target of violence by forces linked to state security; after an engineered traffic accident, Sudanese philosopher 'Abd al-Salam Nur al-Din Hammad left for Aden University. There was even an attempt in 1986 to raise *hisba* claims against the head of Sanaa University, literature professor and poet 'Abd al-'Aziz al-Maqalih, for verses in one of his poems.

The second half of the 1980s saw consolidation of the military-security state of President 'Ali 'Abdullah Saleh, bolstered from 1988 and throughout the 1990s, by revenue from oil and gas production in Yemen. In Yemen, as in Jordan, the ideological fusing of the tribal institution and the security state found expression in sociology. One figure of the General Congress Party (Saleh's party), later appointed minister of education, Fadl Abu Ghanim, wrote two books (1985, 1990) on the tribe-state relationship in the 1980s.[33] Abu Ghanim was a civilian, but an officer from the police, Rashad al-'Alimi in Sanaa, like Ahmad 'Uwaidi al-'Abbadi of the Bedouin

---

31. In an afternoon gathering with university colleagues in late April 1980, 'Abdo 'Ali 'Othman came carrying a revolver, as he too had received threats.

32. Al-'Awdi published an account of the *hisba* trial as *Muttaham bi-l-Kufr Yabhath 'an Mahkama* (1988) and *al-Tuhma wa-l-Difa': Min Mahkamat al-Samt ila Mahkamat al-Ta'rikh* (1989). See the short biography at https://www.khuyut.com/blog/6877.

33. Abu Ghanim served as minister of education from 2001 to 2003.

police in Amman, went on to complete a doctorate in sociology/anthropology writing on customary tribal law. Although al-'Abbadi's doctorate was from Cambridge,[34] and that of al-'Alimi from 'Ain Shams,[35] the latter proved the more gifted, stable, and subsequently successful in politics.[36] Other 'Ain Shams sociologists also belonged to the ruling party: Qa'id al-Sharjabi, who went into local politics, and Khalid 'Abdullah Tamim, a criminologist, who served as head of Sanaa University from 2006 until 2012 when protests forced his resignation. 'Ain Shams was also where two senior women sociologists trained, Wahiba Ghalib al-Faqih in the sociology of education and Nuriya 'Ali Hummad in sociology of the family, gender, and poverty.[37]

The union of the two Yemens in 1990 led to a reopening of political debate; charges against Hamud al-'Awdi were finally formally dropped in

34. Al-'Abbadi's 1982 PhD, examined by P. Dresch and R. B. Serjeant, titled "Bedouin Justice in Jordan (the Customary Legal System of the Tribes and Its Integration into the Framework of State Polity from 1921 Onwards)," is distinguished by an absence of documentation and an ego-centered sociology. Al-'Abbadi went on to publish tomes on the Jordanian tribes in 1984, 1986, 1989; he was lionized in a study by a student of P. Dresch (Shryock 1997). Elected to the parliament from the small circumscription of the 'Abbad near Amman, he was debarred after biting the ear of a fellow parliamentarian (https://www.albawaba.com/news/jordanian-mps-strive-peace-following-ear-biting-incident). Today al-'Abbadi acts as a regime opponent and was last detained in 2020.

35. Al-'Alimi received his MA and PhD in 1984 and 1988 from 'Ain Shams University and returned to Sanaa University in 1989 before taking posts in government administration. He published *Al-Qada' al-Qabali fi al-Mujtama' al-Yamani* (n.d.).

36. In 2001 al-'Alimi became the minister of the interior; he was injured in the assassination attempt against 'Ali 'Abdullah Saleh in 2011, in 2014 was appointed adviser to 'Abd Rabbuh Mansur Hadi, and in 2019 headed the meeting of major political parties in Sai'yun. His son 'Abdu al-Hafiz, a government employee, is the subject of investigative reporting for his investment in an offshore company; see https://en.arij.net/investigation/the-mysterious-company-of-a-former-ministers-son/. In April 2022 al-'Alimi was appointed chairman of the newly formed Presidential Leadership Council by outgoing president Hadi in Riyadh.

37. Al-Faqih supervised two PhDs for the department before going on in 1996 to establish the private university Queen Arwa and to serve in 2001 as minister of human rights; Hummad taught, did research, and supervised five PhDs for the department.

1992. But simultaneously, and well beyond university politics around sociology, senior figures in the Socialist Party became targets of assassination in a struggle that led in 1994 once again to a renewed alliance of the Saleh regime with Islah/the Muslim Brotherhood in the military seizure of the South. At the level of university politics, a separate institutionalization of higher education appears to have provided a focus and to have eased ideological battles inside Sanaa University.[38] In 1993 the Islah leader ʿAbd al-Majid al-Zindani established the party's center of higher education in Sanaa, al-Iman University; President ʿAli ʿAbdullah Saleh laid a foundation stone for the university.[39] Teaching began a year later. In the social sciences, al-Iman University opened departments of political studies and Islamic economics, not sociology. From the early 1990s, government regulations both increased the number of state universities (in Hadramawt, Taʿiz, Ibb, al-Hudayda, and Dhamar) and permitted the establishment of private universities.

In Sanaa University, sociology colleagues continued to teach and train students. Titles of fifty master's theses awarded between 1997 and 2013 and twenty-six PhD dissertations awarded between 1994 and 2008 are given online.[40] By definition, they reflect the concerns of both teaching staff and students. The topics of master's theses are a testimony to the work

38. See the account of an abortive debate in 1992 at Sanaa University between Abu Bakr as-Saqqaf and Shaykh ʿAbd al-Majid al-Zindani available at https://shabwaah-press .info/news/65477.

39. The occasion as filmed is available here: https://www.youtube.com/watch?v=lT QKgGfxcSY.

40. For the MA theses, see the National Information Center listing of library holdings of student dissertations: https://yemen-nic.info/db/studies/section.php?SHOWALL _1=1&SECTION_ID=1164. This compilation would permit a fuller analysis as it includes theses from Aden University and universities abroad (notably Egypt, Russia, Bulgaria, Morocco, Syria, Jordan, and the United Kingdom). I have restricted my remarks to Sanaa University, but for intellectual training of Yemenis as a whole, a wider analysis would be necessary. For PhD dissertations with supervisors, I have used the search engine for the libraries of institutions of higher education in Yemen, specifying Sanʿaʾ University and the Sociology Department; see https://oliye.net/home/.

of the department, covering central issues in education, politics, women's rights, kinship, poverty, administration, work, demography, development, and law in society. That said, only some 10 percent of the master's studies focus on rural areas (or on rural/urban comparison) in a country where two-thirds of the population live in villages. This urban focus contrasts with the master's topics in geography at the university. Among the PhDs awarded in the department between 1994 and 2008 (some twenty-six for which the supervisors are given), the situation is better; some 30 percent deal with rural zones. The major supervisors were 'Abdo 'Othman (seven), Nuriya Hummad (five), and Hamud al-'Awdi (four), with other faculty members appearing to have supervised one or two students.

Given the difficult atmosphere surrounding sociological research, the Yemeni work is impressive. Yet clearly, there were limits: topics such as the changing social structures of trade ("Who owns Yemen?") or agrarian studies (linking landholding, household forms, and labor) are nowhere evident. For the latter question, I turned to the theses of the agriculture faculty. In Sanaa University, as in most agricultural faculties of the Arab world, an extended field project with farmers has not formed a part of undergraduate training.[41] In the Faculty of Agriculture there is a section of extension and economics but not one of rural sociology, nor do there appear to have been any joint programs between the agricultural and the sociological faculties. This lack is unfortunate given the interest evident from thesis titles in issues of agricultural cooperatives, the raising of local breeds of animals, and the varied regions of the country. Although government policy in Sanaa did not prioritize agriculture, the number and titles of master's and PhD dissertations in agriculture at home and abroad indicates that Yemenis have been keen students of the subject in universities.

41. See the roundtable on training in faculties of agriculture: https://www.youtube .com/watch?v=cr8IskU8WnU&list=PLMdFKTfMSzdsvlG0UNH4i8eU56sE2aY6I&index =17, part of a meeting held in September 2016 in Beirut concerning measures and catego- ries in the production of knowledge about rural transformation (http://athimar.org/en /articles/details/measures-and-categories-in-the-production-of-knowledge-about-rural-tra).

## Research by Non-Yemenis and the Interface
## of the "Local and Global"

As described earlier, in the 1970s and early 1980s, foreign doctoral students and researchers came to the YAR through the national research
institutes. In those years, access to most areas of the countryside was relatively unfettered. The growth of the security state from the mid-1980s
and the war with the South in 1994 rendered that work more difficult. In
Yemen as elsewhere, the 1990s was a decade of Western-directed privatization. As noted, private universities opened in Yemen from 1994 onward.
In the name of "good governance and civil society," nongovernmental
organizations became a primary conduit for Western development aid.
From the 1990s, non-Yemeni researchers appear to have come to know
rural Yemen through work with NGOs or the major agencies (see Destremau 2006, 1–86),[42] an institutional affiliation with "development institutions" permitting access to the countryside. Only Socotra seems to have
been something of an exception.[43] In the same period, as part of neoliberal
"good governance," Yemeni consultant researchers and expertise came to
be organized corporately so as qualify to bid for project contracts.

In terms of disciplines, from the 1990s political science began to out-
strip other social sciences as the favored training for the study of the Arab
East. In terms of "words," Islam came increasingly to be the key concept
to open research funds and posts in Western academe. Political scientists
who could provide analyses of Islamic or Islamist thought or movements
proved particularly well placed. France, where the circle of scholarship
is smaller than in the English-language publishing world, is exemplary

42. Valuable work by F. Pelat was conducted in that context—see Pelat and al-Hakimi
(2003)—as was that of Lichtenthäler (2003). Marieke Brandt (2017) also entered Yemen
through work with a German development agency.

43. The exact timing of the securitization of the countryside needs documentation.
The first seizure of tourists for ransom took place in 1996 and continued over several
years. The demands made of the central government often reflected rural distress or marginalization. The conflict of the Sanaa government with the Houthis in the far North
extended between 2004 and 2009. On Socotra in this period, see the work of Peutz (2018)
and Elie (2020a, 2020b).

in this regard.[44] In English too, political science outdid development economics, anthropology/sociology, legal studies, and geography in the number of monographs and articles published in the 2000s. This fact is in itself a problem. In my opinion, even one brief independent economic analysis teaches the reader more than the many political analyses and development reports of the years running up to the 2011 protests and 2015 war.[45]

Since the war began, Western and Yemeni social scientists have launched NGO think tanks with Western funding (CARPO, Sanaa Center for Strategic Studies, Yemen Polling/Policy Center) or have gone to work with established think tanks (Crisis Group, Carnegie, Chatham House, and Washington, DC–based centers). The publications of these researchers and centers may touch upon the distribution of wealth and poverty as drivers of corruption and conflict (see Alley 2008; Salisbury 2011; Phillips 2011; and Hill et al. 2013). Yet they are restricted not only by the vocabulary and policy dictates acceptable to Western funders, but also by the restricted "facts" they can assemble institutionally. None reflect extended, independent experience of rural areas.

## Allies for Documenting Agrarian Transformation and Class Formation

The mass uprisings across the Arab region from 2011 all had rural distress as a central driver (see Ayeb and Bush 2019). Those uprisings in North Yemen were noteworthy for two great marches across the country between major cities, something seen nowhere else in the region. The invocation of President Ibrahim al-Hamdi by quite a different generation reflected his engagement in the cause of rural development and of unity with the South on a different basis than that brought about in 1990 and 1994 (see figure 2). Figures within the protests were far from unaware of the rising

44. A first generation includes Gilles Keppel and Olivier Roy, followed by François Burgat and Laurent Bonnefoy. This is not to say that there has been no textual and author-based research on Islam published in French; see Dorlian (2013).

45. See Colton (2010). This short piece can be compared to World Bank (2007). In spite of the distinguished authors of the report, the published version manages to present a remarkably upbeat picture when set beside Colton's account.

2. The image of Ibrahim al-Hamdi (d. 1977) held aloft in a 2011 protest march in Sanaa. "We are not of your generation . . . yet we love you." Credit: Creative Commons license 4.0, https://alakhbar.com, 2011.

class inequality and the intimate links between state-familial corporations and outside powers (see figure 3).

That said, there is, to my knowledge, no sustained study by Yemeni scholars documenting the changing political economy of the country and the structure of trade. For the agrarian sector, the promise of 'Abdullah Nu'man's 1989 critical analysis of the 1983 agricultural census and reasoned argument for agrarian reform remains without successor. Beyond concerns about the political sensitivity of such questions,[46] it appears that the character of the central state under 'Ali 'Abdullah Saleh and his successor, 'Abd Rabbuh Mansur Hadi, has impeded development of a statistical base adequate to document either agrarian change (landholding and labor) or class formation (structures of trade, urban industry, and remuneration).

46. The obituary of Dr. 'Abdullah Nu'man (see notes 13, 33, and 44) laments the repression exercised on him by the security forces; see https://almoaten.net/2020/05/18/30678/.

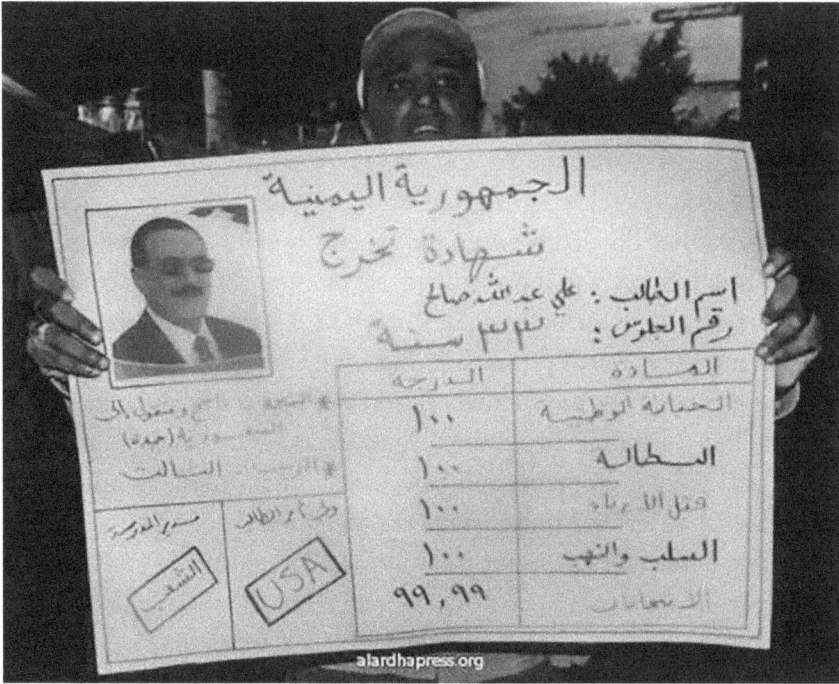

| Yemen Republic |
| --- |
| Graduation Diploma |

**Student's Name:** ʿAli ʿAbdullah Saleh
**Number of Session\*:** 33 Years
**Result:** Passed and moved to
Saudi Arabia (Jeddah)
**Rank:** Third

| Subject | Grade |
| --- | --- |
| Treason | 100% |
| Unemployment | 100% |
| Killing of Innocents | 100% |
| Plunder | 100% |
| Elections | 99.99% |

*A pun in Arabic: it also means years on the throne.

| Pupil's Guardian | Director of the School |
| --- | --- |
| USA | The People |

3. A participant in the 2011 demonstrations in Sanaa holding "The Graduation Diploma of ʿAli ʿAbdullah Saleh." Credit: Source unknown.

And given the securitization of the state, even where facts may exist—for example, tax records of qat sales—access for research by Yemenis can be refused as a matter of state security. Through the privatization of research, Western development agencies are complicit in this failure.

These issues matter for Yemen's future. At present, the authorities in Sanaa strive to revitalize agriculture drawing upon expertise of agronomists, themselves divided between proponents of state-sponsored mechanized wheat farming and those individuals pleading for a revival of native grains, be they sorghum, millet, barley, or wheat. It is a very welcome change that the ministry awards prizes to farmers (albeit all to men, no women). Yet how can planners "see" Yemen's agriculture without documentation of landholding (including ownership), land degradation, water allocation, earlier and present cropping, and labor organization (notably household and hired labor forms)? Indeed, how can the Ministry of Economy judge ownership in the modern sector without systematic survey? Only doing so would permit a grounded debate concerning what the socially destructive policies of the decades of 'Ali 'Abdullah Saleh's rule wrought.

Relentless bombardment and ground fighting have damaged much of agriculture and urban life. Yet could this physical destruction offer an opportunity to build a Yemen more lasting, more inclusive, more socially just? Capacity is greater than in the 1970s, with labor in abundance—if one includes women—and technical competence.[47] If the political will can be found, then the conceptual project could be constructed with "facts" and institutions: a knowledge of Yemen by Yemenis for Yemen.

## References

Al-'Abbadi, Ahmad 'Uwaidi. 1982. "Bedouin Justice in Jordan (the Customary Legal System of the Tribes and its Integration into the Framework of State Polity from 1921 Onwards)." PhD diss., Univ. of Cambridge.

Abu Ghanim, Fadl. 1985. *Al-Bunyat al-Qabaliyya fi al-Yaman Bayn al-Istimrar wa-l-Taghayyur.* Damascus: Matba'at al-Katib al-'Arabi.

———. 1990. *Al-Qabila wa-l-Dawla fi al-Yaman.* Cairo: Dar al-Manar.

47. Early during the war years, Yemen saw the development of solar energy: see Conflict and Environment Observatory, Mytholmroyd (2021).

Ajl, Max. 2020. "Does the Arab Region Have an Agrarian Question?" *Journal of Peasant Studies* 48, no. 5: 955–83.

Al-'Alimi, Rashad. n.d. *Al-Qada' al-Qabali fi al-Mujtama' al-Yamani.* Cairo: Dar al-Wadi.

Alley, April L. 2008. "Shifting Light in the Qamariyya: The Reinvention of Patronage Networks in Contemporary Yemen." PhD diss., Georgetown Univ.

Al-'Ariqi, Fawzi 'Abd al-Baqi. 2020. "Haraqat 13 Yuniyu wa-l-Ma'ahid al-'Ilmiyya: Nash'at-ha wa Nufudh al-Ikhwan al-Muslimin fi Silk al-Ta'lim." June 15, 2020. https://www.khuyut.com/blog/06-14-2020-09-43-pm.

Al-'Awdi, Hamud. 1988. *Muttaham bi-l-Kufr Yabhath 'an Mahkama.* Beirut: Dar al-Haqiqah.

———. 1989. *Al-Tuhma wa-l-Difa': Min Mahkamat al-Samt ila Mahkamat al-Ta'rikh.* Beirut: Dar al-Haqiqah.

Ayeb, Habib, and Ray Bush. 2019. *Food Insecurity and Revolution in the Middle East and North Africa: Agrarian Questions in Egypt and Tunisia.* London: Anthem Press.

Bédoucha, Geneviève. 1987. "Une tribu sédentaire: La tribu des hauts plateaux yéménites." *l'Homme* 27: 139–49.

Blumi, Isa. 2018. *Destroying Yemen: What Chaos in Arabia Tells Us about the World.* Oakland: Univ. of California Press.

Brandt, Marieke. 2017. *Tribes and Politics in Yemen: A History of the Houthi Conflict.* London: Hurst.

———, ed. 2021. *Tribes in Modern Yemen: An Anthology.* Sammlung Eduard Glaser XVIII. Vienna: Austrian Academy of Sciences Press.

Bujra, Abdullah. 1971. *The Politics of Stratification: A Study of Political Change in a South Arabian Town.* Oxford: Clarendon Press.

Carapico, Sheila. 1985. "Self-Help and Development Planning in the Yemen Arab Republic." In *Public Participation in Development Planning and Management: Cases from Africa and Asia,* edited by Jean-Claude Garcia-Zamor, 203–34. Boulder, CO: Westview.

———. 2007. "No Quick Fix: Foreign Aid and State Performance in Yemen." In *Rebuilding Devastated Economies in the Middle East,* edited by Leonard Binder, 182–208. New York: Palgrave Macmillan.

Chaudhry, Kiren A. 1997. *The Price of Wealth: Economies and Institutions in the Middle East.* Ithaca, NY: Cornell Univ. Press.

Colton, Nora A. 2010. "Yemen: A Collapsed Economy." *Middle East Journal* 64, no. 3: 410–26.

Conflict and Environment Observatory, Mytholmroyd. 2021. *Groundwater Depletion Clouds Yemen's Solar Energy Revolution.* https://ceobs.org/groundwater-depletion-clouds-yemens-solar-energy-revolution/.

Delgado, L. Elena, and Rolando J. Romero. 2000. "Local Histories and Global Designs: An Interview with Walter Mignolo." *Discourse* 22, no. 3: 7–33.

Destremau, Blandine. 2006. "Global Discourses, Local Applications: Debating Issues around Transformative and Relational Impacts of Gender-Concerned Development Projects." In *Women and Civil Society: Capacity Building in Yemen*, edited by Blandine Destremau and Maggy Grabundzija, 1–86. Sanaa: CEFAS. https://books.openedition.org/cefas/1675?lang=en.

Dorlian, Samy. 2013. *La mouvance Zaydite dans le Yémen contemporain: Une modernisation avortée.* Paris: l'Harmattan.

Douglas, Leigh. 1987. *The Free Yemeni Movement, 1935–1962.* Beirut: American Univ. of Beirut Press.

Egli, Ernst. 1978. "Landnutzung und Landnutzungsveräderung in der Region Wādī Mawr Arabische Republik Jemen." Master's thesis, Univ. of Zurich.

Elie, Serge D. 2003. "The Anthropological Discourse on Yemen: A Critique of the Intellectual Vestiges of Orientalism." *Journal of the Yemen Center for Studies and Research* 69, no. 2: 1–32.

———. 2013. *State and Qāt Consumption in Yemen: A Cultural Means to Political Socialization.* Sanaa: Yemen Center for Studies and Research.

———. 2020a. *A Post-exotic Anthropology of Soqotra.* Vol. 1, *A Mesography of an Indigenous Polity in Yemen.* Cham: Palgrave Macmillan.

———. 2020b. *A Post-exotic Anthropology of Soqotra.* Vol. 2, *Cultural and Environmental Annexation of an Indigenous Community.* Cham: Palgrave Macmillan.

Escher, Hermann. 1975. "Wirtschafts- und Sozialgeographische Untersuchungen in der Wâdî Mawr Region (Arabische Republik Jemen)." PhD diss., Univ. of Zurich.

Gerholm, Tomas. 1977. *Market, Mosque and Mafraj: Social Inequality in a Yemeni Town.* Stockholm Studies in Anthropology 5. Stockholm: Univ. of Stockholm.

Golovkaya, Elena. 1994. *Al-Tatawwur al-Siyasi li-l-Jumhuriyya al-'Arabiyya al-Yamaniyya 1962–1985.* Sanaa: Markaz al-Dirasat wa-l-Buhuth al-Yamaniyya.

Hill, Ginny, Peter Salisbury, Léonie Northedge, and Jane Kinninmont. 2013. *Corruption, Capital Flight and Global Drivers of Conflict.* London: Chatham House.

Al-Jawi, 'Umar. 1975. *Hisar Sana'a', Ripurtaj Sahafi.* Aden: Matabi' al-'Ummal.

Kopp, Horst. 1981. *Agrargeographie der Arabischen Republik Jemen. Landnutzung und Agrarsoziale Verhaltnisse in einem Orientalisch-islamischen Entwicklungsland mit alter Bauerlicher Kultur.* Erlanger Geographische Arbeiten, Sonderband 11. Self-published, Erlangen.

Lackner, Helen. 1985. *P.D.R. Yemen: Outpost of Socialist Development in Arabia.* London: Ithaca Press.

Lichtenthäler, Gerhard. 2003. *Political Ecology and the Role of Water: Environment, Economy and Society in Northern Yemen.* London: Routledge.

Makin, M., ed. 1977. "Yemen Arab Republic Montane Plains and Wadi Rima Project: A Land and Water Resources Survey; Irrigation and Agricultural Development in Wadi Rima." Project Report No. 16. 2 vols. Surrey: Ministry of Overseas Development, Land Resources Division Project Team.

McCullock, Neil. 2021. "Tackling Lebanon's Electricity Crisis: Lessons from Yemen." Policy Brief, no. 67. Beirut: Lebanese Center for Policy Studies, Nov. 2021. https://lcps-lebanon.org/publication.php?id=444&category=700&title=700.

Meneley, Anne. 1996. *Tournaments of Value: Sociability and Hierarchy in a Yemeni Town.* Toronto: Univ. of Toronto Press.

Mitchell, Brigitta, Hermann Escher, and Martha Mundy. 1978. *Yemen Arab Republic Feeder Road Study, a Baseline Socioeconomic Survey of the Wadi Mawr Region.* Washington, DC: Regional Development Unit, World Bank.

Mundy, Martha. 1980. *Tihama II Project: Monitoring and Evaluation Report.* [Washington, DC]: Ministry of Agriculture, Yemen Arab Republic, and World Bank/Kuwait Fund.

———. 1995. *Domestic Government: Kinship, Community and Polity in North Yemen.* London: I. B. Tauris.

———. 2015. "Yemen as Laboratory: Why Is the West So Silent about This Savage War?" *Counterpunch*, Sept. 23, 2015. https://www.counterpunch.org/2015/09/23/yemen-as-laboratory-why-is-the-west-so-silent-about-this-savage-war/.

———. 2018. *The Strategies of the Coalition in the Yemen War: Aerial Bombardment and Food War.* Somerville, MA: Tufts Univ., World Peace Foundation, 2018. https://sites.tufts.edu/wpf/files/2018/10/Strategies-of-Coalition-in-Yemen-War-Final-20181005-1.pdf.

———. 2021. "Beyond Legal Referent: The Yemen War." In *The Condition of Democracy*, vol. 2, *Contesting Citizenship*, edited by Jürgen Mackert, Bryan S. Turner, and Hannah Wolf, 105–24. London: Routledge.

Mundy, Martha, Amin al-Hakimi, and Frédéric Pelat. 2014. "Neither Security nor Sovereignty: The Political Economy of Food in Yemen." In *Food Security in the Arab World*, edited by Zahra Babar and Suzi Mirgani, 137–59. London: Hurst; New York: Oxford Univ. Press.

Mundy, Martha, and Frédéric Pelat. 2015. "The Political Economy of Agriculture and Agricultural Policy in Yemen." In *Rebuilding Yemen: Political, Economic and Social Challenges*, edited by Noel Brehony and Saud al-Sarhan, 98–122. Berlin: Gerlach Press. Available in Arabic at http://www.athimar.org /Article-74.

Nuʻman, ʻAbdullah Ahmad. 1975. "Al-Numuw al-Iqtisadi fi al-Yaman wa-bi-Shakl Khass fi al-Qitaʻ al-Ziraʻi." PhD diss., Budapest Univ.

———. 1987. "Al-Taʻawuniyat al-Ziraʻiya fi al-Shatr al-Janubi min al-Yaman." Candidate diss., Hungarian Scientific Academy.

———. 1989. *Qadaya wa-Mushkilat al-Tanmiya al-Ziraʻiya: Al-Hiyazat al-Ziraʻiya fi al-Jumhuriyya al-ʻArabiyya al-Yamaniyya*. Beirut: Dar al-Farabi.

ʻOthman, ʻAbdo ʻAli, and Hamud al-ʻAwdi. 1982. "The Yemeni Cooperative Movement and Development: Participation of Local Development Cooperative Associations in the Projects of the First Five-Year Development Plan." In Arabic, paper presented to the CPO, Sanaa, Jan. 1982.

Pelat, Frédéric, and Amin al-Hakimi, eds. 2003. *Savoirs locaux et agriculture durable au Yémen, Les Cahiers du CEFAS*. https://books.openedition.org/cefas /2777?lang=en&format=toc.

Peutz, Nathalie. 2018. *Islands of Heritage: Conservation and Transformation in Yemen*. Stanford, CA: Stanford Univ. Press.

Phillips, Sarah. 2011. *Yemen: Developmental Dysfunction and Division in a Crisis State*. Research Paper 14. Canberra: Developmental Leadership Program.

Pratt, D. 1977. "Yemen Arab Republic Montane Plains and Wadi Rima Project: A Land and Water Resources Survey; An Investment and Development Plan for Wadi Rima." Project Report No. 17, YAR-01-30/Rep-17/77. Surrey: Ministry of Overseas Development.

Al-Qasir, Ahmad 1987. *Sharkh fi Bunyat al-Wahm: al-Hijrah wa-l-Tahawwul fi al-Yaman*. Cairo: Dar Thabit.

Roussillon, Alain. 1999. "Durkheimisme et réformisme: Fondation identitaire de la sociologie en Égypte." *Annales E.S.C.* 54, no. 6: 1363–94.

Salisbury, Peter. 2011. *Yemen's Economy: Oil, Imports and Elites, Chatham House*. Paper 2011/02. London: Middle East and North Africa Programme.

Al-Saqqaf, Abu Bakr. 2020 [1988]. *Al-Jumhuriyya Bayn al-Saltana wa-l-Qabila fi al-Yaman al-Shamali*. Cairo: Dar al-Amal.

Al-Sayyad, Ahmad. 2013. *Al-Yasar al-Yamani: Zalim am Mazlum?* Beirut: Riad El-Rayyes Books.

Seif, Huda A. 2003. "Moralities and Outcasts: Domination and Allegories of Resentment in Southern Yemen." PhD diss., Columbia Univ.

Sha'lan, Tha'ira. 1993. *L'Interférence entre les concepts de classe et de catégorie sociale dans la société Yéménite*. Paris: Paris Nanterre University.

Shami, Seteney. 1989. "Socio-cultural Anthropology in Arab Universities." *Current Anthropology* 30, no. 5: 649–54.

Al-Sharjabi, Qa'id. 1986. *Al-Shara'ih al-Ijtima'iyya al-Taqlidiyya fi al-Mujtama' al-Yamani*. Beirut: Dar al-Hadathah.

Shryock, Andrew. 1997. *Nationalism and the Genealogical Imagination: Oral History and Textual Authority in Tribal Jordan*. Berkeley: Univ. of California Press.

Swagman, Charles F. 1988. *Development and Change in Highland Yemen*. Salt Lake City: Univ. of Utah Press.

Tutwiler, Richard. 1987. "Tribe, Tribute and Trade: Social Class Formation in Highland Yemen." PhD diss., State Univ. of New York at Binghamton.

———. 1990. "Agricultural Labor and Technological Change in the Yemen Arab Republic." In *Labor and Rain-Fed Agriculture in West Asia and North Africa*, edited by Dennis Tully, 229–51. Dordrecht: Springer.

Tutwiler, Richard, and Sheila Carapico. 1981. *Yemeni Agriculture and Economic Change: A Case-Study of Two Highland Regions*. Yemen Development Series 1. DeKalb: American Institute for Yemeni Studies/Northern Illinois Univ.

Al-'Uqqab, 'Abd al-Wahhab. 2011. *Al-'Alaqat al-Yamaniyya al-Sa'udiyya 1900–1970*. Damascus: Dar Raslan.

Varisco, Daniel. 1982. "The Adaptive Dynamics of Water Allocation in al-Ahjur, Yemen Arab Republic." PhD diss., Univ. of Pennsylvania.

Walters, Delores. 1987. "Perceptions of Inequality in the Yemen Arab Republic." PhD diss., New York Univ.

Weir, Shelagh. 1997. "A Clash of Fundamentalisms: Wahhabism in Yemen." *MERIP* 204.

Williams, J. 1977. "Yemen Arab Republic Montane Plains and Wadi Rima Project: A Land and Water Resources Survey; Physical Aspects of Water Use under Traditional and Modern Irrigation/Farming Systems in Wadi Rima

Tihama." Project Record No. 27, YAR-01-40/REC-27/79. Surrey: Ministry of Overseas Development, Yemen Arab Republic, Land Resources Division.

World Bank. 2007. Report 34008-YE. *Republic of Yemen: Country Social Analysis.* Washington, DC: World Bank.

# 4

## Honor

*Beyond Glorious Deeds, an Ethos
of Ordinary Insecurity*

Luca Nevola

In 2009, when I reached Sanaa for my first fieldwork, I brought with me a few books and far less certainty about the research I wanted to pursue. To find inspiration, I clung to a classic: Paul Dresch's *Tribes, Government, and History in Yemen* (1989). The second chapter of Dresch's book, titled "The Language of Honour," appealed to me for the straightforward and enlightening characterization of the tribal ethos. Dresch's prose engraved in my mind the idea of the tribesmen (*qaba'il*) as an armed aristocracy distinguished by the possession of *sharaf* and devoted to the protection of valued *sacra*.

The word *sharaf* is commonly translated in standard Arabic as "honor,"[1] and Dresch glosses it as "honor as presented to the outside world" (1986, 310; 2006, 75–84). Honor gave a new perspective to my experience of Yemen, connecting it with a familiar universe of epic and heroic quests that I projected onto the *qaba'il's* glorious deeds and "heroic actions" (Dresch 1989, 43). However, this ideal-typical portrait of the *qaba'il* and the related interpretation of *sharaf* as honor started crumbling as soon as I began conducting interviews. For instance, in September 2009, during

---

1. In pre-Islamic Arabia and early Islam, the verbal noun *sharaf*, like *majd*, indicated "elevation, nobility, and pre-eminence in the physical and the moral senses," based on prestigious origin (Fahd 1991, 313).

a conversation with a *qabili* living in Sanaa, the man observed (in a mixed English and Arabic language), "*Sharaf* is a word that indicates that you're not a thief, you don't make sex in a bad way. . . . [That] the girls don't go with other boys, [that] people don't say that you're a bad person. An honorable man (*insan sharif*) doesn't do bad things. If you're not honorable you steal, you accept corruption. Conversely, if you're not a thief, or an adulterer, this is *sharaf*. . . . And it's said that your wife is your *sharaf* (*'aylatak sharafak*). You're responsible for your wife." This interview is but one among dozens of similar conversations I collected in more than ten years of research. These dialogues leave *sharaf* devoid of some of the main characteristics attributed to the concept by scholarly literature: there is no reference to weapons, ancestors, glorious actions, land, and so forth, only the elicitation of ordinary, everyday ethically loaded behaviors. Interestingly, no general definition of the term is ever offered, only contextual examples of what it means to be (or not to be) an "honorable" man. Whenever the concept itself is defined, it is by pointing to an "extension" of it (for example, "*sharaf* is your wife"), rather than elaborating on its "intension."[2] Finally, the term—if not solicited by an anthropologist—is rarely used in everyday language (cf. Wikan 1984; 1991, 150), being reserved to a few specific contexts and tied to a peculiar linguistic register.

In conducting a comparison between the anthropological discourse around honor, my own personal and scientific assumptions, and everyday discursive practices around *sharaf* in Yemen, I was left with the incontrovertible feeling that "*sharaf*" exceeded "honor," that some sort of conceptual mismatch brought about a profound misunderstanding. This chapter is an attempt to "emphasize and potentialize" this misunderstanding, arguing that the aim of anthropological discourse is to "avoid losing sight of the difference concealed within equivocal 'homonyms'" (Viveiros de Castro 2004, 7). Accordingly, rather than assuming that the anthropologist and his interlocutors are looking at the same thing—that is, honor—from different perspectives, I will assume that we are looking at different things

2. The "extension" of a concept is a definition by direct reference, while the "intension" is "a relation between concepts that define each other's meaning" (Holbraad and Pedersen 2017, 188).

through the same concept, thus exploring the heuristic power of "equivocation" (Viveiros de Castro 2004).

One of two approaches is presumed in every analysis of "honor"—the "most elusive of social concepts" (Patterson 1982, 80). The "conceptual approach" moves from a general idea of honor as a system of values and explores its features in a given historical society (Stewart 1994, 5); this approach entails a preestablished idea of what honor is, and it requires an intentional definition of the concept.[3] The "lexical approach," on the other hand, focuses on a small cluster of interrelated words and aims at navigating their meaning and contextual use (Stewart 1994, 5), thus leaving room for equivocation.

In this chapter, I shall opt for the "lexical approach" and scrutinize the use of *sharaf* and a few other words related to it by context of usage (for example, *'ird, karama, asl, rajula,* and so forth) in everyday discursive practice, thus interpreting their meaning by bringing it "into the daylight of ordinary understanding" (Jackson 1996, 1). This approach is underpinned by discursive analysis and ethnographic fieldwork conducted between 2009 and 2013 in the urban context of Sanaa and the tribal areas of Bani Matar and Sanhan.

Overall, the chapter is organized around three sections, each exploring the mismatch between *sharaf* and honor using different types of sources. The first section reviews scholarly literature, considering how different authors conflated honor and *sharaf* to construct an object of anthropological reflection. The second section investigates how *sharaf* emerges from everyday discursive practices in contemporary Yemen. First, it presents conversations with a tribesman (*qabili*) from Bani Matar, stressing how he resorted to *sharaf* across different stages of his life. Second, it addresses a corpus of interviews recorded between 2009 and 2013, focusing on the anthropologist's role in soliciting the emergence of *sharaf*'s contextual meaning. The concluding section considers how *sharaf* is constructed in a recent document, *The Tribal Charter of Sharaf,* produced during the

---

3. For instance, Peristiany and Pitt-Rivers argue that "it is an error to regard honor as a single constant concept rather than a conceptual field" (1992, 4). In analyzing "honour-linked values," Abu-Lughod adopts a similar approach (2016, 88).

ongoing Yemen war that erupted in March 2015, showing how the concept was rationalized and formalized in Houthi discourse.

This chapter will deal with Yemeni men affiliated with tribal corporate groups, the so-called *qaba'il*[4] (s. *qabili*). "Tribal" masculinity—the "social constructions of what it means 'to be a man'" (Kimmel and Bridges 2014)—is hegemonic in Upper Yemen; in fact, the *qaba'il* are the vast majority of the population, and their form of manhood is normative and "culturally exalted" (Connell 2005). Obviously, other forms of masculinity coexist with the tribal ethos (for example, Islamic masculinities,[5] to mention the more obvious) and often overlap with it (Caton 1990, 26). In particular, notions of manhood associated with "protected" low-status groups and women are relevant in shaping tribal masculinities (cf. Vom Bruck 1996; Nevola 2020a). However, the perspective of "protected" people is beyond the scope of this chapter. Women, in particular, are represented only from a male perspective: my interlocutors' and mine. Unfortunately, in my experience, there is no way around this methodological shortcoming for a male ethnographer of contemporary Yemeni society.

## Honor and Anthropology

### The Allochronic Homo Honorabilis

"Native" concepts are always interpreted through our own personal and disciplinary biases. The "fieldworker's culture, upbringing and previous experience" have the potential to shape the construction of ethnographic realities (Pitt-Rivers 1992, 133, quoted in Shryock and da Col 2017), yet is rarely made an object of reflection. Honor is a commonsense notion for most Western scholars, and, as such, it is loaded with cultural biases. As Unni Wikan observed, honor's "spell derives from its archaic and poetic overtones: it harks back to more glorious times when men were brave,

---

4. The term *qaba'il* is traditionally applied to southern Arabs belonging to a tribal corporate group. However, in this chapter, it also extends to tribesmen of Hashemite origin (cf. Nevola 2020b).

5. For a well-researched study of Islamic masculinities in Yemen, see, for example, Vom Bruck (2005).

honest and principled" (1984, 635). This remark applies to my own experience of the term, crafted by some juvenile readings of *The Lord of the Rings* and Homer's *Iliad* into a mixture of battles, heroic quests, and beyond-reach worlds of fantasy. Honor never played a role in my lifeworld, yet it shaped my "allochronic" and exoticizing experience of the Yemeni Other, producing an actual "denial of coevalness" (Fabian 1983).

This brief and sketchy biographical portrayal is meant to foster one question: What kind of cultural biases influenced the anthropology of honor? This anthropological domain of inquiry was inaugurated by J. G. Peristiany in the 1966 edited volume *Honour and Shame: The Values of Mediterranean Society*.[6] Testifying to the experience-near dimension of the concept, Peristiany remarked that early anthropologists "could with difficulty envisage the 'savage' as having honor such as they themselves possessed" (1966, 35). Similarly, sociologist Peter Berger argued that anyone using the term revealed "himself to be hopelessly European" (Berger 1970 quoted in Pitt-Rivers 2017, 105). In sum, honor was too high a value to recognize it in the non-European Other. Julian Pitt-Rivers—one of the contributors to the 1966 volume and a leading theorist in the study of honor—was, undoubtedly, a "man of honor." As cogently noted by Shryock and da Col, he inherited an illustrious surname and an aristocratic upbringing, along with the attraction for concepts—such as honor, grace, and hospitality—that were "part of the sociopolitical world of class that produced his sensibilities and his scholarship" (2017, xviii).

Pitt-Rivers famously defined honor as "the value of a person in his own eyes, but also in the eyes of his society" (1966, 21), and he argued for a distinction between "honor = precedence" and "honor = virtue" (2017, 109). He theorized the two main axes around which honor is still debated: the internal/external axis (Stewart 1994, 12), broadly depicting honor as "reputation" versus honor as "embodied disposition," and the agonistic/protective axis, distinguishing competition in honor from the defense of

---

6. As cogently noted by Stewart (1994, 1–2), though barely untouched by the social sciences, the concept of honor had been the focus of a wide number of other disciplines long before the 1960s.

an individual's socially recognized *sacra* (cf. Bourdieu 1966). Both these perspectives contributed to Yemen's scholarship through Paul Dresch's work (cf. Dresch 2006, 75–84).

The 1966 volume and subsequent publications (cf. Gilmore 1987; Peristiany and Pitt-Rivers 1992), turned honor into an anthropological metonym for the circum-Mediterranean area (Appadurai 1986, 357). Thereby, the alleged "constant preoccupation" of the Mediterranean people for the "complementary codes of honor and shame" (Gilmore 1987, 2) was translated into a disciplinary boundary. Simultaneously, to sustain anthropology's comparative effort, the honor/shame dichotomy was put at work to interpret northern African societies and translated into Arabic language.

In *Honour and Shame among the Bedouins of Egypt* (1966), Abou-Zeid glossed the Arabic word *sharaf* with the English "honor" and defined "shame" (*'ayb* or *'ar*) as its opposite; he posited honor's "ranked quality" and its "individual" versus "collective" dimensions, and, eventually, he translated the term *'ird* as "the honour of woman" (247). Albeit contested by Abu-Lughod—who, like Abou-Zeid, studied the Awlad 'Ali Bedouins—these features were later translated into the Yemeni context. Abu-Lughod put forth two fundamental arguments: first, that the "critical" term, when referring to Middle Eastern contexts, is *asl*[7] (that is, root, origin, ancestry) rather than "honor" (2016, 86–87); and, second, that there is no such thing as "honor" in itself, but rather a network of "honour-linked values"[8] (88).

Drawing on her fieldwork in Cairo and in Sohar, Wikan (1984) advanced an even more substantial critique of the anthropological understanding of honor, observing that the literary fortune of the term is linked to the evocative power it retains in the West, especially among men; in Egypt, honor is an experience-distant concept, while "shame" is an experience-near one; and shame is not the binary opposite of honor. Concurrently, Wikan unveiled the importance of the neglected concept of manhood, affirming that "the person who behaves properly . . . is not

7. On the concept of *asl* in Yemen, see Nevola (2020a).

8. In the Yemeni tradition, a similar approach is exemplified by the usage of *qabyala* for *sharaf* (cf. Caton 1990; Adra 1982).

said to possess honour (*sharaf*) or even to be honourable . . . ," he must be a man (1984, 637).

This brief survey exemplifies how a crossover of biographies and discursive traditions produced an anthropological definition of honor that migrated from the Mediterranean to North Africa, translating a variety of local experiences into a theoretically and culturally loaded concept. In the next section, I shall consider how this concept emerged on the Yemeni scene and how it shaped the description of Yemen's social organization.

*Honor in Yemen*

As cogently noted by Abu-Lughod (1989), Yemen was turned into a "zone of theory of the Middle East" by Dresch's work on segmentary lineage theory. The idea of segmentation was first introduced into modern anthropological theory[9] by Edward E. Evans-Pritchard in his masterpiece, *The Nuer*, and further elaborated in *African Political Systems* to describe the social organization of stateless, or acephalous, societies (Evans-Pritchard 1974; Fortes and Evans-Pritchard 1970).

Segmentary lineage theory never succeeded in empirically describing—let alone predicting—the behavior of social actors. This shortcoming pushed Dresch (1986) to rephrase it, setting aside the solid bodies that constituted the "segments"—that is, corporate groups and individuals—and moving its premises to the structural level of values and reflective discourse. By combining Louis Dumont's structural approach and Michael M. Meeker's cultural interpretations, Dresch conceived a highly nuanced and original revision of classic segmentary lineage theory, grounding it in the domain of honor.

In a nutshell, Meeker conceived of *sharaf*—defined as honor "in its broadest, most encompassing sense" (1976, 244)—as the structuring feature of Near Eastern cultural systems of meaning and distinguished the concept from *'ird* (or *namus*), namely, "sexual honor." Drawing on Schneider's work (1971), he posited a correspondence between nomadic

---

9. A prominent precursor of segmentary lineage theory was Scottish orientalist William Robertson Smith, whose work contained *in nuce* many of the principles of the African model of segmentation (Dresch 1988, 53; Robertson Smith 1903).

"segmentary societies," based on the idiom of *sharaf*, and sedentary "communal societies," based on the idiom of *namus* (264). With regard to "segmentary" *sharaf*, he stressed three core features: its relational dimension (250), its connection with glorious acts (251), and its dependence on the legacy of the ancestors (260). Dresch revisited Meeker's theory of *sharaf* and, combining it with a dose of Dumontian structuralism (cf. Dresch 1986, 313), translated it into the Yemeni context. He posited that *sharaf*, or honor, "presented to the outside world" (310), depended on the protection of *'ird*, or "honor defended" (311). Hence, he depicted tribal "segments" as the relational units of an overarching ideological system "opposed to each other in terms of honor."

Dresch's theory also incorporated the decisive influx of Robert B. Serjeant's oeuvre that reflected a wartime experience of Yemen. In the 1940s, Serjeant, a Scottish Arabist who was resident in Aden, was tasked with creating a tribal force of irregulars to invade Somaliland. Later, in 1963, he gained access to the North of Yemen where he traveled with the Royalist forces for a couple of months during the civil war. It is thus not surprising to find that he described the *qaba'il* as an armed aristocracy.

Serjeant introduced the notion of *sharaf* in the academic discourse around Yemen in an essay titled "South Arabia," included in *Commoners, Climbers, and Notables: A Sampler of Studies on Social Ranking in the Middle East* (1977). As the book title suggests, Serjeant represented the hierarchical order of the Highlands in terms of stratified classes, drawing on a language borrowed from the European culture of the ancient regime. He qualified the tribesmen as an "aristocracy" distinguished by the possession of "the quality called *sharaf* or honour" and emphasized "the tradition of bearing arms and being capable of defending oneself and one's dependants" as honor's core feature (227). He overtly restated the binary opposition of honor and shame (228) and individuated *sharaf* as a core principle of social ranking, asserting that "those without *sharaf* are termed *naqis*, that is 'deficient.'"

*Tribes, Government, and History in Yemen* (1989) incorporates all these elements: the warrior-like component of the tribesman's identity (41), the role of weapons in the definition of honor (39), the connection between shared ancestry and shared *sharaf* (44), and the binary opposition of *sharaf* and *'ayb* (39). Interestingly, the same principles are pillars of most contemporary approaches to the social organization of the Yemeni tribes (cf. Brandt 2017, 19; Heinze 2014, 81). The value of Dresch's theory is not at all in doubt, but rather than searching for a coherent and encompassing theory of social organization, I'd rather investigate gaps and misunderstandings in emic self-descriptions of Yemen's society.

## Honor and Lives

### A Case Study from Bani Matar

As cogently observed by Michael Herzfeld (1980, 349), the "reductionist generalisation" of glosses (for example, "honor" and "shame") risks obscuring the significance of local terms and concepts. Acknowledging this call to "ethnographic particularism" (349), in this section I shall try to analyze how the term *sharaf* was used and given significance in the context of my relationship with Qays, one of my closest Yemeni friends. In 2006, when I first met him, Qays—a *qabili* from Bani Matar—was married, with two daughters. He lived in Sanaa and worked as a tour agent, but his family also cultivated almond and qat trees in their village of origin.

One day, at the beginning of my research, I proved inexperienced enough to investigate the meaning of the word *sharaf* in a public *diwan*. Qays immediately urged me to be quiet and postpone the topic. Later, in private, he wrote a short note and asked me to recopy it in my notebook to hide his calligraphy. Titled "A girl's *sharaf* in Yemeni society," the small piece of paper listed the moral characteristics of a girl with a good reputation (*sum'a tayyiba*). While writing, my friend commented, "These characteristics preserve the real *sharaf*: virginity." He continued, "A girl's hymen (*ghisha' al-bakara*) is her family's gate, because a girl's *sharaf* is her family's *sharaf*." "The crown of *sharaf*," he concluded, "is women."

In 2011—when Qays's daughter Layla entered puberty—he involuntarily offered me an exemplification of the significance of *sharaf* in his life. Layla opposed the idea of wearing the *niqab*, and even Qays's wife thought it could wait at least another year. However, Qays—an open-minded person who used to work with tourists and foreigners—felt profoundly insecure, almost paranoid. He told me that his daughter had grown up and

developed breasts, that he saw her "talking with two boys." A neighbor
even suggested to him to "cover her, and dress her up with wider clothes."
Qays commented, "*Sharaf* is important, your reputation (*sum'a*) is important. It's *'ayb* to talk with a woman in the street."[10]

In an attempt to justify his decisions, Qays put the blame on the behavior of "modern male teenagers": "These days, the *niqab* will protect her
from harassment. Because people's gaze (*nazr*) is worse than their words,
and the second gaze equals adultery (*zina'*)." He continued by justifying
his decision in Islamic terms. And eventually he concluded, "I must protect her from herself. . . . She's got her head in the clouds, doesn't watch
cartoons anymore, and listens to music all day long." *Sharaf* was but one
conceptual tool among many (including Islamic discourse) mobilized by
Qays to rationalize and explain what he conceived as his daughter's need
for protection. However, the main drive of his action was emotional: he
felt vulnerable because his daughter's behavior was being judged by his
peers (*kalam an-nas*). Overall, this story exemplifies the internal/external
axis of honor (Stewart 1994, 12): indeed, Qays's subjective experience reflected his awareness of living in a world of Others (Duranti 2015).

In years of conversations, Qays always used *sharaf* to refer to a man's
womenfolk. It was, therefore, with great surprise that in 2020 I heard him
using the concept in an unprecedented way, owing to the war context.
During an interview, taking a political stance, Qays affirmed: "When
you ask, 'Does the Hadi[11] government have any *sharaf* or any *karama*?'
you'll find that it is below zero."[12] Hence, he added: "Recently, I became
on the side of Ansar Allah. You know the reason? That I have found my
dignity (*karama*). When I go to Marib [which was IRG-controlled], *wallah*
I'm insulted. At least the Somali refugees have the UN cars and they can
go through. And I am Yemeni, I will go to al-Mahra to the border with
Oman, and they insulted me while I'm going, they investigated me, and

10. Recorded interview, Nov. 2, 2011, Sanaa.

11. In the context of the ongoing Yemen war, the internationally recognized government (IRG) is led by 'Abd Rabbu Mansur Hadi, while the de facto authority in control of
Sanaa is led by Ansar Allah, or the Houthi movement.

12. Recorded interview via Skype, Apr. 6, 2020.

they checked my bag and they checked my pocket. Like they suspected that I had stolen something."

I asked: "Is this an insult to your *sharaf*?" And he replied, "No, to your *karama. Sharaf* can be hurt if the man gets raped." This passage hints at the polysemous nature of *sharaf*: first, it is used as a synonym of *karama*, subsequently with reference to sexuality. I continued asking, "During the war, did the way people defend their *sharaf* change?" And Qays replied: "Yes. For example, the people suffered these airstrikes. . . . At first, we were shocked. Then, we prepared for the defense. And then it's like, defend the *sharaf* of the nation, the *sharaf* of the country. Because the rocket was not targeting men; it was for everyone, women and children."

He continued, "When you talk with them, people say, 'If I have no *sharaf* I don't need to live, because *sharaf* is the main thing.'" In this second excerpt, *sharaf* assumes yet another meaning. The nation's women and children are considered *sharaf* because an external enemy is targeting them.

A few lines earlier I referred to *sharaf* as a polysemous word, but semantic explanations tend to obscure the power of language. During my fieldwork, I came across *sharaf* in fragmentary and incoherent bits of discourse as the ones presented above. Perhaps I never found a folk philosopher, a Yemeni Ogotemmeli,[13] capable of weaving together a global and coherent theory of honor. However, I am prone to believe that no overarching theory of *sharaf* exists in Yemen as elsewhere, and, to put it into Keesing's terms, anthropologists took "the unconnected bits and pieces manifest in . . . what native actors do and say" and constructed a "coherent philosophy that no informants articulate themselves" (1985, 202).

Indeed, *sharaf* resembles what Claude Lévi-Strauss would term a "floating signifier" (1987, 63). Like the Maori word *mana*, floating signifiers function to "fill the gap between the signifier and the signified," thus

---

13. Ogotemmeli famously recounted the cosmology of the Dogon people to French anthropologist Marcel Griaule. Griaule's rendition of Ogotemmeli's words has been extensively critiqued, revealing the power dynamics inherent in the ethnographic encounter and their connection to the rhetorical devices employed in constructing anthropological narratives (see Clifford 1988).

becoming devoid of meaning in themselves and "susceptible of receiving any meaning at all" (55–56).[14] *Mana*-notions appear to be "empty" and undefinable (Boyer 1986, 60) because individuals acquire and learn them "into situations in which a term is used long before they have beliefs concerning the corresponding concept" (63).

Two observations descend from these general assumptions. First, people know how to use *mana*-terms in concrete situations—that is, they know when *sharaf* is at stake—but they can hardly define them in purely semantic terms. In fact, "floating categories are embodied in human experience. People feel them and enact them" (Littlewood and Reynolds 2020, 112). Second, the vagueness of *mana*-terms makes them particularly apt to "cope with the addition of new information" (Boyer 1986, 52) and thus a vector for cultural change. Indeed, *sharaf* can maintain its relevance despite historical transformation precisely because it has no substantial meaning: it works as a linguistic index, pointing to a set of virtuous behaviors that change across time and place.

*The Messy but Rich Fields of Everyday Honor*

The dialogues I shall present below are sketchy, incoherent, and at times inherently contradictory. It is the substance of the anthropological encounter. In this paragraph I aim to represent the "messy but rich fields" of everyday experience (Schielke 2010, 6) within which my interlocutors lived and interpreted the concepts of *sharaf* and *'ird*.

In February 2013, I recorded the life story of Ahmad, a soldier of Hashemite origin[15] in his mid-thirties, hailing from the village of Kuthreh

---

14. Lévi-Strauss's theory is useful for our purposes inasmuch as it individuates a general category of linguistic symbols (that is, the *mana*-terms or floating signifiers) capable of exceeding the signified. However, the structuralist conclusions drawn by Lévi-Strauss from his analysis, and in particular the comparison between *mana*-terms and "zero-value" symbols, like the French word *truc*, go in a direction that we shall not partake.

15. As noted above, although genealogically a *sayyid*, Ahmad—as all other *sada* (pl.) in Kuthreh—also considered himself a *qabili*. This status means that he paid *ghurm* and actively joined the activities of Kuthreh's corporate group. For more on "sayyid tribesmen," see Nevola (2020b).

in Sanhan. While reflecting on his biography, Ahmad depicted the choice of serving in the army as a strategy to gain freedom and independence from his father's household. At the age of sixteen, he was serving in al-Jawf governorate, and the following episode occurred to him: "I was offered a sum of 60,000 Saudi riyal to let them [unspecified] enter the area and blow up the soldiers inside. The Saudis offered this corruption through one of al-Jawf shaykhs. I refused such an offer. They made an attempt, and I said, 'If I agree with this, it is to the detriment of my *'ird* and my *sharaf.*' Because the betrayal of your country (*balad*), your homeland (*al-watan*), implies betraying (*yikhun*) your *sharaf* and your *'ird.*"

According to Ahmad, "betraying the homeland" reflects on one's own *sharaf* and *'ird*. Yet the meaning of the two terms remained implicit during the conversation. Consequently, at the end of the interview, I tried to clarify this point:

> LUCA: You told me that it is a duty to defend *sharaf* and *'ird*. Would you explain to me what is *sharaf* and what is *'ird*?
>
> AHMAD: When someone talks about your *'ird* is when he insults you, when he speaks about your *'ird*, meaning your wife, your mother, your sister. . . . And *sharaf* is the same, it's tied to *'ird*. . . . Any person, any Muslim, any person on earth is nothing but his *sharaf*, his *'ird*, his blood (*dammeh*) and his land (*maleh*). . . . If he loses anything else it doesn't matter. But *'ird*, *sharaf*, blood and land, if you leave them (*tifukkeh*) you are considered nothing, not even a human being. [These things] are more precious than life (*a'azz min al-hayya*). It is better to die, than leaving these four things.
>
> LUCA: And *karama*?
>
> AHMAD: The same. It comes from *sharaf* and *'ird*.

In this passage, *sharaf* and *'ird* are treated as synonyms. Again, there is no extensional definition of the two terms, only the indication that *'ird* comes into being when a man's womenfolk are insulted. Together with land and blood, *sharaf* and *'ird* are described as constitutive elements of any human being worth the name. In this excerpt, *sharaf* is never used as an umbrella term—as "encompassing honor," thus also embracing land, blood, ancestry, and so on—but rather it points to a specific form of relationship (that is, with women).

Let me consider another case. In April 2013, I interviewed a shaykh *mashaykh* hailing from one of Kuthreh's neighboring villages. He told me the story of his great-grandfather who killed an assaulter who was trying to steal his *janbiyya*.[16] After the incident, the shaykh's grandfather was forced by his lineage group (*badana*) to abandon his own village and properties, and so he moved from the Khawlan at-Tiyal tribe to Sanhan, where he gained prestige and economic influence.

The shaykh's renown conveyed to my humble *diwan* several guests, and the general conversation touched upon different aspects of the tribal ethos. At one point, one villager recalled that Kuthreh's corporate group once forgave a blood price (*diya*) owed to them. The shaykh commended the good deed, shouting, "This is considered respect (*ihtiraman*), and esteem (*taqdiran*), and *sharaf* for you."

All these terms clearly vehiculated a generic sense of "prestige." I took the chance and asked, "What's this *sharaf*?" To my bewilderment, the shaykh's reply seemed completely unrelated: "*Sharaf* is an attack against my *janbiyya* or my daughter." He continued: "If you attack my *sharaf*, it is my wife, my daughter, my sister, my niece (*bint 'ammi*) or from my tribe (*qabilati*), or even from Kuthreh. A woman is a daughter to the whole place of Armil [the shaykh's village]. Or the whole Bani Matar, or the whole Sanhan. The attack against a woman. This is *sharaf*. . . . When someone talks about her, insults her, or beats her up, this is *sharaf*. But the greatest *sharaf* is an attack."

This excerpt hints at the segmentary nature of *sharaf*, a point we shall tackle below. In addition, it discerns a "big" *sharaf* (that is, a sexual attack on a woman) and a "smaller" one (that is, insulting her, or beating her up). The shaykh also noted, "The other kind of *sharaf* is when I take someone's *janbiyya* or something like that, or I beat someone up while he

16. The *janbiyya* is a traditional dagger worn by a large portion of the male Yemeni population.

is safe (*amin*). This is considered breaking the *sharaf* (*kasr ash-sharaf*), . . . and it is black shame (*'ayb aswad*)."[17] Interestingly, the broken *sharaf* is the perpetrator's who is labeled *maksur ash-sharaf*.

The shaykh, in accord with his expert role, provided a more systematic and comprehensive description of *sharaf*, also including references to tribal customary law.[18] This expertise is consistent with Boyer's observation that the specialist's linguistic register often includes "definite" and "reliable" statements around a *mana*-term (1986, 57). Nonetheless, even the shaykh still explained *sharaf* in ostensive terms, by pointing to concrete cases and instances.

By the end of 2012, a land conflict erupted in Kuthreh, bringing to the foreground several other *sharaf*-related concepts. Tribesmen from Rada' demarcated some land overlooking Kuthreh's valley. This operation pushed the villagers to patrol the border and triggered a morbid curiosity for the land whose value had recently increased following the construction of a state road. My host, 'Ali, saw an opportunity in the impending conflict and claimed a plot of land in the area.

One morning, I came across a villager—'Abdullah, a man involved in the land sale—who told me in front of many others, "Tell *'ammak* 'Ali that he is a fool (*majnun*) to claim those lands. His grandfather already sold the sun and the wind." When I got back home, I delivered the message. 'Ali picked the mobile and called 'Abdullah, who laid it on thicker. In an outburst of rage, 'Ali grasped a stick and walked down the valley toward his opponent's house. Several villagers joined him along the road, owing

17. In this context, *'ayb* is an infringement of tribal customary law that requires an increased compensation. This meaning is more specific than the everyday usage of *'ayb*, which covers situations ranging from minor mischiefs (for example, scolding a child) to the most despicable behaviors (for example, insulting women, stealing, killing, and the like). For a sample of the language used in tribal customary law, including the usage of the word *'ayb*, see Dresch (2017) and Rossi (1948).

18. While comprehensive definitions of *sharaf*, such as the one put forth by this shaykh, still exist within a world of floating signification, they do not represent a total social vision, as per Serjeant's classic approach.

to 'Abdullah's suspicious role in the land sale. In a few minutes, some ten angry people gathered outside the man's door, willing to confront him. 'Ali shouted, "[Come out] you drunk!" The man replied, "What do I owe you?" The men held 'Ali back from assaulting the house. Eventually, he challenged 'Abdullah to meet him on the contested plot of land and returned home.

When 'Ali recounted these events to me, he commented, "If a person sells what belongs to other people (*haqq an-nas*), the people insult his *'ird*, his *sharaf*, and his *karama*." I replied, "What's with his *'ird*?" And he said, "His *'ird* is himself." During the following days, I heard similar expressions referred to 'Abdullah, including the recurrent, "He's not afraid of his *'ird*." When I asked 'Ali to comment on this last sentence, he explained: "It means that it doesn't bother him if people curse him; it's normal for him." 'Abdullah, unlike most men, seemed not to care for his *'ird*, and this had a consequence: the other villagers assumed that he would show no respect for other people's. 'Ali further deepened this point, explaining to me the meaning of the attribute *sharif*. "He who preserves women (*muhafiz 'ala al-makalif*) is *sharif*." He added, "A *sharif* does not threaten or insult anybody, not even as a joke, because he preserves (*muhafiz*) his *sharaf*. If you insult a person, he will reply (*yijawib 'aleyh*). I mean, [the *sharif* is someone] polite (*mu'addab*), okay? He does not accept any bad talk. This [person] is preserving his *sharaf*."

*Sharif* is the man who fears for his *sharaf* (or *'ird*) and preserves it by disciplining his everyday behavior and weighing his words and actions; he avoids insulting his peers so as not to be insulted, his action being preemptive; and he is a *mu'addab* person, someone "polite" or "educated." It is worth stressing that the latter terms, less "exotic" and "theoretically loaded," better hint at the ordinary ethics of *sharaf*, a lifeworld within which "right" and "wrong" are expressed by means of everyday gestures rather than in relation to a transcendent scheme.

Also, the meaning of *sharif* is context bound. 'Ali al-Sharqi, a pious man in his late seventies who served in the army and worked as a farmer, observed: "The *sharif* person keeps to himself (*ba'd haleh*). He worships God and His Prophet; he loves God and the Prophets, all of them. He is respectful (*muhtaram*)."[19] His nephew, a fanatic supporter of Ansar Allah in his late twenties, added that a *sharif* avoids "haram things, like adultery and fornication, alcohol, the religiously forbidden things (*al-muharrama wa-l-makruha*), and the shameful ones (*'ayb*)." These two perspectives are clearly informed by a religious discourse, and the meaning of *sharif* slightly differs from the one we just analyzed above, adding a further semantic layer.

Let me now consider one last case. As recalled above, by the end of 2012, some outsiders made a move to control the lands overlooking Kuthreh. The village shaykh urged the aggressors not to build over the land and appointed men from each *badana* to protect it. My host, 'Ali, his shotgun on his shoulder, climbed his way to the lands with me. When we reached the highlands, while I was taping, he explained: "This is mine (*haqqi*)! Someone came from Rada'! . . . He wants to build here, over what is mine (*haqqi*)! What belongs to my grandfather and my great-grandfather! I swear (*amana*) I will die the worst death here, but he won't have what is mine (*haqqi*)!" (Nevola 2015, 202).

In the Yemeni dialect, *haqq* is a claim, a demand, a right, something that is due (also in ritual occasions), and a property. In everyday language, *haqq* works as a personal pronoun, combined with a possessive suffix (cf. Piamenta 1990, 100). In this excerpt, it means "it's mine," or "it's my right," and it establishes an indexical connection between self and property. The term is loaded with thick cultural assumptions around the value of land, yet assumptions embodied in practice rather than explicated in cosmologies or expert discursive traditions. A few days later, when we returned to the highlands to build a guardhouse, 'Ali continued his explanation in response to my questions.

> LUCA: Why are we building a guardhouse (*deyma*) over here?
> 'ALI: So that we can protect our land. No one comes to bother; no one comes to take what is mine (*haqqi*). . . .
> LUCA: What did you tell me before? This way, people will see what?
> 'ALI: Our resolution (*'azima*) and the strength of the man! . . .

---

19. Recorded interview, Dec. 2012, Kuthreh.

LUCA: Can I say that your land is your *karama*?

'ALI: No.

LUCA: Okay, maybe your *sharaf*?

'ALI: No. *Haqqana* (it belongs to us)! If anyone takes it from us, how can I say that, people will feel that we are weak (*du'afa'*). If someone takes it, we are weak.

LUCA: You are not men . . .

'ALI: It's not that we are not men. . . . I mean, we are weak. Or you can say that we have no manliness (*rajula*). I mean, poor people (*masakin*) who cannot defend their belongings. (Nevola 2015, 203–4)

This dialogue is an outstanding example of equivocation. 'Ali immediately frustrated my attempts to link our risky enterprise to an honor-related discourse, reducing my theoretical constructions to the taken-for-granted reality that "what is yours must be defended," for reasons so obvious (and so implicit) that he deemed them not worth an explanation. The last passage—"defending what is yours not to appear weak"—is a reminder that our social identity is always an allusion to the "voices of others" (Irvine 1990, 130): in this case, the so-called *du'afa'* (or *masakin*) (cf. Serjeant 1977; Bujra 1971), people who cannot defend themselves.

'Ali concluded our dialogue by glossing the same concepts in a religious register. "I told you the Prophet said that your blood, your *a'rad* and your lands are *haram* for you. The meaning of *haram* is that abandoning these things is not licit. Your *a'rad* means your *sharaf*: your wife, your sister, your mother. This is *'ird*" (Nevola 2015, 205).

*Challenge and Offense: Two Separate Domains of Honor*

Before continuing our analysis of *sharaf*, we shall first clarify how challenge and offense are interrelated in the domain of honor. In *The Sentiment of Honour in Kabyle Society*, Pierre Bourdieu makes a distinction between "point of honour" (*nif*) and "honour" (*h'urma*). *Nif* would point to the order of challenge, "the game of outbidding the other," *h'urma* to the category of "offence" that involves the most sacred values controlling the mythico-ritual system of the Kabyle society (1966, 216).

This distinction is fundamental to understand key aspects of the Yemeni case. In the highlands, the order of challenge is pervasive yet seldom analyzed. The "dialectic of challenge and riposte" (197) is particularly evident in the context of hospitality. In this ambit, a man gains *qidr* (esteem or, more simply, social capital) by "honoring" (*taqdir*) a guest (Nevola 2015). This ritual implies practices of self-depletion: giving honor involves "diminishing oneself" (cf. Keating 1998, 407), and serving (*yikhdum*) a guest is a way to gain a symbolic credit while showing respect to him.

At times, practices of self-depletion trigger competition (*qimr*) that must be kept within customary boundaries. For instance, a man is expected to "honor" his affines by slaughtering bulls (*ru'us baqar*) at their wedding. However, this depletion of one's possessions must be kept within limits, in order to be reciprocated. The same holds for the quantity and type of food offered during wedding ceremonies (Nevola 2015, 285). As noted above, this kind of competition takes place between peers. The dialectic of challenge and riposte (*da'wa w-ijaba*) is so pervasive that it also invests poetry, and men can be challenged in verse concerning anything in their life (Caton 1990, 28).

One would expect practices of challenge and riposte to increase or decrease a man's symbolic capital, his reputation (or his "honor"). And indeed, a man's *qidr*, *karam*, or *muruwwa* would be heightened by such practices. However, these practices would not increase (or disgrace) a man's *sharaf*. In fact, in most cases, the latter term refers only to women, and its meaning is even narrower than that of Bourdieu's *h'urma*. Indeed, as seen above, in my interlocutors' reading, *sharaf* is only a subset of what is haram.

According to Bourdieu, the *h'urma* is preserved through a double movement grounded into two general principles: be respectful to be respected; never abandon the *sacra*. This ethnographic account is strikingly similar to what emerged from the Yemeni dialogues presented above. The deterrent function of a peer's reaction is recognized by my interlocutors as the fundamental mechanism structuring a man's expectations. In most cases my interlocutors would simply state that a man does not "abandon" (*yifallit* or *yifukk*) his *sharaf*, reinforcing this assertion with references to death. In my interlocutors' words, "[The *sacra*] are more precious than life"; "I swear (*amana*) I will die the worst death here, but he won't have what is mine (*haqqi*)!"; and so forth. Offense and preservation of the *sacra* are thus linked in a reciprocal mechanism. However, this mechanism is not necessarily conceptualized in terms of a mythico-ritual system; neither is it solely expressed in terms of tribal customary law or Islamic piety: this discourse is how the lived immediacy of experience is socialized and elaborated upon at the anthropologist's request. As also noted by Bourdieu, "In practice, the system of values of honor is lived rather than clearly conceived" (1966, 231).

Having pulled the domain of "offense" apart from a general theory of honor, we are now in the position to address the core theme emerging from the above dialogues, namely, the idea that "*sharaf* is women." During my fieldwork, most of my male interlocutors were deeply concerned with the idea of "covering" (*satar*) their womenfolk, especially their daughters and sisters. The root *s t r* often occurs in the hadith with the meaning of isolating an individual from the multitude to avoid disturbing him (for example, during prayer), and *sitr* was the curtain by which the Prophet Muhammad "concealed women from the gaze of the world" (Wensinck 1991, 902). Similarly, in Yemen, the verb *satar* conveys the idea of a proactive "nonexposition" of women, both in physical and in symbolic terms, to be achieved through several different means: preemptively, through an "appropriate" education, but also through impositions aimed at preserving women from allegedly compromising situations.

This idea is staged through the "apparatuses of everyday life" (Das 2012, 145), and it pervasively shapes a Yemeni man's lifeworld. Indeed, a man never directly refers to women in public. When talking about his wife, he uses the expression "my house (*bayti*)" or "Fulan's mother." Most men even avoid writing their wife's name on their mobile phone (Nevola 2016), suggesting a conception of female names as an "ontological extension of the self" (cf. Mahmood 2013, 72). This idea is rooted in Yemen's history: during the time of Imam Ahmad (1918–48), women of elite families would bear male names, and addressing them by their female name was deemed inappropriate for the non-*mahram* (Vom Bruck 2019, 69).

This point is better understood if we look at female bodies in the public domain. The *sharif* man is expected not to talk with unrelated women in public or to look at them—it would be considered '*ayb*. When boarding a public minivan (the so-called *dabbab*), a man always leaves an empty seat between himself and a woman. If the woman is young or if she feels shy, the whole backseat can be reserved for her. Whenever a man meets a woman he knows in public, he is expected to ignore her presence—even though in a private context he would be allowed to talk with her.

Even staring at women is deemed inappropriate. A look (*nazra*) retains the performative force of an action. Women in the street would often shy away from a man's stare, hiding their eyes behind the *niqab*. Looking at a woman with envy (*hisd*), without pronouncing the ritual "*ma sha' Allah*," amounts to casting the evil eye to her husband (or male guardian). When building a house, placing a window in front of a neighbor's courtyard or in front of his windows can lead to strong disagreements: women must be protected from prying eyes. A friend named Ibrahim—who was *sharif*, but clumsy—once got into trouble because of his stare. While chewing qat with me and other friends in a small office room he was caught, three times, staring at the neighbor's wife through her window. As she complained, her son demanded apologies, threatening to close down the office. It was in these trivial everyday cases that people experienced the immediate meaning of *sharaf*, its practical dimension. Rather than being a call to war in defense of the *sacra*, the idea of *sharaf* shaped a pervasive form of segregation of the sexes, disciplining actions—but also words (*kalam*), gazes (*nazra*), and bodies—and working as a "total" social fact.

Given the concept's sensitive nature, peeking behind the curtain of *sharaf* required an intimate relationship with my interlocutors. For instance, 'Ali, my widowed host from Kuthreh, started addressing such a topic after months of coresidency, and even then he would whisper as if someone could hear us talking. A Hashemite, son of a teacher who served both Imam Yahya and Imam Ahmad, 'Ali joined the Republican army and embraced a dazzling career. Unfortunately, during the mid-1990s, his wife passed. Challenging social expectations, 'Ali refused to remarry: at first, as he confessed, because affection bound him to his wife and, later, because he enjoyed his bachelor life. For years, he took care of his two daughters as a single father, thus challenging another pillar of manhood.

In spite of this "liberal" attitude, 'Ali was obsessed with his daughters' virginity, and he never allowed them to visit female friends until they got married. He told them, "If you want to see your friends, you can invite them home. Here's the television; there is popcorn and juices. I will go to the other room." In case of a wedding or a childbirth (*wilad*), or any other *mawjib*,[20] he prohibited his daughters from coming home after sunset and explained: "Once, a girl was groped in the darkness. How would you know who did that?" An offense to a woman's *'ird* calls for a reaction: How to react, if the perpetrator remains unknown?

When 'Ali's daughters got married, both on the same day, he described the occasion as one of paramount tension and danger—"I was scared to death (*kunt akhaf al-mawt*)." As he told me, he did not calm down until his daughters were "delivered" by the wedding procession (*harawa*) to their husbands' houses. Related womenfolk are all considered a man's *sharaf*. Daughters, however, retain a distinct place. The proverb says: "Whose daughter is the whore? And whose wife is this naked girl? (*qahba bint man wa-'ariya marat man?*)." A daughter's misbehavior, in fact, always falls upon her father, even if she is married. The man who reported this proverb explained to me: "I say that my daughter is my *'ar*, because her behavior falls upon my reputation. People will say, 'She's Fulan's daughter.'"

Whenever men recounted to me their daughters' usage of the term *sharaf*, it was always to emphasize the control their daughters had over them. When a young *sharifa*—a Hashemite's daughter—fell in love with an "ordinary" tribesman (*qabili*) from Kuthreh, she told her father, "I'm your *sharaf*; I won't misbehave. But I won't marry anyone but him." This simple sentence sufficed to remind the father that, in the end, he had no control over her. He gave his consent, and he fixed the date of the engagement. Another *sharifa* from the village practiced sexual intercourse with quite a number of men before marriage, and when she got pregnant she indicated her favorite lover as her child's father. In order to preserve the *sharaf* of the girl's family—that is, preventing rumors from spreading—the shaykh of the village coerced the lover to marry her. This episode

---

20. A *mawjib* is a semimandatory social gathering related to lifecycle celebrations (weddings, funerals, childbirths, and the like). Every adult member of the society is expected to at least "show up."

was recounted to me by one of the woman's relatives who stressed men's extreme vulnerability to women's behavior. From these dialogues, *sharaf* emerges as a relation of dependence and a dangerous one for men.

Moving from the same case, we shall consider one last example. After a few years of marriage, the male lover of the above story—whom we shall call Fulan—took a second wife while still married to the first one. Fulan had another child and stopped practicing sexual intercourse with his first wife. As a reaction, she left the marital house and returned to her father's house, to put pressure on her husband. By nighttime, her brothers ambushed Fulan and beat him up, and so he screamed "*ant taliq*" three times, thus irremediably divorcing his wife. In response, she fled with her brother to their in-laws' village, in another tribal confederation. They asked for refuge and protection and eventually even joined the new tribe through a ritual called *mukhuwwa* (Nevola 2015).

These actions spread the rumor of the scandal to another tribe, and the story became one of public domain. A man from the village, concerned for his own reputation, commented, "They are damaging our *sharaf*." When asked to further explain the matter, he stated, "In Khawlan they will not say, 'She's *bint Fulan* or from *Bayt Fulan*'; they don't even know it. They will say, 'She's a girl from Kuthreh.'" In sum, this woman's behavior interpellated all Kuthreh's men, who felt their *sharaf* was at stake.

*Segmentary Proclivity and Sharaf*

This last point raises the thorny issue of the individual versus collective dimension of *sharaf*, and it speaks to its segmentary nature. I've never heard any of my interlocutors describing *sharaf* as a quality of the line of descent or as prestige passed down from one generation to another. Rather, origin (*asl*) is what defines the essence of an individual, both in moral and in physical terms. It defines what the individual *is* and how his qualities and prestige are inherited "from father and grandfather (*ab 'an jadd*)" (Nevola 2020b). *Sharaf* and *asl* are clearly related and overlap, inasmuch as an individual who claims *asl* is expected to care for his *sharaf* and to avenge it, and the *asil* is considered *sharif* until proven otherwise. This said, is it possible for a group or a descent line to *have* a shared *sharaf*?

The answer to this question lies in the notion of segmentary proclivity. M. Herzfeld cogently observed that segmentation is an idiom, and it "does not necessarily entail a unilineal descent system" (1984, 655), nor does it necessarily refer to political organization. Rather, segmentation can take various forms in different societies, and it works as a "practical relativity. It marks the level of social, cultural, and political differentiation that are salient for a given community" (661).

The notion of *sharaf* qualifies the relationship of a man with his *sacra* in terms of proximity. This "closeness" to the *sacra* can be expressed in terms of descent, kinship, shared territory, nationality, or even religion, and it is always differential: ego is "closer" to his *sacra* than an "alter" who—in a given circumstance—is threatening them. It follows that, under specific circumstances, a group of men with a shared identity (genealogical, territorial, and so on) could qualify the attack against his *sacra* as *sharaf* and thus react in a corporate way. However, *sharaf* cannot be possessed or lost as a substance, given its indexical nature.

For instance, dynamics of proximity can interpellate a tribesman to consider a woman his *sharaf*, if she hasn't got anyone closer to protect her. Consider this excerpt from a broader interview with a young *qabili* from Sanhan:

> In sum, *sharaf* is *'ird*, nothing else. I mean, your *'ird* from your female relatives. This is my *sharaf*. I mean, it's impossible that one attacks you, or your daughter, or your wife or your sister or your female relatives. . . . If we consider the level of the village, only the brother defends his sister, because we are in the village. And if we are in Sanaa, and a girl from Kuthreh goes to Sanaa, I will be her relative (*al-qarib*). So I will preserve my *sharaf*, which is the *sharaf* of the village. And if I were in another province, or in another place, like 'Aden, and I knew that she is from Sanaa, it's possible that I would feel *ghira* and defend her. Even if I were in a European country and she were Yemeni: she's my *sharaf*, she's Yemeni, and I will kill for her. This is *sharaf*. Only what is related to the woman. (Nevola 2015, 267)

This last excerpt eventually introduces us to the notion of *ghira* and to the embodied nature of *sharaf*.

*Sharaf as an Embodied Emotional Structure*

In 2013, while heading toward lunch after a Friday prayer, I witnessed a man from Kuthreh emptying his AK-47 on another villager's car in reaction to a disagreement over land. In a similar vein, a few months later, I observed another villager quivering in rage while eradicating his nephews' qat trees that trespassed by less than one meter on his land. I could provide countless other similar examples, including the above-mentioned anecdote of how 'Ali raged down the valley to avenge a mild insult.

These outbursts of "rage"—for lack of a better word—always echoed in my mind Steven Caton's remarks on symbolic power and his anecdote on how the sanctuary where he lived was targeted by bullets in a farcical "game of violence" (1990, 12). It is beyond doubt that, at times, violent performances are instrumentally staged to restore the balance of power without resorting to a harmful physical assault. However, in many other cases, violent reactions are clearly "spontaneous"—seemingly "natural"—because triggered by bodily *hexis*, "a set of body techniques or postures that are learned habits or deeply ingrained dispositions that both reflect and reproduce" the objective structure of a society (Abu-Lughod and Lutz 1990, 12; Bourdieu 1977). From this perspective, *sharaf* can operate as a "floating signifier" by bridging the domain of embodied experience and that of cultural discourse.

A pertinent example of how emotions, conceived as cultural products and embodied habits, are produced by and reproduce social structure is provided by Wikan in *Behind the Veil in Arabia* (1991). In discussing how Sohari women adhere to "the dictates of sexual segregation," Wikan observes that they do not conceptualize segregation or modesty in general terms, but rather enact a "feeling of shyness" (*yitkhayil* or *yistihi*) that pushes them to proactively avoid men in specific contexts. In particular, the verb *yistihi* (or *yitkhayil*) points to the experience of "a clear and strong emotion within oneself" inhibiting the acts in question (1991, 68). Otherwise stated, the habitus of Sohari women structures their dispositions in accord with an overarching social organization, orchestrating individual interests and objective societal structures (69).

Reflecting on Wolof village society, Judith Irvine pushes this argument even further, positing a direct connection between social ranking and bodily hexis. Central to the Wolof hierarchical system is the idea that people are inherently unequal and that one's genealogically inherited constitution (biological, emotional, and moral) is the source of his "temperament (*naw*)" or "capacity for emotionality": "Persons of the same rank are *nawlé* 'castemates,' who resemble one another in temperament and moral status" (1990, 133).

A similar idea lies at the core of highland Yemen's hierarchical system. The notion of *asl* delimits several domains of power and crafts human subjects who are inherently unequal, their constitution inherited from father and grandfather along the line of descent. Having *asl* implies a distinctive emotional *habitus* that is perceived as "natural" and "essential" to one's origin. The tribesmen should be "light-blooded" (*khafif al-dam*) or "red-eyed" (*ahmar al-'ayn*): mercurial, fearless, and impulsive (Dresch 1989, 42). Light blood can and must be limited by self-control (Caton 1990, 29) and patience (*sabr*), but nonetheless it guarantees the proper reaction with regard to *sharaf*.

Seemingly, the *qaba'il* are expected to feel *ghira* when *sharaf* is at stake. This emotion is canonically translated as "jealousy," but the glossing is misleading and downplays the reach of the concept: *ghira* can also be felt for the nation or for Islam. Moreover, it does not only cover—as it would in Western countries—the reaction to another man's interest for one's partner. Rather, it extends to any woman who could be considered a man's *sharaf*. It is, in sum, an emotional trigger that pushes men to "cover" their women (physically and symbolically), to care for their reputation and integrity, and to react whenever they are endangered, but also to protect their *sharaf* in a broader sense that is constantly redefined.

According to Irvine (1990), hierarchical systems are characterized by complementary affectivities that exert different functions within the system. Accordingly, in highland Yemen, low-status groups are described by the dominant groups as lacking in origin (*nuqqas al-asl*), and their temper and moral status is believed to depart from the *qaba'il*'s one (Vom Bruck 1996). In particular, they are believed not to feel *ghira* of their womenfolk, and this emotional disposition would allegedly translate into a more libertine attitude. Discourses on emotions and *sharaf* are, thus, also discourses on the Other. Interestingly, Yemeni laymen also believe that the capacity to feel *ghira* also distinguishes Muslim believers from Christians. In fact, the latter's capacity to feel *ghira* is allegedly inhibited by pork consumption, leaving Christians indifferent to their womenfolk's behavior.

## Conclusion: Ordinary Ethics, Wartime Morality

"Honor" entered the anthropological discourse as a tool for comparison, a theoretical metonym for the circum-Mediterranean area. In Arab-speaking countries, the alleged homology between Western notions of "honor" and local understandings of *sharaf* yielded opposite effects: on the one hand, a conflation of distinct local concepts into one English umbrella term; on the other hand, a reduction of *sharaf* to a normative form of social ranking or a feature of warlike contexts. By adopting a lexical approach, I have attempted to equivocate the notion of *sharaf* and "run with it," letting the ethnographic material reveal itself (Holbraad and Pedersen 2017, 2).

Going through this journey, *sharaf* came into view as a domain of everyday ethics in which the protection of the *sacra* was performed through the cultivation of embodied sensibilities (Das 2012; Lambek 2010). But *sharaf* also belongs to the public domain: its subjective experience is embedded in our "being-with-others" (Duranti 2015, 232) and translated into the domain of language. Indeed, "naming" an ethical domain is always already an act of "objectification" (Keane 2016, 182), and *sharaf's* public nature offers the possibility to "back up individual ethical intuitions with ethical descriptions" (Mattingly and Throop 2018, 480). However, in my ethnography these descriptions remained fuzzy, unsystematic, and the word *sharaf* seemed to operate as a floating signifier, pointing to embodied experiences rather than elaborated "native cosmologies."

By way of contrast, in this last section I shall precisely focus on a formalized native cosmology, namely, *The Tribal Charter of Sharaf*, and consider how Yemen's present brings to the fore a number of pertinent questions concerning the future words and worlds of honor. Indeed, the ongoing civil war offers the chance to observe a "revolutionary morality" in the making (Keane 2016). This emerging formalized code is bringing the meaning of *sharaf* closer to the classic anthropological notion we have examined—an umbrella term apt to describe an "encompassing" moral system—departing from the ordinary ethics of *sharaf*.[21]

Since March 2015, the Houthi movement, also known as Ansar Allah, has controlled Yemen's capital, Sanaa. The Houthis refer to their opponents—namely, the Saudi-led coalition backing the IRG—as the "aggression ('adwan)." Starting from October 2015, the pro-Houthi Council of Tribal and Popular Cohesion has promoted a manifesto titled *The Tribal Charter of Sharaf*[22] and fostered tribesmen to adhere to it. In this manifesto, the word *sharaf* refers to a "permanent" code of conduct, a sort of "honor in its most encompassing sense," and the charter is defined as valid "in war and peace, in all circumstances and times, embodying the tribal principles, values, and foundations."

The principles contained in the charter are thus intended to be constitutive of *sharaf*. However, classic tribal values—like generosity, bravery, self-reliance, and so on (Caton 1990)—do not appear in the document. Rather, the main focus of the charter is the so-called declaration of innocence, through which the adherents affirm that their conscience is "innocent and their faces whitened from the perpetrators of the aggression." He who betrays the charter is labeled an *'a'ib*, literally a "disgracer." The language of shame (*'ayb*) is thus mobilized and applied to the supporters of the "aggression," labeled as "traitors" and "agents[23] (*'umala'*)," and described as "armored in *'ayb* and clothed in crime and *'ar*." According to the charter, the *'a'ib* is "excluded from the rights of brotherhood

---

21. Although scholars tend to disagree on the distinction between ethics and morality, I will adopt Bernard Williams's definition (1985) and refer to "ethics" as pertaining to "desires, motivations and embodied sensibilities" and to "morality" as concerning "public and systematized descriptions, norms, rules, and agreed-upon values" (Keane 2016, 18; cf. Fassin 2015, 176).

22. The text of the document is available at this address: https://www.taiz-news .com/4966/. The translation from Arabic to English is mine.

23. The word "agent" (*'amil*, pl. *'umala'*) refers to the alleged agents working in Yemen as "spies" on behalf of Israel and the United States. These words, along with others mentioned in the text, pertain to a vocabulary shared by the members of the so-called Axis of Resistance, an anti-imperialist movement led by the Iranian regime.

(*akhuwwa*), companionship, defence, and joint expenses (*ghurm*), protection of the neighbor (*al-mujawara*), and citizenship."

This Houthi-sponsored morality of *sharaf*, which is spread by Houthi ideological state apparatuses, stands in stark contrast to the ordinary ethics I've described through ethnography, and it compels us to formulate a few questions related to Yemen's present and future. First, I have described the subjective experience of *sharaf* as characterized by a double emotional movement: a feeling of vulnerability and fear related to the protection of the *sacra* and a feeling of "outrage" (*ghira*) that the *qabili* is supposed to "naturally" feel when *sharaf* is at stake. It is worth asking: Is the Houthis' "morality of *sharaf*" capable of mobilizing this very same emotional configuration in defense of an imagined community of tribesmen and citizens threatened by the aggression?

Second, like most emotional configurations, the one triggered by *sharaf*-bound contexts is also dialogical and complementary (Irvine 1990, 155). Not only does the *qabili* always experience his world as if his fellow *qabili* could be aware of him and judge him, but he is also always "naturally" aware of a more distant Other: for example, the low-status servant or the Western foreigner we have mentioned. This Other is often defined in genealogical and essentialist terms (Nevola 2015, 2020a). The Houthi morality of *sharaf* focuses on a different level of distinction: the Other is defined by his political affiliation with the aggression, while the Self is identified with the "resistance." Will this new distinction overshadow the values that used to organize the traditional hierarchical order of the highlands?

Last, let me tackle a potential value conflict implied by the morality of *sharaf*. In the domain of ordinary ethics, the *qabili* is called to discipline the "apparatuses of everyday life," and the "rightness" of his actions is constantly "judged by the cultivation of a moral sensibility that is able to detect the 'human'" within habits and customs (Das 2012, 140). The word *sharaf*, functioning as an index or a floating signifier, gives meaning to these ethical intuitions without ever crystallizing them. As such, it enables cultural change: ordinary ethics leave room for maneuvering and are open to redefinition. Quite to the contrary, in *The Tribal Charter of Sharaf*, moral choice is reduced to political affiliation, and no room is left for divergence: dissenting equals betraying. The choice between "right" and "wrong" is removed from the ordinary domain and enforced by a hegemonic discourse, backed up by the use of political violence. The *qabili* is potentially embroiled in a value conflict (Robbins 2016, 776) between tribal bonds—the classic principle of *'asabiyya* or the Yemeni idea of *akhuwwa* (cf. Nevola 2020b)—and political affiliation.

Interestingly, this value conflict cannot be solved in the domain of ordinary ethics. Rather, it refers to normative definitions of "rightness," and it calls for public declarations of loyalty. Is this new focus compatible with the structure of tribal corporate groups? Or will it ultimately weaken the corporate bond of the tribes? To conclude, I shall ask with Joel Robbins: Is it possible for moral ends to be "merely a matter of duty or obligation" (2016, 779)? The morality of *sharaf* seems to relocate the possibility of choice—and, ultimately, of freedom—in the "troubled waters" between ethics and politics (Fassin 2015, 207). Approaching *sharaf* through equivocation leaves the door open to future investigations in this contested domain.

## References

Abou-Zeid, Ahmed. 1966. "Honour and Shame among the Bedouins of Egypt." In *Honour and Shame: The Values of Mediterranean Society*, edited by John G. Peristiany, 243–59. Chicago: Univ. of Chicago Press.

Abu-Lughod, Lila. 1989. "Zones of Theory in the Anthropology of the Arab World." *Annual Review of Anthropology* 18: 267–306.

———. 2016. *Veiled Sentiments: Honor and Poetry in a Bedouin Society*. Oakland, CA: Univ. of California Press.

Abu-Lughod, Lila, and Catherine A. Lutz, eds. 1990. *Language and the Politics of Emotion*. New York: Cambridge Univ. Press.

ACAPS. 2020. "Tribes in Yemen: An Introduction to the Tribal System." Thematic report, Aug. 2020. https://www.acaps.org/sites/acaps/files/products/files/20200813_acaps_thematic_report_tribes_in_yemen_0.pdf.

Adra, Najwa. 1982. "Qabyalah: The Tribal Concept in the Central Highlands of the Yemen Arab Republic." PhD diss., Temple Univ.

Appadurai, Arjun. 1986. "Theory in Anthropology: Center and Periphery." *Comparative Studies in Society and History* 28, no. 2: 356–61.

———. 1988. "Putting Hierarchy in Its Place." *Cultural Anthropology* 3, no. 1: 36–49.

Berger, Peter. 1970. "On the Obsolescence of the Concept of Honor." *European Journal of Sociology* 11, no. 2: 339–47.

Bourdieu, Pierre. 1966. "The Sentiment of Honour in Kabyle Society." In *Honour and Shame: The Values of Mediterranean Society*, edited by John G. Peristiany, 193–241. Chicago: Univ. of Chicago Press.

———. 1977. *Outline of a Theory of Practice.* Cambridge and New York: Cambridge Univ. Press.

Boyer, Pascal. 1986. "The 'Empty' Concepts of Traditional Thinking: A Semantic and Pragmatic Description." *Man*, n.s., 2, no. 1: 50–64.

Brandt, Marieke. 2017. *Tribes and Politics in Yemen: A History of the Houthi Conflict.* London: Hurst.

Bujra, Abdalla S. 1971. *The Politics of Stratification: A Study of Political Change in a South Arabian Town.* Oxford: Oxford Univ. Press.

Caton, Steven C. 1990. *"Peaks of Yemen I Summon": Poetry as Cultural Practice in a North Yemeni Tribe.* Berkeley: Univ. of California Press.

Clifford, James 1988. *The Predicament of Culture: Twentieth-Century Ethnography, Literature, and Art.* Cambridge, MA: Harvard Univ. Press.

Connell, Raewyn W. 2005. *Masculinities.* Cambridge: Polity.

Das, Veena. 2012. "Ordinary Ethics." In *A Companion to Moral Anthropology*, edited by Didier Fassin. Hillsdale, NJ: Wiley-Blackwell.

Dresch, Paul. 1986. "The Significance of the Course Events Take in Segmentary Systems." *American Ethnologist* 13, no. 2: 309–24.

———. 1988. "Its Roots in Arabia and Its Flowering Elsewhere." *Cultural Anthropology* 3, no. 1: 50–67.

———. 1989. *Tribes, Government, and History in Yemen.* Oxford: Clarendon Press.

———. 2006. *The Rules of Barat. Tribal Documents from Yemen: Texts and Translation.* Sanaa: Centre Français d'Archéologie et de Sciences Sociales. http://books.openedition.org/cefas/853.

———. 2017. "Rossi's Kitāb al-Sinna: A Seventeenth-Century Note of Tribal Law in Yemen." *Arabian Humanities* 9. http://journals.openedition.org/cy/3489.

Dumont, Louis. 1970. *Homo Hierarchicus: An Essay on the Caste System.* Chicago: Univ. of Chicago Press.

Duranti, Alessandro. 2015. *The Anthropology of Intentions: Language in a World of Others.* Cambridge: Cambridge Univ. Press.

Evans-Pritchard, Edward E. 1974. *The Nuer: A Description of the Modes of Livelihood and Political Institutions of a Nilotic People.* New York: Oxford Univ. Press.

Fabian, Johannes. 1983. *Time and the Other: How Anthropology Makes Its Object.* New York: Columbia Univ. Press.

Fahd, T. 1991. "Sharaf." In *The Encyclopaedia of Islam.* Vol. 2, C-G, edited by Bernard Lewis, Charles Pellat, and Joseph Schacht, 313–14. New ed. Leiden: Brill.

Fassin, Didier. 2015. "Troubled Waters: At the Confluence of Ethics and Politics." In *Four Lectures on Ethics: Anthropological Perspectives*, edited by Michael Lambek, Veena Das, Didier Fassin, and Webb Keane. Chicago: Hau Books.

Fortes, Meyer. 1953. "The Structure of Unilineal Descent Groups." *American Anthropologist*, n.s., 55, no. 1: 17–41.

Fortes, Meyer, and Edward E. Evans-Pritchard. 1970. *African Political Systems.* London: Oxford Univ. Press.

Gilmore, David D., ed. 1987. *Honor and Shame and the Unity of the Mediterranean.* Washington, DC: American Anthropological Association.

Heinze, Marie-Christine. 2014. "On 'Gun Culture' and 'Civil Statehood' in Yemen." *Journal of Arabian Studies* 4, no. 2: 70–95.

Herzfeld, Michael. 1980. "Honour and Shame: Problems in the Comparative Analysis of Moral Systems." *Man*, n.s., 15, no. 2: 339–51.

———. 1984. "The Significance of the Insignificant: Blasphemy as Ideology." *Man*, n.s., 19, no. 4: 653–64.

Holbraad, Martin, and Morten Axel Pedersen. 2017. *The Ontological Turn: An Anthropological Exposition.* Cambridge: Cambridge Univ. Press.

Irvine, Judith T. 1990. "Registering Affect: Heteroglossia in the Linguistic Expression of Emotion." In *Language and the Politics of Emotion*, edited by Lila Abu-Lughod and Catherine A. Lutz. New York: Cambridge Univ. Press.

Jackson, Michael. 1996. *Things As They Are: New Directions in Phenomenological Anthropology.* Bloomington: Indiana Univ. Press.

Keane, Webb. 2016. *Ethical Life: Its Natural and Social Histories.* Princeton, NJ: Princeton Univ. Press.

Keating, Elizabeth. 1998. "Honor and Stratification in Pohpnei, Micronesia." *American Ethnologist* 25, no. 3: 399–411.

Keesing, Roger M. 1985. "Conventional Metaphors and Anthropological Metaphysics: The Problematic of Cultural Translation." *Journal of Anthropological Research* 41, no. 2: 201–17.

Kimmel, Michael, and Tristan Bridges. 2014. "Masculinity." In *Oxford Bibliographies.* Oxford: Oxford Univ. Press. https://www.oxfordbibliographies.com/view/document/obo-9780199756384/obo-9780199756384-0033.xml.

Lambek, Michael. 2010. *Ordinary Ethics: Anthropology, Language, and Action.* New York: Fordham Univ. Press.

Lévi-Strauss, Claude. 1987. *Introduction to the Work of Marcel Mauss.* London: Routledge and Kegan Paul.

Littlewood, Roland, and Ellie Reynolds. 2020. "The Embodiment of a Floating Signifier." *Anthropology & Medicine* 27, no. 1: 110–23.

Mahmood, Saba. 2013. "Religious Reason and Secular Affect: An Incommensurable Divide?" In *Is Critique Secular? Blasphemy, Injury, and Free Speech*, edited by Talal Asad, Wendy Brown, Judith Butler, and Saba Mahmoud, 64–100. Berkeley: Univ. of California.

Mattingly, Cheryl, and Jason Throop. 2018. "The Anthropology of Ethics and Morality." *Annual Review of Anthropology* 47: 475–92.

Meeker, Michael E. 1976. "Meaning and Society in the Near East: Examples from the Black Sea Turks and the Levantine Arabs (I)." *International Journal of Middle East Studies* 7, no. 2: 243–70.

Nevola, Luca. 2015. "Blood Doesn't Lie: Hierarchy and Inclusion/Exclusion in Contemporary Yemen." PhD diss., Univ. of Milano-Bicocca.

———. 2016. "Love, Mobile Phones and the Codification of Intimacy in Contemporary Yemen." *Middle East Journal of Culture and Communication* 9, no. 2: 147–64.

———. 2020a. "'Black People, White Hearts': Origin, Race, and Colour in Contemporary Yemen." *Antropologia* 7, no. 1: 93–116. https://www.ledijournals .com/ojs/index.php/antropologia/article/view/1626/1526.

———. 2020b. "Houthis in the Making: Nostalgia, Populism, and the Politicization of Hashemite Descent." *Arabian Humanities* 13. http://journals.open edition.org/cy/5917.

Patterson, Orlando. 1982. *Slavery and Social Death.* Cambridge, MA: Harvard Univ. Press.

Peristiany, John G. 1966. *Honour and Shame: The Values of Mediterranean Society.* Chicago: Univ. of Chicago Press.

Peristiany, John G., and Julian Pitt-Rivers, eds. 1992. *Honor and Grace in Anthropology.* Cambridge: Cambridge Univ. Press.

Piamenta, Moshe. 1990. *Dictionary of Post-Classical Yemeni Arabic: Part 1.* Leiden: E. J. Brill.

Pitt-Rivers, Julian. 1966. "Honour and Social Status." In *Honour and Shame: The Values of Mediterranean Societies*, edited by John G. Peristiany, 19–77. Chicago: Univ. of Chicago Press.

———. 1992. "The Personal Factors in Fieldwork." In *Europe Observed*, edited by João de Pina-Cabral and John Campbell, 133–47. London: Palgrave Macmillan.

———. 2017. "The Malady of Honor." In *From Hospitality to Grace: A Julian Pitt-Rivers Omnibus*, edited by Andrew Shryock and Giovanni da Col, 105–18. Chicago: Hau Books.

Robbins, Joel. 2016. "What Is the Matter with Transcendence? On the Place of Religion in the New Anthropology of Ethics." *Journal of the Royal Anthropological Institute* 22, no. 4: 767–808.

Robertson Smith, William. 1903. *Kinship and Marriage in Early Arabia*. Boston: Beacon Press.

Rossi, Ettore. 1948. "Il Diritto Consuetudinario delle Tribù Arabe del Yemen." *Rivista degli Studi Orientali* 23: 1–36.

Schielke, Samuli. 2010. "Seconds Thoughts about the Anthropology of Islam; or, How to Make Sense of Grand Schemes in Everyday Life." ZMO Working Papers 2.

Schneider, Jane. 1971. "Of Vigilance and Virgins." *Ethnology* 9: 1–24.

Serjeant, Robert B. 1977. "South Arabia." In *Commoners, Climbers, and Notables: A Sampler of Studies on Social Ranking in the Middle East*, edited by C. A. O. van Nieuwenhuijze, 226–47. Leiden: Brill.

Shryock, Andrew, and Giovanni da Col, eds. 2017. "A Perfect Host: Julian Pitt-Rivers and the Anthropology of Grace." In *From Hospitality to Grace: A Julian Pitt-Rivers Omnibus*, edited by Andrew Shryock and Giovanni da Col, xiii–xxxix. Chicago: Hau Books.

Stewart, Frank Henderson. 1994. *Honor*. Chicago: Univ. of Chicago Press.

Viveiros de Castro, Eduardo. 2004. "Perspectival Anthropology and the Method of Controlled Equivocation." *Tipití: Journal of the Society for the Anthropology of Lowland South America* 2, no. 1: 3–22.

Vom Bruck, Gabriele. 1996. "Being Worthy of Protection: The Dialectics of Gender Attributes in Yemen." *Social Anthropology* 4, no. 2: 145–62.

———. 2005. *Islam, Memory, and Morality in Yemen: Ruling Families in Transition*. New York: Palgrave Macmillan.

———. 2019. *Mirrored Loss: A Yemeni Woman's Life Story*. London: Hurst.

Wensinck, Arent J. 1991. "Sutra." In *The Encyclopaedia of Islam*. Vol. 2, C–G, edited by Bernard Lewis, Charles Pellat, and Joseph Schacht, 902–3. New ed. Leiden: Brill.

Wikan, Unni. 1984. "Shame and Honour: A Contestable Pair." *Man*, n.s., 19, no. 4: 635–52.

———. 1991. *Behind the Veil in Arabia: Women in Oman*. 1982. Reprint, Chicago: Univ. of Chicago Press.

Williams, Bernard. 1985. *Ethics and the Limits of Philosophy*. Cambridge, MA: Harvard Univ. Press.

# 5

# The State

*Metaphorical and Material*

Susanne Dahlgren

> How does one define the state apparatus . . . and locate its limits? At what point does power enter channels fine enough and its exercise become ambiguous enough that one recognizes the edge of this apparatus? Where is the exterior that enables one to identify it as an apparatus?
>
> —Timothy Mitchell, "Society, Economy, and the State Effect"

Studying the state in Yemen has always been a tedious task. Over the past century, its states have been many, and their reach, territorially and socially, has been of varied success. Taken the circumstances, political scientists have agreed that the Weberian perspective is not particularly fruitful in the Yemeni case, especially considering how many rulers have actively sought to foment tension in state-society relations as a matter of course.[1]

---

1. Political scientists have engaged prolifically in defining the various states that, during the past century, have numbered almost fifty in the territory that today forms the Republic of Yemen and have pointed out repeatedly the futility of defining the state in Weberian terms of a monopoly on the legitimate use of violence and territorial control (Carapico 1985, 203). In the North, they have shown how a tribal order controls territory in a state-like manner (for example, Peterson 2016), while the state fails to act in its basic functions of a tax collector and provider of services and security (Chaudhry 1989, 1997). Similarly, scholars have highlighted the variegated state experiences in the South during

My interest here is not to engage in that discussion but to approach the state from the logic that Timothy Mitchell proposes regarding the limits of the state and the ambiguities of its power. I am particularly interested in seeing what we can learn about the state in Yemen when looking at it through the eyes of an outsider. Here, I argue that such a perspective is fruitful taken that the current Yemeni "state" is the product of two earlier sovereign administrations—that of the Yemen Arab Republic (YAR or North Yemen) and the People's Democratic Republic of Yemen (PDRY or South Yemen), which united in 1990. However, the formation of the current Republic of Yemen (RoY) that year did not constitute a clearly articulated unifying state project between the two administrations. Following the 1994 war between the two Yemens, the new state administration became solidly rooted in the structures inherited from the North Yemeni state, while southerners who joined it were compelled to operate within its parameters. The state outsider in this case, whom I will introduce shortly, is a man who joined an administration that was completely new to him, having come from the civil service of the losing side in the war: the South. With the help of political anthropology and its focus on everyday practices of state agencies (Sharma and Gupta 2006, 11), in this chapter I seek to trace the "thingness" of the state in relation to "society" and the logical and functional relations that serve to abstract the former from the latter. I follow Marilyn Strathern's (1996) suggestion that categorical boundaries (in this case, the limits of the state) do not always coincide with the complexity of people's actions or the networks that they enfold.[2]

---

the British Protectorate era, as a territory patterned by a mosaic of larger and smaller sultanates, emirates, and other one-family autocracies without actual sovereignty (Halliday 1975; Stookey 1982). Lisa Wedeen has called for studying postunity Yemen as a political system wherein "substantial representation," as evident in the various fora of the public sphere, must be taken into account (2007, 63), while Phillips (2008) and Longley (2010) characterize the Republic of Yemen as a patronage system.

2. As Strathern elaborates, the language of boundaries raises expectations in social scientific analysis that might not meet the needs of cultural translation. As she states, "Such expectations are both superfluous and insufficient: the complexity of people's interactions as they might be apprehended sociologically does not find a simple substitute

I correspondingly suggest that when studying the "effects" of the state in Yemen, in Mitchell's terms, we must be sensitive to its distinctive languages (Hansen and Stepputat 2001). For the period in question, we encounter a variety of historically specific configurations of "stateness," each with its own symbolic, performative, and practical expressions that serve to perpetuate the state apparatus that unified Yemen inherited from the North.[3] As Hansen and Stepputat put it, in studying the state it is illustrative not only to show how it becomes "tangible through symbols, texts and iconography . . . but also to move beyond the state's own prose" and see how it "appears in everyday and localized forms" (05). This conceptualization they call the "languages of stateness." As for this language, in the Yemeni case, the particular word that is on the lips of every Yemeni when discussing the state is "corruption" (*fasad*). However, instead of discussing corruption in reference to the usual regime/elite suspects, here I instead focus on how corruption plays out in what I call the everyday state. The setting for this study is the state administration in the capital, Sanaa, a few months following Yemeni unity, in the very moment that eligible civil servants from the former PDRY assumed positions in the RoY's state administration.

To study the constitution of the state through the lens of everyday practice requires that we think not only about humans who *make* the state (cf. Ortner 1996), but also the material objects that drive administrative practices and thereby communicate the state's agency in specific ways. In the ethnographic case that follows, the material object in question is that of a whiskey bottle. To highlight the everyday nature of state work, I leave leaders and political elites aside and, instead, focus on the experiences of a middle-rank official from the South who joined the postunity

---

in the subtlety with which categorical boundaries may be re-thought. For a start, the concept of boundary is one of the least subtle in the social science repertoire" (1996, 520).

3. By "state apparatus," I am relying on an Althusserian understanding of the state as a force of "repressive execution and intervention 'in the interests of the ruling classes'" (2006, 90). While I understand that Yemen is not a class society in the classical sociological meaning, it has a ruling system that represents the interests of the ruling "class."

administration in Sanaa. I show that in making this move, he crossed not just the physical border that had existed between the two Yemens, but also a border that persisted from then on as a moral threshold, separating, in turn, two languages of stateness (Dahlgren 2010). This man, whom I shall call Hamid, is someone who gradually acquired a practical mastery of the language of the state through the careful deployment of its nonhuman "thingness." While gaining this mastery, Hamid was able to act as my guide to the secrets of the North Yemeni bureaucracy. I discuss Hamid's story against the background of my own experiences while working within the state administration as an aid worker, first during the PDRY and later in postunification Sanaa.[4]

### New State, New Capital

By the time of unity in May 1990, the majority of civil servants who had worked in the South Yemeni bureaucracy were given the chance to join the ranks of the civil service in Sanaa. While most declined the offer, for one reason or another, and stayed to run the "Aden branch," one of those individuals who took the chance was Hamid. After a decade of working in the PDRY administration, he was an experienced civil servant and much liked by his colleagues. In Sanaa, he entered an administrative system and political culture that was strange to him and, even after an initial trial-and-error phase over the first several months, remained alien to him. He is, I suggest, "an outsider" in the sense Mitchell alludes to in the earlier quote, who is able to make visible the limits of the state apparatus from a position of relative exteriority. Such outsiders are correspondingly able to make visible (in this case, for the ethnographer) the mechanisms

4. I initially traveled to southern Yemen when the country was the PDRY to work in a Finnish health-care project located in al-Ghaydha, the center of the easternmost governorate of al-Mahra. As the coordinator of the project stationed in the erstwhile capital, Aden, I spent most of my time working with people in the ministries and other government agencies. When unity came, and with the centralization of all ministries in Sanaa, my tasks were moved to the North even though our office remained in Aden. While working in this capacity during 1991 and 1992, I experienced firsthand the change in administrative culture.

and narratives that many who work as insiders in the bureaucracy may take for granted.[5]

In discussing the eternal question of the boundary between state and society, Mitchell suggests that such a distinction should not be taken as a boundary between two discrete entities. Instead, he calls for a perspective where a line is drawn internally within the *network* of institutional mechanisms through which a social and political order is maintained. In such a perspective, the state is not an abstraction somewhere "out there"—even though it is made to appear as such—but rather an assemblage of institutions, sites, procedures, techniques, and practices (Mitchell 1991, 78; see also Benhabib 2004 and Navaro-Yashin 2002). In analyzing the networks that participate in "making the state," vis-à-vis Mitchell, it is useful to simultaneously consider Bruno Latour's actor-network theory (ANT) (Latour 2005) and its broader anthropological engagements (for example, Strathern 1996, 2018). ANT allows us to see how nonhuman elements can exist alongside human actors as part of an agentive network. I find this approach critical in making sense of the various material practices that make the (former) southern and (current) northern state apparatus so distinct from each other, as we will see. Here, "network" is not indicative of classical sociological webs but, rather, is a total outcome of making, whatever such making involves, be it scientific inquiry, religious festivals, or state bureaucracy (Candea 2018). Nonhuman elements, such as tangible, exchangeable objects—in our case a whiskey bottle—have, to an extent, lives of their own and thus form an essential part of how the everyday state works. However, paying heed to Caroline Humphrey's (2008, 358) warning not to let the individual agent be eclipsed in the jungle of networks that take center stage in ANT analyses, we will see that Hamid, as our outsider, makes key decisions about how best to harness the affective potential of nonhuman actants.[6] We need to bear in mind in this discussion that

5. In my forthcoming book I discuss other cases of southerners in the labyrinth of Sanaa bureaucracy.

6. As Humphrey ascertains, "It is necessary to think about how a singular human being might put him- or herself together as a distinctive subject by adding to, or

power is not equally distributed within the network. For James Ferguson and Akhil Gupta (2002), the state has a distinct spatiality through which its agents attempt "to secure their legitimacy, to naturalize their authority, and to represent themselves as superior to, and encompassing of, other institutions and centers of power" (982). Such spatiality facilitates Hamid's position as an outsider "within" the network, while also constituting the very lexicon that he sought to acquire and master.

States are "made" in much larger networks of agency (human and nonhuman, material and immaterial, communicative, and processual) than earlier studies on Yemen have explicitly maintained, centered as they are predominantly on the personality of the former president, his entourage, rival political parties, or a combination thereof. When reviewing earlier studies on the state in Yemen(s), it is evident that we need to pay much more attention to the different material and immaterial "workings" of the state beyond such a confined lens (see also Mathur 2016). This elaboration, I suggest, both complements and challenges the idea of the state as finely drawn by many political science accounts on Yemen.[7] Following this more expansive approach to the state and its languages, we see that states are not only bureaucratic apparatuses or playgrounds for elites (even though certainly they may be made to appear as such), but powerful sites of symbolic and cultural production that represent themselves in specific cultural ways (Ferguson and Gupta 2002, 981).

**Rulers, Regimes, States**

The state has always been a topical theme in Yemeni studies. The troubled relationship between the people and the state and its inability to protect and provide are two persisting topics. Along with this problem, we find a considerable body of scholarship addressing the interplay of state

---

subtracting from, the possibilities given by culture as it has been up to that point, through the very process of taking action" (2008, 358).

7. Among others, see Carapico (1998); Chaudhry (1997); Clark (2004); Halliday (1975, 1990); Ismael and Ismael (1986); Kostiner (1990); Longley (2010); Peterson (1984); Phillips (2008); Schwedler (2006); Stookey (1974, 1982); Wedeen (2008); Wenner (1991); and Yadav (2013).

sovereignty, nationalist politics, and a regionally vibrant tribal society, as well as the maneuverings and machinations of leaders, elites, and activists across party lines. During the past decade, however, this multi-disciplinary discussion that came to be typical of late-twentieth-century Yemeni studies has been eclipsed by a form of knowledge production that is overtly driven by policy-oriented agendas, largely reflective of post 9/11 co-optations of Middle East studies. The result has been that the terminology used to describe the state in Yemen has become analytically vague and theoretically empty. Concepts such as "legitimate government," "secessionists," and "rebels" accompany memes used to describe the country, such as "the poorest country in the Arab World" and "the host of Al-Qaeda in the Arabian Peninsula,"[8] thereby contributing to a form of knowledge production in which outside interference in Yemeni internal affairs somehow becomes understandable and even desirable. This laxing of diverse scholarly discussion pertaining to the nature(s) of the state in Yemen is partly the result of the country becoming a privileged zone of theory for "strategy studies," "terrorism studies," and "failed-state studies," the new subdisciplines that receive disproportionately high levels of private and public funds in Western academia and the think-tank world.

Such obfuscation is further entrenched when the state is perceived, or at least discussed in both academic and policy circles, as being interchangeable with a sole political figure (cf. Lakoff 1991). Although it may be accurate to describe Yemeni politics during 'Ali 'Abdullah Salih's rule as a patronage system (Longley 2010; Phillips 2008, 45), this rendering fails to account for the larger state apparatus—the "everyday state." The state-as-ruler metaphor certainly resonates with how Yemenis discuss the state in history, with each era typically inviting the name of the ruler, such as the "Salim era" and "'Ali Nasir time."[9] Rulers have also, of course, used such metaphorical substitutions to their own ends as a means to legitimate

---

8. Take any news report on Yemen in international media, and these terms appear.

9. Salim Rubai' 'Ali acted as the leader of the PDRY during 1969–78 and 'Ali Nasir Muhammad held various state and party positions during 1980–86. While the followers of these two leaders often tended to coincide with the regional origin of the leader, the networks of power were more complex than this rendering would suggest.

their power. In both the YAR and the PDRY (and in the latter beginning with imperial newsreels under the British), daily TV news broadcasts would typically present the respective leader opening development projects, receiving foreign dignitaries in the airport, and distributing material goods to citizens. This orchestrated father-of-the-nation play reinforced the image of the president not only as *the* state, but also as the guardian of the state coffers.[10] Still, ask almost any Yemeni and she or he will tell you that the image that the leader aims to disseminate is rarely taken at face value. The "father of the nation" narrative is but one of several narratives of the state, and one that is often reproduced with a level of sarcasm, while at the same time competing with other languages of stateness, such as the "corruption" narrative and, specifically among southern citizens, the "looter" narrative.[11]

In what follows, I seek to bring complexity to the study of the state in Yemen by observing the routines of a state agent for whom "the state" becomes material in those tasks and duties in which he must complete his administrative duties. Necessarily, there is a difference in degrees of agency between higher presidential echelons and civil servants like Hamid, whose task is merely to operate in the labyrinth of the state administration. It is the latter's world of state bureaucracy that I want to make visible.

## The Northern State

While getting to know the northern state after moving my administrative activities to Sanaa in the early 1990s, I began to understand the major differences between the states of the PDRY and the YAR. Such differences failed to make sense within the standard reference in the literature to the

---

10. Cf. Borneman (2004), who calls such states as 'Ali 'Abdullah Saleh's Yemen "patricentric."

11. This accusation resonates with Sami Hermez's (2015) discussion of how cynicism constitutes a mode of resistance in Lebanon and also Navaro-Yashin's (2002) discussion of cynical agency in Turkey. See also Wedeen's (2008, 100) discussion of the spectacle as a moment of national unity making. Similarly, in discussing colonial-era Hadhramaut, Gilsenan (1982, 264) talks of the act of kissing the sharifs' hands by people of lower social strata as being "feigned."

PDRY as a "Marxist state" (Bidwell 1983)[12] and the YAR as a state led by "a governing coalition composed of tribal and military leaders" (Stookey 1974, 410). To start with, the Sana'a'ni bureaucracy hired a manifold of civil servants in contrast with the rather slim bureaucracy in Aden. Part of the reason for this swelling of civil servants in the North naturally had to do with the fact that southerners who were willing to join the Sana'a'ni administration were simply brought there without redesigning anyone's duties.[13]

After spending some time in the government offices of the new capital, I realized that the number of such employees whose only job appeared to be sitting in front of an office desk and smoking cigarettes was much higher in Sanaa than it ever had been in Aden. Furthermore, many of the employees in Sanaa came from outside the capital, a fact that became evident in and around public holidays as the absentee levels in Sanaa ministries skyrocketed. A regular 'id holiday led to three to four days' absence in Adeni offices, whereas in Sanaa the breaks, even among lower-ranking officials, tended to be seven to eleven days depending on how far away one's village is located. Coemployees of serial absentees would kindly inform me when a public holiday approached, so I could prepare accordingly. One could say that working discipline tended to be better in Adeni offices, but that explanation is only part of the story.

The composition of the staff in the Adeni offices also differed markedly from the Sana'a'ni staff. Once the British colonial power withdrew in 1967 and local people were hired as civil servants, women were granted opportunities in the workplace alongside men, thereby replacing the British and Indian civil-service ranks that the empire had brought to the colony.

12. Manfred Wenner (1984) criticized the idea of analyzing the PDRY as a "Soviet satellite," emphasizing that the two states' interests should not be blurred.

13. Chaudhry explains that in comparison to the imamate era, the Republic experienced a rapid growth in bureaucracy, with the number of civil servants swelling from three thousand in 1962 to thirty-one thousand in 1975. This happened in a period when tax revenues in fact declined owing to heavy labor migration and the consequent parallel economy that the remittance system generated (Chaudhry 1997, 200). My own experience in working with the bureaucracy of both the PDRY and the postunity RoY also attests to an ever-increasing bureaucracy in Sanaa, with unity adding to the number of civil servants performing similar, and often parallel, tasks.

PDRY male white-collar employees typically dressed in shirt and slacks, a legacy of British colonial rule. Those workers who had already assumed office during colonial rule simply continued in the same style following independence in the late 1960s. Female office employees and members of the administration typically wore dresses, and some wore a headscarf. But covering the face was never the case before unity and, indeed, would not have been allowed by the authorities. The alienating factor of a covered face (from the perspective of anyone who must communicate with a covered face) emerged in Adeni offices during the late 1990s, a factor that in the onset of unity was an overwhelming practice in Sana'a'ni offices. In the Sana'a'ni ministries that I frequented, I never saw a female face. In general, women tended to have secretarial jobs or acted as tea makers and cleaners. As the civil service, since the time of the imamate (pre-1962), tended to be a male prerogative, it seemed natural to me that the few females working in offices wanted to protect themselves with the face veil if for nothing else than to avoid sexual harassment.[14] In Aden, women occupied high administrative posts, and a female head of section was a rule rather than an exception during the late 1980s. The monotony of gender variety struck me once I started to engage with the Sana'a'ni bureaucracy and made me consider my own position as a foreign aid worker who happens to be female (a question I never had considered during the PDRY era). These two capitals also differed in terms of movement outside the workplace. During the PDRY, no woman was required to have "her guardian" to accompany her on a business trip, a practice that also emerged within Aden following unity. These issues affected Hamid, too, as he had moved to the city with his professionally active wife and their small child, as I will shortly discuss. Suffice it to say here, as I have elaborated in my earlier work (Dahlgren 2010), female civil servants exhibited a stronger work ethic than their male colleagues during the PDRY era, a fact evident not only in their keeping to hours but also avoiding side jobs or entertaining relatives during the workday.

14. Even though veiling has many contexts in Yemen, here I am referring specifically to how the face veil acts as a communicative border line that the carrier draws and maintains (see Dahlgren 1999).

By contrast, long absences from the workplace turned out to be a rule rather than an exception in Sanaa. Not only did public holidays provide an excuse for longer-than-expected absences, but workdays also tended to be shorter, with most men hurrying to their favorite qat[15] dealer at midday. Indeed, following noon prayers, the long corridors of Sanaa's ministries were practically empty of civil servants. I was informed that some of the many absentees were taking care of their side jobs during office hours. As an absent person's colleague in a ministry once told me, the civil-servant job was to his colleague itself a side job. Thus, while working in Sanaa, I found that taking care of my necessary paperwork was far more difficult and time-consuming than it had ever been in Aden, primarily because of widespread absences. However, this fact turned out not to be the only reason for the delays, as will be revealed through the case of Hamid and his explorations of the jungle of the Sana'a'ni bureaucracy.

### Out of a Different Past

The two Yemens entered into unity from two very distinct, though inter-linked, trajectories, a brief account of which is necessary for understanding the challenges faced by our man of the state, Hamid. If in the South, the independent state formed in 1967 was patched together from a plethora of family dynasties that joined the state administration built during the colony (and later state) of Aden, the situation was equally complicated in the North, although prior to unity only two states, the Mutawakkilite Kingdom of Yemen (1918–62) and the Yemen Arab Republic (1962–90) formed state apparatuses. In Euro-American political science, the establishment of the Republic in the North is typically referred to as a coup (*inqilab*) (see Peterson 1984, 99), while Yemenis in both the North and South generally

---

15. Qat, *Catha edulis*, is a mild stimulant that is consumed in afternoon social gatherings (see, for example, Wedeen [2007]). Today everyman's habit, during the imamate its consumption was limited to affluent sectors of society. In the 1950s, the British unsuccessfully attempted to ban its sale in the colony. During the PDRY, qat sale was restricted to Thursdays and Fridays. Unity expanded its use even to the eastern governorates of Hadhramaut and al-Mahra, where it was not the custom earlier.

call it a revolution (*thawrat 26 sibtambar*).[16] Clearly, in terms of public governance, even when new republican ministries were established following the 1962 revolution, the state apparatus changed little. Once the Egyptian "advisers" arrived in the early 1960s to "modernize" the administration and the army, their social and geographical composition barely changed from what had been drawn up prior to the Republic. Both were dominated by northern highlanders, while southern lowlanders (active in the British colony of Aden) formed the economic dynamo (Chaudhry 1997). Once the oil boom that benefited North Yemen in the form of labor export and remittances came to an end, the recession sealed the political exclusion of southern business elites. As Kiren Chaudhry (1989, 142) informs us, the economic reforms of 1986 evidenced a dramatic shift in favor of northern tribal elites who received all the state subcontracts for public imports. Among the beneficiaries of import licenses in grain, sugar, and flour (that is, key food imports) were notable tribal shaykhs from the North, such as 'Abdullah al-Ahmar and Sinan Abu Lahum, who were also notable figures in republican politics (142). The oil wealth that was meant to substitute the dwindling remittance economy failed to trickle down to the rural population, and its beneficiaries, overwhelmingly, comprised a few individuals associated with the government (Colton 2010, 411). As the Hamid al-Din family was evicted from power in 1962, the authoritative system of governance that centralized power around a ruler who governed through carrot-and-stick policies continued in the presidential system of the YAR, while the imamate-era chosen social stratum, the *sada*,[17] lost its monopoly, if not access to power.[18]

16. The term *inqilab* points to a perceived absence of deep-rooted economic, social, or cultural transformation following this event. In the minds of many Yemenis in the North, however, the new national vision and language of stateness embarked upon by the Republic is better conceived through the emic concept of revolution (*thawra*).

17. *Sada* is the plural of *sayyid*, a descendant of the Prophet Muhammad, who under the imamate formed the ruling stratum as an educated class. The imam could come only from the male members of this stratum.

18. During the presidency of 'Abd al-Rahman al-Iryani (1967–74), tribal shaykhs were invited to Sanaa to take up high state offices, substituting the ones that members of

For those foreign scholars who initially carried out fieldwork during the YAR, unity in 1990 was not a leap into the unknown. The initial unity agreement, a two-page document signed in Sanaa by 'Ali 'Abdullah Saleh and 'Ali Salim al-Bidh on April 22 that year, centralized all powers to a five-member Presidential Council, but said little about how the administration was to be restructured or the army reassembled.[19] As Sanaa was crowned the new capital, state administration came to be concentrated within its environs. Top ministerial posts were distributed evenly between northern and southern members of the joint cabinet, with respective deputy ministers coming from the other part of the earlier divided country. In principle, this division meant that some former PDRY ministers began to administer the entire country. In practice, however, this even division meant very little; the ministries that southerners came to lead functioned as if nothing had changed since the YAR. As Salwa Amber (1999) who, throughout the 1990s, worked in the office of the Presidential Council ascertained (and corroborated by my own experience), southerners were granted neither full access to necessary documents nor administrative support that, on top of administering a new territory, rendered their work impossibly difficult. During the post-unity thirty-month "transitional period," old Adeni ministries and government offices became "Aden branches" with jurisdiction over the southern governorates, only now they were dependent on fiscal policies determined in Sanaa. While practical state work continued to be carried out in the Aden branches, decisions were made in the new capital where many top politicians had little or no knowledge of the problems prevalent in the South. It is illustrative that, in the long corridors of the Sana'a'ni ministries, I met officials who did not know that al-Mahra was part of Yemen.

---

the *sada* occupied during the imamate. This measure was aimed at securing the collaboration of regions beyond state control and to expand republican grip in the countryside (Brandt 2017, 57).

19. The Agreement on the Establishment of the Republic of Yemen, signed on April 22, 1990, in Sanaa, English-language translation with introduction by Nassib G. Ziadé, is available at https://www.cambridge.org/core/journals/international-legal-materials /article/yemen-arab-republicpeoples-democratic-republic-of-yemen-agreement-on-the -establishment-of-the-republic-of-yemen/DB7E7AF47B349CC2AEC9F690BC2A9687.

The northern state persisted throughout the early 1990s, bringing in minor changes, such as allowing political parties and civil-society organizations to open, and introducing a free press, all of which was articulated under the banner of "democracy."[20] The RoY became democratic in terms of freedom of speech, assembly, and association, although it was a freedom that throughout the 1990s would be increasingly curtailed.[21] By the time of the war in 1994 in which the North vanquished the South, any previous political opening had now firmly closed. The war shattered the remnants of the southern state, including its public sector, army, and political organization and limited the possibilities for anyone wanting to democratize the system beyond the parameters imposed by Sanaa. Throughout the South, people felt these changes in the deterioration of state services, the loss of employment opportunities in the public sector and the army, and the loss of control over their resource wealth. The discourse of "northern occupation" (al-ihtilal al-shimali), as it continues to be known, began to spread among southerners when talking about state rule.[22]

## The Happy State Official

While many Adeni civil servants who were called upon to join the new administration in Sanaa following the establishment of RoY declined the offer, Hamid, a middle-level officer in a ministry, took up the call and moved with his family to the new capital. Hamid was a smiling guy, always making jokes about whatever situations we encountered while roaming the corridors of the Adeni government offices. His positive attitude and joyfulness made taking care of dull bureaucratic work pleasurable. As

20. The PDRY regime allowed for a free press six months prior to unity in the winter of 1989, and in doing so reissued the license of the famous Adeni newspaper, al-Ayyam.

21. See Law No. 66 of the 1991 Governing Parties and Political Organizations (including Republican Resolution of 109/1995 issued after the 1994 war) on the regulation of political organizations and parties. The official English translation of this law is available here: https://www.refworld.org/docid/3ae6b5288.html.

22. There is little doubt that all of Yemen has suffered from an absence of state services. Still, the unity narrative that cites "equal suffering" in the North and the South fails to address the very different trajectories of state building and state absence in al-Mahwit (North) and al-Mahra (South).

with so many others like him who mastered a foreign language, Hamid had studied abroad in one of those "friendly countries" that accepted South Yemeni students.[23] His Arabic was sprinkled with foreign words in a manner he had learned while studying abroad. My involvement with the PDRY administration began in the year preceding unity when I was the coordinator of a small Finnish health-care project. My "office" comprised my living room in a block of flats in Aden, a building that hosted many Yemenis working in different governmental posts. While our project was based in al-Ghaydha in al-Mahra Governorate, a thousand kilometers to the east, my Adeni colleagues working in government offices became close to me as I met them almost daily. One of them was Hamid.

With the Aden Branch of the Ministry for Public Health continuing to take care of health care in al-Mahra, our office remained in Aden postunification. From Aden it was easier to fly to al-Ghaydha, a trip that took one day with a change of planes in Riyan, on the Hadrami coast. All the earlier facilities, such as the al-Mahra Office—the outpost of the governorate in Aden—continued to work here. Still, managing our project's paperwork now took place in Sanaa, which was a new town for me. I had left Aden in late 1989, only six months prior to unity, and when I came back in early 1991, the ministries in the new capital were already busy at work managing the territories in the South. Already, the functions in the Aden Branch had been cut down, and very little now took place there besides core functions pertaining to health administration.

Hamid was a street-smart guy who was quick to establish large social networks after moving to Sanaa. From his new colleagues he learned all the tricks of the trade for navigating the strange administrative culture. It was he who also introduced to me these tricks, and had it not been for Hamid I would have certainly been in trouble, so different was the paperwork in the bureaucracy of Sanaa as compared with Aden or al-Ghaydha. To start with, bribes (*rishwa*, sing.) came into the picture as soon as I started to handle our project affairs. During the PDRY, I recall only once being asked for a

23. Many graduates with medical degrees had studied in China or the German Democratic Republic, for instance, while those students who went to Bulgaria, Cuba, Hungary, and the Soviet Union typically studied agriculture, administration, or military science.

kickback.[24] Still, there were moments when project supplies vanished while storing them in Aden or in al-Mahra. If nobody guarded the boxes and containers, the opportunity became too much to resist for anyone hanging around to collect "his share." Indeed, once unity came, Adeni civil servants began to inform me of a culture of opportunism allegedly prevalent in Sanaa where each official was expected, at least, to exploit the chance of taking his or her slice from the communal cake. Such behavior, it was explained to me, culminated in the figure of President Saleh as looter in chief with his vast shares in the lucrative qat market and the black-market economy, not to mention cashing foreign development funds. Many believed that Saleh, himself from a modest tribal background, had become one of the richest men in the world over the course of his tenure. As a junior officer in the army, it was rumored he controlled the illicit whiskey trade on the road to Sanaa through Manakha in the highlands.[25] According to this narrative, the president was the father of the nation and from whose pockets all who acted in his favor received their "share."[26]

Throughout the many months working in the new capital prior to my arrival, Hamid had gained a certain fluency in the "language" of this state. In introducing me to the Sana'a'ni bureaucracy, he became my "language tutor," as it were, so considerably at odds was this world from that of the Adeni bureaucracy.

### First Visit to Sanaa

When I arrived for the first time in Sanaa to do the project paperwork, Hamid invited me to his home. I had booked a room in one of the shabby hotels near Tahrir Square and was not in a position to ask him to visit me.

---

24. I elaborate the entry of bribing in Adeni public administration in my longer text (Dahlgren forthcoming). Suffice to say here that it was a new phenomenon in the South.

25. As Stewart and Strathern (2004) have suggested, rumor and gossip work covertly, outside of formal mechanisms of social control and thus cannot easily be checked or verified through explicit means. They can nevertheless produce results in themselves regardless of verification (29). WikiLeaks cables came many years after the period I discuss here.

26. While I am narrating a story about dishonesty and a corrupt civil service, I must add that while working in the Sana'a'ni bureaucracy, I met many honest civil servants, too.

Being a female traveling without a chaperon, I was considered by many in Sanaa to be a suspicious person.[27] The authorities whose task was the relocation of southerners in Sanaa had given Hamid and his family a small but practical apartment not far from the ministry where he worked. When they lived in Aden, ʿAʾisha, his wife, had done office work, while here she now acted as a housewife, at least in the beginning before they could find a job for her. The couple's only son was about to start school. Maysaʿ, ʿAʾisha's mother, lived with them, and together they took care of the household and child care. The relatively new flat was situated in a block of apartments meant for state employees and had "modern" furnishings—that is, sofas and armchairs rather than cushions on the floor, as is typical in most homes throughout Yemen.

I was sitting on the sofa in the living room chatting with Maysaʿ and ʿAʾisha when Hamid called me into the kitchen. I expected him to show me the cooking he and ʿAʾisha had prepared, but, instead, he opened a cupboard below the sink and, to my great amazement, revealed a shelf full of alcohol: whiskey, vodka, cognac, gin, rum, and other liquors. During the years I had lived in Yemen, never had I seen any alcohol available except beer (local and imported), Russian vodka, and, rarely, Johnny Walker, not to forget the *baladi*, local home brew. Before traveling to Sanaa, my Adeni friends advised me about the alcohol situation there: "Sanaa is a dry place." This advice gave me some perspective on how great the demand for a bottle of any alcohol was in this part of the country.[28] My first reaction in seeing the well-equipped "mini bar" was feeling sorry for Hamid for starting to drink. While some South Yemeni men who had studied abroad had adopted the habit, Hamid was not one of them. Quickly, I reasoned it to be a result of the struggles he had faced resettling

---

27. A Yemeni friend of mine, who as a woman worked as head of her department after unity and regularly visited Sanaa for business, told me that she felt pressure to have her husband or adult son accompany her as a chaperon in her visits to the new capital, despite the fact that she had a company car and driver to take her there.

28. Any item that is rendered illegal has a market in an underground economy. Whiskey has a demand among qat chewers who want to balance the excitement the stimulant creates.

in the often-hostile environment of the new capital. While I felt sorry for him, I could nevertheless sympathize that he had found solace in the bottle. I also speculated that the northern hosts of the Adeni newcomers in the state service had purposely made alcohol easily available for them so that they would refrain from taking proactive roles in public affairs. All such speculation was quickly interrupted by Hamid, smiling at my startled expression. He went on to explain how he had obtained the bottles from a special storage for civil servants of rank working in ministries and government offices. He told me that he had not paid a shilling[29] for the exceptionally large collection of booze. It was a "benefit of the job." His tone quickly became excited as he proceeded to inform me of the bottles' purpose: for making the wheels of the Sana'a'ni bureaucracy run smoothly.

Initially, I did not fully grasp the extent of Hamid's meaning. The chains of internal corruption that ran through the administration became evident to me only the following day when we went together to the Ministry of Finance to clear a permit for the Finnish project. Hamid had all the documents signed and ready on behalf of his ministry (seven signatures with seven stamps) accompanied by a bottle of Johnny Walker in his briefcase. As we entered the ministry, Hamid led me to an office where several officials sat at their desks. He knew beforehand whom we were to meet, and even though this official knew Hamid from prior business dealings, he did not ask us to sit down, something we had become accustomed to while working in the Adeni administration. Standing in front of the official's desk, Hamid handed over not only the papers but also the bottle of whiskey, first glancing around to check that the coast was clear. With an air of routine to his movements, the official, a man in his thirties and wearing a long white *thawb* and a scarf, surreptitiously slipped the bottle into his desk drawer. He then took my papers to review—permits to import hospital equipment. His task now was to get the required signatures from his superiors in the ministry. He never smiled or exchanged the

29. The South Yemeni currency dinar as distributed in twenty shillings was still in use in the early years of unity.

usual compliments that Yemenis exchange when encountering a person, even a stranger. When leaving the office, Hamid commented to me, "This is how it is here." Shocked, I walked with him down the long corridor and out into the street, contemplating along the way how my work, from then on, would be difficult to manage.

It took me some time to understand why a government official needs to bribe another government official so that the latter does his work. While, of course, I knew that in many countries public servants receive such low salaries that they are inclined to supplement their income with bribes, my experience in the South had not prepared me for what I was to encounter in the North. Besides, I thought that it was primarily foreigners and the wealthy companies and agencies they represent that are the targets of such practices. What amazed me the most, however, was that Hamid needed to anoint his colleague in the other ministry for a matter that was by no means a special favor but merely routine paperwork. As I have mentioned, absences during working hours were very frequent in Sana'a'ni ministries, much more than I had, to my great irritation, experienced in Aden. For the Ministry of Finance official, it might take several attempts and many hours of waiting to get the signatures from his superiors. Hence the necessity to pique his interest so that the job be finalized swiftly rather than my papers left on his desk. The transaction manifested a hierarchy; while Hamid formally was the same rank as the colleague in the other ministry, as a southerner he had been granted access to the store. The other man's rank in the northern hierarchy was not high enough to grant access. Clearly, this sparked the speculation in my mind that southerners even of low rank were granted admission to the booze store to corrupt them.

Still, it was not clear to me why Hamid provided the bottle on my behalf. Should it not have been me, a foreign aid worker, who would been expected to hand over the bottle? Clearly, Hamid was acting on my behalf. Perhaps he was seeking to save me the embarrassment of engaging in such a practice myself. Perhaps he was also considering the delicate situation in an office in which several persons worked (even though it was clear that others in the room acted as though they were buried in their work during the exchange). And, possibly, Hamid was aware that his colleague would not pay any attention to me as a (foreign) woman. It is also likely that Hamid wanted to spare his colleague the embarrassment of receiving illicit goods from a woman. I asked Hamid if I should compensate him for the price of the bottle, but he laughed, telling me that after he moved to Sanaa he had been invited to the secret booze store and told that he may take whatever he wants. As he was not a drinker himself, he stashed the bottles and used them for making the running of his errands smoother. The necessity of such smoothing he had learned not only though experience but through discussions with his northern-born colleagues who were kind enough to enlighten him on how things were done in the new capital. That the whiskey bottle acted as a lucrative bribe meant that the official, in this case, located in a different ministry, did not have access to the elusive store, a matter that indicates a system of favoritism based not on rank but on a more complicated design, which I will explain shortly.

It was in such brief transactions that manifested, for Hamid, the "language" of the northern state. For him, to become a skillful civil servant in this domain, like his northern-born colleagues, he must go along with the prevailing system. But bribery was not the only difference he experienced. The northern bureaucracy was far vaster in terms of how many vertical steps a single piece of paperwork needed to ascend in order for it to fulfill its function. In Aden, depending on the number of agencies and jurisdictions involved, such steps tended to comprise two to three senior officials, whose signatures I was required to collect. These signatures were normally accompanied by further instructions, handwritten on the same page, for the next level. The final step was to get the required stamps, which in Aden equaled the requisite number of signatures. In Sanaa, a similar process could require up to seven signatures, sometimes all within the same ministry. The difference came from the fact that in Sanaa since the early years of the Republic, it was the Egyptian administrative system that prevailed, albeit often quite unsuccessfully, as Joshua Rogers (2017) has shown. This system replaced the premodern imamate-era system that, more often than not, functioned without paperwork in face-to-face receptions, *diwans*, of the governor or another state representative.[30] In the

---

30. Rogers (2017) states that the number of Egyptian advisers to the civil administration of the YAR grew from three to four hundred during the years 1962–67, which equates

South, the Socialists had maintained the British administrative system that since 1839 had been introduced in the British-held Aden. That arrangement had less red tape than the Egyptian system.[31] Upon unity the Egyptian system was allowed to prevail and now caused additional problems to people like Hamid and me.

Hamid was critically aware that the system was very dissimilar to the one he had learned while working in Aden and knew, owing to my experience working in the southern system, that I would share his understanding that what we saw was not morally right. He also understood that to be able to work in the state administration in Sanaa, there were only two options available to him: adapt or leave. While he decided to stay, he understood that he could neither publicly criticize the system nor work against it. At home with his wife, and with like-minded friends, he talked about his experiences at work.

### A Precious Good, Full of Agency

The secret booze store forms part of the state apparatus in Sanaa in its capacity to divide officials into those individuals who have access and those individuals who do not.[32] Alcohol was a precious, albeit illicit, good in this part of the country; it was not available for purchase but was made available only to selected members of the state administration.[33] As Hamid and

---

to one Egyptian to ten Yemeni civil servants. See also Messick (1992) on how remnants of the imamate system functioned in the 1970s in his field site of Ibb in lower Yemen. On imamate rule, see also Willis (2018).

31. As Amber (1999, 188) suggests, the Egyptian administrative system was overcentralized and involved much more paperwork. As an example, each paper in a ministry needed not only the minister's signature but also the signatures of the deputy minister, department director, and section chief.

32. At one stage during the 1970s, a similar exclusive store existed in Aden. Instead of alcohol, which was freely available, the store had consumer goods and some foodstuffs. The store had to be closed and the system of exclusive rights for the party apparatus canceled once its existence became a public outcry.

33. During the early years of unity, Aden had some restaurants and bars serving beer and vodka, while other parts of the South were serviced through liquor outlets, often a hole in the wall of the store, located in governorate centers. The famous Seera Beer of the

I soon came to learn, a system of "shares" formed a vertical practice where the president was understood as standing at the top rung of the ladder, thus being the entitled recipient of the greatest share. In discussing the fiscal policies of the YAR, Chaudhry (1989, 114) explains that the rationality in public spending was informed more by primordial networks and political considerations than by economic rationalization.[34] With its victory in the summer of 1994, the northern apparatus could continue, unhindered, to service those sectors of society that had benefited in the past, while incorporating willing southerners into the public administration and the system of "shares." Across the country, Yemenis recognize that such configurations of social mobility and access to wealth are indicative of a state that is corrupt—this fact, of course, being the key driver behind both regional and national revolutionary upheavals in past decades. As Salwa Amber—the southern civil servant who, as I mentioned, joined the Presidential Council as a top administrator following the unity agreement—characterized the administration in Sanaa: "The tribally-dominated power centre did not encourage a change in the administrative setup and the two sides wanted to impose their former systems on the national administration. As the capital, Sanaa, was in the ex-YAR territory, the central administration was predominantly characterized by the latter's system which was cumbersome and corrupt" (1999, x). The sentiment resonates with the revelations of the late editor in chief of the Sanaa-based *Yemen Times* newspaper, 'Abd al-'Aziz al-Saqqaf, who, in a 1998 editorial accused

---

Aden Brewery was produced with a West German license. It was made to terminate its business following bazooka fire on its factory a few weeks after the 1994 civil war. While official rhetoric blamed "Islamic pressure" for its closure, Adenis tended to agree that termination of the highly popular product favored importers of foreign beer and was thus commissioned by these circles.

34. Chaudhry suggests that the problems were exacerbated by inadequate information-collecting systems and that the bureaucracy lacked numbers to compensate for the effects of its distribution policy (1989, 114). The problems in data gathering improved little if at all after unity. One reason was the need to hide the PDRY's lead in providing health care, education, and a longer life expectancy. This practice happened in line with the unity narrative of "equal suffering" in development as allegedly prevalent in the two former states, as discussed in footnote 22.

leading politicians of "robbing the state in broad daylight" (1998), threatened to publish the names of the accused. The precious goods robbed included large plots of agricultural land, industrial properties, palaces, and villas, mostly located in the southern territories.

**Conclusion**

In this chapter I have approached the everyday state as a network of different agencies, human and material. Through the bodies of the civil servants, the state works and produces the outcomes of state rule, be it in the form of documents, projects, or policies. But as we have seen, by himself Hamid is incapable of operating in his role, especially considering his lack of connections compared to many of his northern colleagues. He needs essential material goods—the whiskey bottle—to lubricate the state machinery. Describing this arrangement merely as "corruption" without any elaboration of what actually happens would conceal much of the social making that takes place in the transaction. As Marilyn Strathern reminds us in discussing networks from the perspective of commoditization, "It is not buying and selling as such, of course, that are at the heart of anthropological understandings of commoditization, but the quality of relationships" (1996, 518). In discussing Melanesian marriage arrangements, the point for her is not that brides are "bought" but that specific social relationships unfold in the process of the arrangement and in its outcome. Similarly, what is interesting about corruption, in this case, is that Hamid is not "buying" the cooperation of the finance office employee but, rather, taking part in an administrative culture in which material objects have relational agency.

When looking at networks and relations from the perspective of what Strathern discusses as a "flow"—which in our case equates to the smooth "flowing" of a civil-service machinery—there is little difference between human and nonhuman participants in the everyday language of stateness. Indeed, here the state becomes visible and material in all its connotations as a hierarchical system of shares the very moment that the whiskey bottle is whipped out from the briefcase. This object, we might say, represents the "thingness" of the state—the thing that makes visible its languages and its limits. But for society at large, the differences are immense: without the nonhuman means, which may be called instruments of corruption, those individuals without are inevitably overlooked when the meager wealth of the public treasury is distributed. While in the Yemeni case the patrimonial system is highly centered around an elite, there is still some room for lower-level agents to become recipients of the public good. It did not take many years before this system of shares also became widespread in the South, with many enthusiastically waiting to receive his or her plot of land, SUV, or offspring's foreign scholarship. As this practice was how the public administration functioned, staying out of the system—refusing to speak the language—meant being drastically incapacitated to complete one's duties at work.

In his *Recognizing Islam*, Michael Gilsenan recalls a moment in 1959 when, in the British Eastern Aden Protectorate, his enchantment with an age-old culture was shattered after meeting two young Hadhrami noble men and being invited to their home. Dressed and acting in the street according to their ancestral standing, once "the front door slammed behind us . . . the spell was broken." Hidden from outside eyes and ears, "a Grundig tape recorder played Western pop music, and the strictly forbidden whiskey came out of the cupboard. Turbans were quickly doffed, and there was no talk of religion but only of stifling boredom, the ignorance of local people, the cost of alcohol, and how wonderful life had been in Indonesia" (1982, 10). In a similar way to the ethnography described in this chapter, a single material object had agency, which in Gilsenan's case caused his enchantment of this ancient culture to shatter and which in Hamid and my case made our trust in the state evaporate.

In Yemeni social life, the whiskey bottle, as a metaphorical frame for prevailing corruption, has played a momentous role in the country's fate. Rumors of the president being drunk in public events began to circulate in the 2000s and played a role in the resolve of so many Yemenis in 2011 to join the change and revolution squares across the country, demanding his resignation.[35] The favorite drink of the ousted president, "everyone knew,"

---

35. A friend of mine who had been compelled to join the ruling party to safeguard the resources of his department recalled to me meeting the president four times, who on each occasion was heavily drunk. According to an anonymous alcohol importer

was nothing else than the same that Hamid used to pave his way through the cumbersome and corrupt administrative system.

## References

Althusser, Louis. 2006. "Ideology and Ideological State Apparatuses (Notes towards an Investigation)." In *The Anthropology of the State: A Reader*, edited by Aradhana Sharma and Akhil Gupta, 86–111. Oxford: Blackwell.

Amber, Salwa Murbarak. 1999. "The Political and Economic Transformation of Yemen, 1968–1998." PhD diss., Durham Univ. http://etheses.dur.ac.uk/4861/.

Benhabib, Seyla. 2004. *The Rights of Others: Aliens, Residents, and Citizens*. Cambridge: Cambridge Univ. Press.

Bidwell, Robin. 1983. *The Two Yemens*. Boulder, CO: Westview Press.

Borneman, John. 2004. *The Death of the Father: An Anthropology of the End of Political Authority*. Oxford: Berghahn.

Brandt, Mareike. 2017. *Tribes and Politics in Yemen: A History of the Houthi Conflict*. Oxford: Oxford Univ. Press.

Candea, Matei. 2018. *Schools and Styles of Anthropological Theory*. Abingdon: Routledge.

Carapico, Sheila. 1985. "Self-Help and Development Planning in the Yemen Arab Republic." In *Public Participation in Development Planning and Management: Cases from Africa and Asia*, edited by Jean-Claude Garcia-Zamor, 203–34. Boulder, CO: Westview Press.

———. 1988. *Civil Society in Yemen: The Political Economy of Activism in Modern Arabia*. Cambridge: Cambridge Univ. Press.

Caton, Steven C. 1990. *"Peaks of Yemen I Summon": Poetry and Cultural Practice in a North Yemeni Tribe*. Berkeley: Univ. of California Press.

Chaudhry, Kiren Aziz. 1989. "The Price of Wealth: Business and State in Labor Remittance and Oil Economies." *International Organization* 43, no. 1: 101–45.

———. 1997. *The Price of Wealth: Economies and Institutions in the Middle East*. Ithaca, NY: Cornell Univ. Press.

interviewed by Reuters in 1991, North Yemen was the biggest importer of Johnny Walker Black Label in the entire Arab world (Reuters 1991). A considerable part of the imports were, of course, smuggled across the border to Saudi Arabia. How the current war has affected the supply routes still needs to be explored.

Clark, Janine. 2004. *Islam, Charity and Activism: Middle Class Networks and Social Welfare in Egypt, Jordan and Yemen.* Bloomington: Indiana Univ. Press.

Colton, Nora Ann. 2010. "Yemen: A Collapsed Economy." *Middle East Journal* 64, no. 3: 410–26.

Dahlgren, Susanne. 1999. "'The Chaste Woman Takes Her Chastity Wherever She Goes': Discourses on Gender, Marriage, and Work in Pre- and Post-unification Aden." *Chroniques Yéménites* 7: 77–86.

———. 2010. *Contesting Realities: The Public Sphere and Morality in Southern Yemen.* Syracuse: Syracuse Univ. Press.

———. Forthcoming. "Different Roads to Modernity: State, Society, and Islam in Yemen" (working title).

Ferguson, James, and Akhil Gupta. 2002. "Spatializing States: Toward an Ethnography of Neoliberal Governmentality." *American Ethnologist* 29, no. 4: 981–1001.

Gilsenan, Michael. 1982. *Recognizing Islam: An Anthropologist's Introduction.* London: Routledge.

Gupta, Akhil. 2006. "Blurred Boundaries: The Discourse of Corruption, the Culture of Politics, and the Imagined State." In *The Anthropology of the State: A Reader,* edited by Aradhana Sharma and Akhil Gupta, 211–42. Oxford: Blackwell.

Halliday, Fred. 1975. *Arabia without Sultans.* Harmondsworth: Penguin Books.

———. 1990. *Revolution and Foreign Policy: The Case of South Yemen, 1967–1987.* Cambridge: Cambridge Univ. Press.

Hansen, Thomas Blom, and Finn Stepputat. 2001. "Introduction: States of Imagination." In *States of Imagination: Ethnographic Explorations of the Postcolonial State,* edited by Thomas Blom Hansen and Finn Stepputat, 1–39. Durham, NC: Duke Univ. Press.

Hermez, Sami. 2015. "When the State Is (N)Ever Present: On Cynicism and Political Mobilization in Lebanon." *Journal of the Royal Anthropological Institute* 21, no. 3: 507–23. https://doi.org/10.1111/1467-9655.12249.

Humphrey, Caroline. 2008. "Reassembling Individual Subject: Events and Decisions in Troubled Times." *Anthropological Theory* 8, no. 4: 357–80.

Ismael, Tareq Y., and Jacqueline S. Ismael. 1986. *PDR Yemen: Politics, Economics, and Society: The Politics of Socialist Transformation.* London: Frances Pinter.

Kostiner, Joseph. 1990. *South Yemen's Revolutionary Strategy, 1970–1985.* Boulder, CO: Westview Press.

Lakoff, George. 1991. "Metaphor and War: The Metaphor System Used to Justify War in the Gulf." *Peace Research* 23, nos. 2–3: 25–32.

Latour, Bruno. 2005. *Reassembling the Social: An Introduction to Actor-Network-Theory.* Oxford: Oxford Univ. Press.

Longley, April Alley. 2010. "The Rules of the Game: Unpacking Patronage Politics in Yemen." *Middle East Journal* 64, no. 3: 385–409.

Mathur, Nayanika. 2016. *Paper Tiger: Law, Bureaucracy and the Developmental State in Himalayan India.* New Delhi: Cambridge Univ. Press.

Messick, Brinkley. 1992. *The Calligraphic State: Textual Domination and History in a Muslim Society.* Berkeley: Univ. of California Press.

Mitchell, Timothy. 1991. "The Limits of the State: Beyond Statist Approaches and Their Critics." *American Political Science Review* 85, no. 1: 77–96.

———. 2006. "Society, Economy, and the State Effect." In *The Anthropology of the State: A Reader,* edited by Aradhana Sharma and Akhil Gupta, 169–86. Oxford: Blackwell.

Navaro-Yashin, Yael. 2002. *Faces of the State: Secularism and Public Life in Turkey.* Princeton, NJ: Princeton Univ. Press.

Ortner, Sherry B. 1996. *Making Gender: The Politics and Erotics of Culture.* Boston: Beacon Press.

Peterson, John E. 1984. "Nation-Building and Political Development in the Two Yemens." In *Contemporary Yemen: Politics and Historical Background,* edited by Brian R. Pridham, 85–101. London: Croom Helm.

———. 2016. "Yemen: Tribes, the State, the Unravelling." In *Tribes and States in a Changing Middle East,* edited by Uzi Rabi, 111–44. London: Hurst.

Phillips, Sarah. 2008. *Yemen's Democracy Experiment in Regional Perspective: Patronage and Pluralized Authoritarianism.* New York: Palgrave Macmillan.

Reuters. 1991. "Islamic Pressure Forces Brewery to Stop Producing Beer." https://www.joc.com/maritime-news/islamic-pressure-forces-brewery-aden-stop-producing-beer_19910624.html.

Rogers, Joshua. 2017. "Importing the Revolution: Institutional Change and the Egyptian Presence in Yemen, 1962–1967." In *Gulfization of the Arab World,* edited by Marc Owen Jones, Ross Porter, and Marc Valeri, 113–33. Berlin and London: Gerlach Press.

Al-Saqqaf, 'Abd al-'Aziz. 1998. "Top Ruling Politicians Rob State Property Openly." *Yemen Times,* Jan. 13, 1998.

Schwedler, Jillian. 2006. *Faith in Moderation: Islamist Parties in Jordan and Yemen.* Cambridge: Cambridge Univ. Press.

Sharma, Aradhana, and Akhil Gupta. 2006. "Introduction: Rethinking Theories of the State in an Age of Globalization." In *The Anthropology of the State: A Reader*, edited by Aradhana Sharma and Akhil Gupta, 1–41. Oxford: Blackwell.

Stewart, Pamela J., and Andrew Strathern. 2004. *Witchcraft, Sorcery, Rumors and Gossip*. Cambridge: Cambridge Univ. Press.

Stookey, Robert W. 1974. "Social Structure and Politics in the Yemen Arab Republic." *Middle East Journal* 28, no. 4: 409–18.

———. 1982. *South Yemen: A Marxist Republic in Arabia*. Boulder, CO: Westview Press.

Strathern, Marilyn. 1996. "Cutting the Network." *Journal of the Royal Anthropological Institute* 2, no. 3: 517–35.

———. 2018. "Relations." In *Cambridge Encyclopedia of Anthropology*. https://www.anthroencyclopedia.com/entry/relations.

Wedeen, Lisa. 2007. "The Politics of Deliberation: *Qāt* Chews as Public Spheres in Yemen." *Public Culture* 19, no. 1: 59–84.

———. 2008. *Peripheral Visions: Publics, Power and Performance in Yemen*. Chicago: Univ. of Chicago Press.

Wenner, Manfred. 1984. "South Yemen since Independence: An Arab Political Maverick." In *Contemporary Yemen: Politics and Historical Background*, edited by Brian R. Pridham, 125–46. London: Croom Helm.

———. 1991. *The Yemen Arab Republic: Development and Change in an Ancient Land*. Boulder, CO: Westview Press.

Willis, John M. 2018. "The Salafi Imamate: Moral Reform and Anti-imperialism in the Mutawakkilite Kingdom." *Journal of Arabian Studies* 8, no. 1: 47–65.

Yadav, Stacey Philbrick. 2013. *Islamists and the State: Legitimacy and Institutions in Yemen and Lebanon*. London: I. B. Tauris.

Yemen Arab Republic–People's Democratic Republic of Yemen. 1991. "Agreement on the Establishment of the Republic of Yemen." English translation with introduction by Nassib G. Ziadé. *International Legal Materials* 30, no. 3: 820–23.

# 6

# Refugee

*Yemenis Navigating Humanitarianism*
*and Human Rights in the Afro-Asian Circuit*

Nathalie Peutz and Angie Heo

> Never before have Yemenis left the country as refugees. This is
> the first time this has happened. Yemen encountered problems,
> demonstrations, civil war, but Yemenis have never had to flee their
> country. . . . Have you ever heard of a Yemeni refugee camp before?
> This is the first time in history.
> —Layla, Djibouti, January 2017

> Imagine, when the Somalis and Syrians were refugees in Yemen, we
> didn't even know what a "refugee" was. We didn't know anything
> about asylum [*al-luju'*]. There were real refugees in Yemen, even
> from Ethiopia. . . . Our neighbors were Somalis and they never felt
> that they were refugees [*laji'in*] or strangers [*ghuraba'*]. We didn't
> even know there was a thing called "refugee." We didn't know the
> term, at all.
> —Karim, South Korea, September 2018

On March 9, 2015, former president of Yemen 'Ali 'Abdullah Saleh warned
his adversaries that they had few avenues for refuge or escape: "Those fleeing to Aden as they did in 1994 [during the previous civil war] . . . will
find only one exit, which is the Red Sea toward Djibouti" (Wakalat Khabr
al-Yamaniyya 2015). Saleh had been taunting his successor, President 'Abd
Rabbuh Mansur Hadi, who, in the wake of the Houthi takeover of the government in 2014, had recently escaped from Sanaa to Aden. Nevertheless,
when the Saudi Arabia–led coalition launched its military intervention

in Yemen two weeks later, thereby closing Yemeni airspace, thousands of Yemenis and foreign nationals would find themselves fleeing the country via the few exits available to them: across land borders into Saudi Arabia or Oman or across the Gulf of Aden and the Red Sea. By the end of 2015, nearly two hundred thousand people had fled to neighboring countries, and among them more than thirty thousand had crossed the sea to Djibouti—the only country in the world that has erected a camp specifically for refugees from Yemen (UNHCR 2015b).

Many of the Yemenis fleeing to neighboring countries traveled onward by air to join their relatives or to seek out urgent medical care in the Middle East, Europe, North America, and Southeast Asia. Eventually, as the war dragged on, more and more Yemenis "stuck" in countries without refugee protections sought out nations that would grant them asylum. In the first months of 2018, a few enterprising young Yemeni men flew from Malaysia—a country with a large Yemeni diaspora owing to centuries-old migratory connections across the Indian Ocean—to South Korea's Jeju Island. By the summer of 2018, more than five hundred Yemenis had landed in Jeju: an unexpected portal that had temporarily allowed Yemeni citizens visa-free entry into South Korea, one of only five nations in East and Southeast Asia signatory to the UN Refugee Convention.

This chapter offers a comparative examination of the legal and political category of the "refugee" in African and Asian circuits of Arabs (Yemenis) seeking asylum. Drawing on fieldwork among Yemeni asylum seekers in Djibouti and Jeju (South Korea), this chapter discusses the experiences of Yemenis seeking and securing refugee status in these two dissimilar host societies.[1] How did these Yemenis conceptualize this word *refugee*, and what does this convey about their expectations of and demands upon the world (Gluck and Tsing 2009)?

---

1. Research for this chapter draws on Peutz's fieldwork in Djibouti, where she interviewed more than one hundred Yemeni refugees between December 2016 and January 2020, and on Peutz and Heo's joint visits to Jeju Island, South Korea, in September 2018 and December 2018, where we interviewed twenty-five Yemeni asylum seekers as well as several Korean officials and volunteers assisting them. All the names of our interlocutors are pseudonyms. Unless specified, all transliterations indicate terms used in Arabic.

As a result of the war in Yemen, more than four million Yemenis—more than 10 percent of the country's population—have been forced to flee their homes owing to hostilities and armed conflict. The majority are displaced within Yemen's borders, making Yemen in 2021 the country with the fourth-largest number of internally displaced persons (IDPs) in the world. In contrast to Yemen's centuries-long yield of predominantly male migrants, nearly 80 percent of these IDPs are women and children (UNHCR 2021). Although many have moved to their natal villages or are hosted by relatives and friends, most of the displaced Yemenis are living in tents or in makeshift shelters in crowded displacement sites—in effect, refugee camps—where they suffer from shortages of food and medicines; COVID-19 and other communicable diseases; limited access to education, water, livelihoods, and income; and further displacement owing to flash floods or encroaching armed conflict (cf. HRW 2021). Despite its alarming level of conflict-induced displacement and its designation by the United Nations as the scene of the world's "largest/worst humanitarian crisis," Yemen is rarely associated, however, with displaced persons seeking international protection—unless as a host to forced migrants and refugees from the Horn of Africa (Betts 2013; de Regt 2014; Thiollet 2014). This lack of association may be because, relative to the millions of Yemenis displaced within the country's borders and to the millions of Syrians who fled Syria, a comparatively small number of Yemenis have managed to escape Yemen since 2015 and request asylum elsewhere. In short, few countries today permit visa-free entry to Yemeni citizens, and even fewer countries have opened their borders to asylum seekers from Yemen. Additionally, as this chapter argues, many of those individuals who have been recognized as asylum seekers or even as refugees struggle to obtain and maintain this slippery status in a world largely indifferent to the conflict in Yemen and in contexts principally inhospitable to young Arab men.

The comparison between Djibouti and South Korea is instructive. Whereas the Republic of Djibouti, a low- to middle-income nation, has officially welcomed and recognized all asylum seekers from Yemen as prima facie refugees and drawn up plans for their long-term integration, the Republic of South Korea, a high-income nation, originally granted refugee status to only 2 out of the approximately 550 Yemenis who applied for asylum in 2018. Nevertheless, in both contexts, Yemenis accustomed to prior pathways of economic migration labor struggled to be recognized and protected as rights-bearing refugees (Arabic, *laji*'; French, *réfugié*; Korean, *nanmin*). In doing so, they are both pushing back against the perception of Yemenis as economic migrants ("fake refugees") and rejecting emic identities associated with other forms of abjection (Peutz 2019). Despite the stigma this "'dirty' word" (Masquelier 2006) bears in both places, the term *refugee* is as liberating as it is constraining. For these Yemenis, being recognized as a refugee stakes their claim to be treated as "deserving" subjects. It also connotes a disruption of past forms of discrimination and displacement and ascendancy to a good life—a future. In what follows, we compare the circumstances of the Yemenis' arrival and reception in Djibouti and South Korea's Jeju Island. In the second section, we discuss how these Yemeni asylum seekers were interpellated as "real" or "fake" refugees, leading many to question one another's legitimacy. Finally, we discuss their resolve to be recognized as refugees even while themselves questioning the legitimacy of this status. In the conclusion, we insist on the import(ance) of the term "refugee" to future scholarship on Yemen.

**Of Ports and Portals**

Situated at the narrowest juncture just twenty miles across the Bab al-Mandab strait, Djibouti was the nearest and most accessible safe haven for those persons fleeing the conflict in Yemen.[2] On March 31, 2015, the first arrivals from Yemen disembarked in Khor Angar, a small port in northern Djibouti from which Ethiopian migrants regularly embark to Yemen on their journey to Saudi Arabia to find work (IFRC 2015). Over the following weeks, Yemenis and other nationals arrived via commercial and privately owned boats at the country's ports in Djibouti (the capital), Obock (in northeastern Djibouti), and Khor Angar (north of Obock) on a

---

2. Yemenis also fled overland to Saudi Arabia, which provided temporary visas, and to Oman, which permitted transit. Foreign nationals were evacuated by charter flights to Ethiopia, Sudan, Somalia, India, and a few other countries. Notably, there were no reported evacuations to the United States, despite the many Yemenis having US citizenship.

near-daily basis. By May 29, Djibouti had received thirteen thousand Yemenis and other nationals, becoming the country with the largest initial influx of arrivals from Yemen since the start of the Saudi-led intervention (UNHCR 2015c, 3).[3] The majority of these initial arrivals originated from Aden, Bab al-Mandab, and coastal villages along Yemen's Red Sea shore (IFRC 2015). Many fled to Djibouti to reach its airport and embassies, transiting through the country on their way home or to one of the few other countries willing to grant visas to Yemeni passport holders: for example, Sudan, Egypt, Malaysia. Others—in particular Yemenis from the coastal fishing villages and those individuals with prior family or business connections to Djibouti—moved in with relatives or acquaintances with the intent of returning to Yemen once the fighting subsided. Some fled to Djibouti because they were in urgent need of medical care, which they were unable to access in Aden or in other parts of Yemen. Others fled to Djibouti to avoid being conscripted by the Houthis, or because they had no electricity or water, or because their apartments and houses were destroyed by the air strikes, or because—as the war dragged on and on—they were searching for income to support their family.

Yemeni citizens who did not have the means, documents, or connections to travel onward, to rent apartments, or to move in with relatives in Djibouti were registered by the United Nations High Commissioner for Refugees (UNHCR) and the Office National d'Assistance aux Réfugiés et Sinistrés (ONARS), Djibouti's national refugee agency, as "refugees." This route to becoming and understanding themselves to be "refugees" (*laji'in*) was a new one for most Yemenis, who had long viewed themselves as citizens of—or even "migrants" (*muhajirin/mughtaribin*) from—a country that had welcomed refugees, but not one that engendered them.

A state party to the 1951 Convention Relating to the Status of Refugees and its 1967 Protocol (since 1977) and a signatory to the 1969 OAU Convention Governing the Specific Aspects of Refugee Problems in Africa

3. On May 29, 2015, the UNHCR reported that more than 545,000 people had been newly displaced in Yemen since March 2015 and nearly 38,000 people had fled to neighboring countries (2015c, 1). By the end of December 2015, more than 168,000 people had fled Yemen, with an estimated 31,500 having arrived in Djibouti (UNHCR 2015b, 1).

(since 2005), the Republic of Djibouti maintains an "open-door" policy toward refugees and asylum seekers.[4] Since 1977, the year of its independence from France, Djibouti has accepted tens of thousands of refugees from neighboring Ethiopia, Eritrea, and Somalia, the majority of whom live in two camps south of Djibouti city. In April 2015, Djibouti began granting prima facie refugee status to all asylum seekers from Yemen, recognizing them on the basis of the objective conditions prevailing in Yemen.[5] Shortly thereafter, the government redoubled its commitment to refugee protection and rights. In January 2017, Djibouti's president, Ismaïl Omar Guelleh, promulgated a new National Refugee Law aiming to ease refugees' access to education, health care, employment, and eventual naturalization (Republic of Djibouti 2017). And Djibouti was among the first countries to apply the Comprehensive Refugee Response Framework laid out by the New York Declaration for Refugees and Migrants in September 2016. In alignment with this framework, the government is now focused on the socioeconomic "integration" of refugees through their inclusion in the national educational and health systems and the reconceptualization of its three refugee camps as "villages" (Peutz 2019).

4. The 1951 Convention and 1967 Protocol define a refugee as someone who is outside of and in need of protection by a country other than the country of their nationality "owing to well-founded fear of being persecuted for reasons of race, religion, nationality, membership of a particular social group or political opinion" (189 UNTS 137, art I [2] and 606 UNTS 267, art I [2], both available at https://www.unhcr.org/3b66c2aa10). The 1969 Organization of African Unity (OAU) Convention, the first binding regional instrument governing refugee protection, adopted this definition but expanded it to include those individuals displaced "owing to external aggression, occupation, foreign domination or events seriously disturbing public order in either part or the whole of his country of origin or nationality" (1969, 1001 UNTS 45, art I [2], available at https://www.refworld.org /docid/3ae6b36018.html). Djibouti was also among the early signatories to the 2009 African Union Convention for the Protection and Assistance of Internally Displaced Persons in Africa ("the Kampala Convention"), the first binding regional instrument seeking to protect those persons displaced internally owing to climate change and natural disasters.

5. Prima facie status determination lowers the standard of proof required of each asylum applicant during large influxes or when the host state's determination procedures are overwhelmed. In 2015, the governments of Somalia, Ethiopia, and Sudan also granted prima facie recognition to asylum seekers from Yemen (UNHCR 2015d, 14).

The Yemeni refugees in Djibouti have been both witness and hostage to these uncertain developments. Many expected to return within weeks if not months to Yemen; they certainly did not expect to end up living in a refugee camp for ten years and counting (at the time of writing in 2021). The first arrivals were housed in an orphanage and sport stadium complex in Obock, both still under construction, or in the nearby Migrant Response Center run by the International Organization for Migration. In mid-April 2015, the UNHCR and the Norwegian Refugee Council began constructing a camp for the Yemeni refugees in an area called Markazi, a barren plain five kilometers southwest of the town. Designed to accommodate 3,000 individuals, the Markazi camp houses mainly vulnerable and lower-income families with children, single men (mostly retired or unable to find work in Djibouti), and female-headed households.[6] Initially, the government of Djibouti required all Yemenis claiming refugee status to move to the camp. As a result, thousands of Yemenis refused to register with the UNHCR, preferring to remain in Djibouti city where they could find undocumented work and hope to live more comfortably. At the end of September, as the number of arrivals from Yemen increased, the government authorized the registration and residence of Yemeni refugees in the city (UNHCR 2015d, 20). Still, just over a third of the 17,749 Yemeni nationals who arrived in Djibouti in 2015 registered as refugees: 2,983 individuals in Markazi camp and 3,393 in Obock and Djibouti city (UNHCR 2015b, 2).[7] Albeit a small number in comparison to other refugee flows, this "open-door" policy toward refugees from Yemen transformed the social landscape in Obock (population 10,000), where the presence of Yemeni refugees had increased the population by nearly 50 percent, as well as in Djibouti city, where the influx of Yemeni entrepreneurs revitalized commercial districts (Lauret 2020).

6. The majority of the Yemeni refugees registered in Djibouti in 2015 were women and children: of the 15,761 Yemeni arrivals by November 1, 2015, 39 percent were children, 25 percent women, and 36 percent men (UNHCR 2015d, 18).

7. This number has fluctuated over the years owing to refugees returning to Yemen as well as new arrivals. As of January 2019 (the latest publicly available UNHCR update at the time of writing in 2021), of the 29,214 refugees and asylum seekers registered in Djibouti, 4,916 were Yemeni nationals (2,264 of whom were living in Obock) (UNHCR 2019).

The Markazi camp has been generously supported by international and local humanitarian organizations as well as Gulf-based charities. Yet its harsh environment and remote setting make daily life there both arduous and monotonous. From June through August, when daytime temperatures regularly exceed 40°C (104°F), hot and sandy windstorms thrash against the refugees' tents. More than half of the refugees left the camp during the 2015 monsoon wind season to rent houses or move in with relatives in Obock or Djibouti city (UNHCR 2015a). Djibouti is an extraordinarily expensive country with one of the highest costs of living in Africa (Jelagat 2020). After draining their savings or social capital, Yemeni refugees had few options but to return to the camp where they receive free shelter and monthly food rations. This shelter has been upgraded significantly over the years. When the winds destroyed the refugees' UNHCR-issued tents in July 2015, "Sahara tents" donated by the Bahrain Royal Charity Organization were erected in their place. Following this contribution, the Qatar Red Crescent donated three hundred Refugee Housing Units designed by the IKEA foundation. Then, Saudi Arabia's King Salman Humanitarian Aid and Relief Center donated three hundred twenty-four-square-meter prefabricated housing units along with a new clinic and school building (Nuryap İnşaat n.d.). Outfitted with an interior shower/toilet, (occasional) running water, electricity, and air conditioners, these one-bedroom units and studios are better equipped than most houses in the region. "The first air-conditioned camp in Africa," a Markazi refugee quipped in October 2018.

Despite these legal and physical accommodations, the Yemeni refugees' opportunities to make a life for themselves in Djibouti were and remain circumscribed. In principle, the government accords refugees their basic rights as enshrined in the 1951 Convention, such as the right to gainful employment, access to public primary and secondary education, and freedom of movement within the country. In practice, refugees have been limited to working in the informal sector and were often confined to living in the camps (UNHCR 2012). Prior to the gradual implementation of the new legislation, refugees seeking formal sector employment in the city were hired illegally on occasion but were paid less than their Djiboutian counterparts. The Yemeni refugees living in Markazi were limited to the few "incentive" jobs they could secure within the camp or to opening small groceries or kiosks. And they were required to obtain permission from the camp managers or the prefect's office to travel to Djibouti city. Even now, refugees in all three "villages" lack opportunities for gainful employment owing to their remote locations in a largely impoverished country that suffers from high unemployment (40–60 percent according to some estimates). Besides, a camp by any other name is still a camp. Few of the refugees Peutz met in Markazi between 2016 and 2020 were interested in their local "integration." Most of the refugees who had endured the harsh conditions in Markazi camp for this long came from fishing villages in coastal Yemen to which they planned to return. The rest were holding out for third-country resettlement, in which case their years in Djibouti will have been one long layover: a "waiting station," as a Yemeni who had passed through Djibouti on his way to Malaysia and eventually South Korea described it to us in Jeju in September 2018.

If Djibouti was a regional transit hub, a "port," for all but the most vulnerable or the already locally connected, South Korea's Jeju Island was an accidental "portal" that provided a few hundred Yemenis direct but temporary access to a high-income country before closing again. Between January and May 2018, 561 Yemenis flew to Jeju Island where the large majority of them requested asylum. Even more surprising than this surge of Yemeni asylum seekers in the Republic of Korea—a country that had received fewer than 50 Yemeni asylum seekers in the three years prior—was the national outcry that followed. The largest island in South Korea, Jeju is a resort destination with a sizable percentage of foreign inhabitants (25,000 out of 650,000 total population) that is inundated with 15 million foreign tourists a year. It is also, since 2006, South Korea's only self-governing province, with extensive administrative powers. The arrival of a few hundred Yemeni refugees in Jeju should have barely registered in Seoul. Yet within months of their arrival, more than 700,000 South Koreans had signed an online petition calling on the national government to revoke the Yemenis' refugee applications and expel them from the island. Compared to the understaffed scramble of nongovernmental organizations (NGOs) supporting the Yemenis, the mass mobilization of antirefugee sentiment was large, swift, and effective. The entire contested affair—soon referred to as the nation's first "refugee crisis" (Korean, *nanmin wigi*)—ignited highly charged debates on the status of migrant rights, antidiscrimination legislation, economic stability, and national security in South Korea (Cho 2018; Heo 2021; N. Kim 2018; D. Kim, Curran, and Kim 2020).

One of the few states in Asia party to the 1951 Convention and its 1967 Protocol (since 1992), the Republic of Korea was also the first Asian country to enact its own standalone refugee law (in 2013).[8] However, since signing the convention and receiving its first (non-Asian) asylum applicants in 1994, South Korea's acceptance rate of these applicants has been notably low: for example, 3 percent in 2018 compared to the global average of 30 percent (Yoon, Fisseha, and Suk 2020, 3). Still, the combination of South Korea's refugee legislation and Jeju Island's visa-waiver program introduced in 2002 to promote tourism captured the attention and hope of Yemenis searching for a viable safe haven. In the first years of the war, thousands of Yemenis fled—many of them via Djibouti—to Malaysia, a country with a large Yemeni diaspora owing to centuries-old migratory connections and one of the only upper-middle-income countries to permit Yemeni citizens visa-free entry. Not being a signatory to the 1951 Refugee Convention, however, Malaysia has barred foreigners with a "social-visit pass" or even its UNHCR-registered refugees from working or attending public schools. Yemenis who had overstayed their ninety-day visit and those persons who worked informally in restaurants to make do lived in constant fear of arrest and imprisonment (Kermeliotis 2019). Several

---

8. South Korea's 2013 Refugee Act's definition of a "refugee" (*nanmin*) aligns with the 1951 Convention/1967 Protocol definition based on "well-founded fear of being persecuted for reasons of race, religion, nationality, membership of a particular social group or political opinion" (Republic of Korea 2013). Although South Korea had received hundreds of thousands of de facto Korean war refugees (*p'inanmin* or "people escaping from a disaster") between 1945 and 1953 and around 3,000 Vietnamese refugees/"boat people" (also *p'inanmin*) between 1975 and 1992, the country "officially became a member of the international refugee regime" upon signing the Convention in 1992 (N. H.-J. Kim 2021, 15). Subsequently, South Korea recognized its first "genuine" refugee (*nanmin*) in 2001: a political asylee from Ethiopia who, in 2010, was also the first refugee to have been granted South Korean citizenship (UNHCR 2010). North Korean "defectors"/refugees do not apply for asylum through the same process; they are granted South Korean citizenship through the Promotion and Resettlement Support Act for North Korean Refugees.

Yemenis we met in Jeju told us that they had been regularly searching online and through social media for an opening—somewhere, anywhere—
with "human rights." When, in December 2017, the budget airline AirAsia
launched its direct flights from Kuala Lumpur to Jeju Island, the Yemenis
feeling stuck in Malaysia took notice.[9]

In early 2018, a few Yemenis tentatively boarded flights from Kuala
Lumpur to Jeju, entered as tourists, and applied for asylum. They then
shared updates and instructions with their friends and relatives via social
media. Marwan, a thirty-year-old computer software engineer from Sanaa
whom we met in Jeju in September 2018, described the bustle among his
compatriots in Malaysia when they received the news: "I was in Malaysia, and, suddenly, people were asking me, 'What are you doing here?' I
said, 'Why are you asking me this?' They said, '*The entire world traveled to
Korea, and you're still sitting here?*' I said, 'What's there in Korea? What's
happening?' Someone told me, 'They opened up for Yemenis.'"

Marwan had moved to Malaysia in 2015 after having been trapped in
Jeddah, Saudi Arabia, where he had been visiting relatives when the war
broke out. Initially, he was optimistic about his prospects in Malaysia, en-
visioning himself following in the footsteps of his grandparents who had
migrated to Ethiopia in the 1950s, where they had fared well prior to their
return to Yemen in the 1970s (de Regt 2014). Instead, he had spent three
years working one seasonal job after another, all without proper authori-
zation. For Marwan, as for others, Malaysia had become "a transit station,
an opportunity for me to go to another place to find my future. Something
more secure." When Marwan heard about the Jeju opening, he settled his
debts and flew to South Korea.

Others traveled to Jeju from as far as Egypt, Sudan, and even Yemen.
Jalal, a young man from a farming family in northern Yemen, described
how he had been sitting in an internet café "looking for a country" when
he read that the Jeju immigration office was processing Yemeni asylum

9. Between 2002 and 2018, Jeju permitted foreigners from all but eleven countries to
stay for thirty days without a visa. From 2014, Yemeni citizens who were no longer permitted visa-free entry to the mainland were still able to enter Jeju directly through its visa-
waiver program, a loophole that became apparent to them when the direct flights began.

claims. Over the next ten days, Jalal and three friends scrambled to collect $3,000 each from relatives for their flights from Aden (the Sanaa airport was closed) to Khartoum to Malaysia to Jeju and for their initial expenses. They arrived in Jeju in mid-May. Rashid, an electrician and youth "revolutionary" from Taiz, recalled being in Cairo that May, feeling depressed after his plan to be smuggled from Sudan through Libya to Europe fell through. A friend who had heard about the Yemenis entering Jeju encouraged Rashid to travel there with him. Upon their arrival in Malaysia on May 28, his friend suggested resting a few days. But Rashid insisted on pressing on. "We entered [Jeju] on the twenty-ninth, and then they closed the borders for Yemenis," Rashid said. "There were two flights after us, and they were sent back from the airport. I am telling you that if this happened to us, if they closed the doors in our faces, I would have died right then." On June 1, 2018, the Ministry of Justice added Yemen to the list of eleven countries excluded from Jeju's visa-waiver policy, effectively ending this "influx." Both Jalal and Rashid told us about other Yemenis they knew who had tried but failed to reach Jeju in time: some never made it past the checkpoints between Sanaa and Aden; others had reached as far as Malaysia, only to be denied onward travel when the "Jeju ban" went into effect (Lee 2018).

The Yemenis fortunate enough to have entered South Korea before the Jeju portal closed encountered a distinct set of challenges. Whereas the Yemenis disembarking in Djibouti's ports were able to draw on prior social networks or to avail themselves of immediate humanitarian aid, the Yemenis landing in Jeju were navigating an unfamiliar environment with little formal assistance—at least initially. Bassam, a thirty-year-old male from Sanaa who had lived in Malaysia for more than two years before venturing to Jeju, explained how he and his friends had relied on the directions of those persons who preceded them. "When we first arrived on the island, no one supported us, not the Red Cross or the government—no one," Bassam told us in September 2018. Most of the Yemenis had expected to fly onward to Seoul; few could afford to live as "tourists" on Korea's resort island for long. (The owner of Jeju Olleh Hotel, where more than a hundred Yemenis had rented rooms, told us how he had received one group of Yemenis after another until finally realizing that they were not merely tourists; he then gave them a discount.) However, on April 30, as inexpensive hotels and guesthouses around Jeju began filling with Yemeni asylum seekers, the Korean Ministry of Justice restricted the asylum seekers from leaving Jeju Island. Faced with this unexpected confinement, several Yemenis created Facebook groups through which to mobilize resources, support, action plans, and media messaging—turning to the same social media platforms they had used to plan their journeys to now facilitate their mandated island stay. By early June, the Jeju People's Coalition for Refugee Rights (a coalition of thirty-nine NGOs), several churches, island-based "expatriates" and local Jejuans, and the government-supported Jeju Migrants Center had come to the Yemenis' assistance.

If the Yemenis in the Markazi camp were subjected to a competitive humanitarianism inflected by regional geopolitics—Bahraini tents, Qatari shelters, and Saudi houses, during the very period that Saudi Arabia and Bahrain had severed diplomatic relations with Qatar—the Yemenis in Jeju found themselves primarily supported by and sometimes also caught between institutions associated with the three locally dominant religions. The Naomi Migrant Pastoral Center of the Jungang Cathedral of the Immaculate Conception of Mary (the "Naomi Center") served as the central leading hub for refugee support, helping the Yemenis to find jobs, shelter, and medical treatment. It also secured and paid for several apartment rentals and opened a canteen providing them with free food and necessities. The Jeju Migrant Center run by an Evangelical Protestant offered a temporary dorm for fifty to sixty refugees. And Global Inner Peace, an NGO supported by Jeju's Buddhist leaders, organized free Korean-language instruction. Other NGOs and volunteers assisted as they could. For example, the Jeju Peace and Human Rights Institute provided free legal counsel and connections with NGOs on the mainland. "Expats" (primarily English-language teachers) donated tents for local campsites, offered housing in their own apartments, and held fund-raisers for the Yemeni asylum seekers at a popular bar. Korean volunteers taught daily Korean-language classes at several locations, including Global Inner Peace, the Naomi Center, and Olleh Hotel. By the summer's end, the NGOs also provided sewing classes for women and school classes for Yemeni children composed of music, painting, and outdoor recreation.

Despite this generous community support, many Yemenis found living in Jeju to be challenging. One of their biggest stressors was employment, or lack thereof. By law, asylum seekers are not permitted to work during the first six months in South Korea in order to prevent illegal stays. When it became clear that nearly 500 Yemenis would have to remain on the island for as long as it would take the government to process their refugee-status determinations, the local government announced that it would permit them to seek employment in specific fields: fishing, food services, agriculture, and aquafarming (Belan 2018). In mid-June, the Jeju Office of Immigration hosted two job fairs that resulted in the short-term employment of approximately 400 Yemenis. But few of the predominantly urban Yemenis had the necessary skill set or temperament to work long hours in farming or at sea. Within the first two weeks, more than 70 of the 180 Yemenis who had found work on fishing boats had quit these jobs owing to the hard, physical labor. Marwan, the computer software engineer, was one of them, having surrendered to seasickness his first day on the job. In other cases, Yemenis found the working terms of their contracts risky or exploitative. Perhaps the most significant obstacles were language and "cultural" differences. Few employers were able to speak English, let alone Arabic, and few Yemenis spoke any Korean; Jalal and his friends showed us how they had used Google Translate on their smartphones to communicate with their boss on an orange farm—a job they soon quit, too. By September 2018, only half of the Yemenis in Jeju were employed (Sŏng-u Pak 2018). Many were anxious, homesick, and frustrated, feeling trapped on the island with the mainland just beyond the horizon. Battling local perceptions that they were lazy and insincere, the Yemenis were criticized both for stealing jobs and for not working enough. On top of this situation, they had to contend with antimigrant demonstrations, Islamophobia, and accusations that they were "fake refugees" (Korean, *gajja nanmin*).

### "Real" and "Fake" Refugees

While the arrivals of Yemeni asylum seekers in Djibouti and South Korea provoked divergent responses, Yemenis in both countries found themselves struggling to prove that they were genuine refugees. In many cases, it was not just their host country's bureaucracy or citizenry that needed convincing; it was also themselves. Time and again, Yemenis we met in Djibouti and South Korea voiced their surprise and humiliation at having become refugees. At the same time, they had to convince others that they were "real" refugees deserving of humanitarian assistance and legal protection, not "economic migrants" trying to capitalize on their country's chaos. They did so by echoing the distinctions drawn between "real" and "fake" refugees. And they did so by claiming repeatedly that the terms "refugee" (*laji'*) and "asylum" (*al-luju'*) were entirely foreign to them. "We are asylum seekers, and honestly, we don't even know what this means," a female shopkeeper from Sanaa told Peutz in Obock in December 2016. "Of course, in Yemen, we don't know anything by the name of *refugee*; we had Somalis there, and we saw them, all of them, just as Yemenis. We didn't know the word, *refugee*. . . . I used to say I could travel or migrate. That was the extent of our knowledge, as Yemenis," Marwan told us in Jeju in September 2018. Of course, such comments cannot be taken simply at face value precisely because they underscore the shame, stigma, and racialization of the term "refugee" in Yemen. Many of the Yemenis who sought refugee status in Djibouti and in South Korea had previously associated the condition of "refugeeness" (Nyers 2006, xv) with the Somali refugees given asylum in Yemen since the early 1990s—if not also with Iraqis and Syrians who sought refuge in Yemen more recently—but not with their relatives or compatriots whose past and often forced migrations put them firmly in the category of "migrants" (*muhajirin*), "(estranged) expatriates" (*mughtaribin*), or persons of "mixed" descent (*muwalladin*) (Peutz 2019). As Noura, a divorced mother of five from Aden living in the Markazi camp put it in March 2017, "I used to see the refugees and displaced persons from Palestine and cry for them. Never did I imagine that I would be in the same situation."

When Yemeni nationals began arriving in Djibouti in the spring of 2015, the Djibouti government instructed its citizens to welcome them (UNHCR 2015d, 19). This push toward reception does not mean that the Yemeni refugees in Djibouti experienced no hostility or discrimination. But the proximity between Djibouti and Yemen, the close cultural and socioeconomic ties between their populations, their shared religious identity, and the preponderance of Yemeni refugees with African and specifically

Djiboutian roots (*muwalladin*) flattened some of the distinctions between refugees and citizens. Several government officials, aid workers, Djiboutian citizens, and Yemenis Peutz met corroborated this hospitable reception. A Djiboutian professor insisted that the Yemenis had been received "with open arms," especially owing to their prior family connections in the country. "It was like they were coming home," he told Peutz in January 2019. A Yemeni merchant from Taiz who had moved to Djibouti in 2012 confirmed this sentiment. "Most of the Arabs in Djibouti are of Yemeni origin," he stated in January 2019. "That is why Djibouti took them in. When you look at the tribes of the Issa [a Somali subclan], the tribe of the president, then you see that their origin is from Yemen."[10] Now a registered refugee with a housing unit in Markazi—his work in Djibouti City dried up in 2017, he explained, so he registered with the UNHCR then—he is esteemed by several other refugees in the camp for having assisted them upon their arrival at the Port of Djibouti, where his father had worked during the French colonial period.

But it was not just the Yemeni residents or Djiboutian citizens with sociocultural ties to Yemen who "welcomed" the refugees. Djiboutians are accustomed to their small country hosting large numbers of refugees, asylum seekers, and migrants—albeit not always hospitably. By the mid-1980s, Djibouti's Ethiopian refugee population had swelled to more than 10 percent of the country's total population. The government's response to this influx included the detention and forced repatriation of Ethiopian refugees in 1981–83 and the forced resettlement of its urban refugees into two camps, first established in 1981 (Crisp 1984). Less than a decade later, Djibouti was the reluctant host to about thirty thousand Somali refugees (IRB Canada 1991). It also received a few hundred Yemenis fleeing from Yemen's 1994 civil war. At the same time, the Djiboutian civil war (1991–94) between Afar guerrilla fighters and the Issa Somali-dominated government had precipitated the internal displacement of tens of thousands

10. Djibouti's multiethnic population is composed of Somalis (of which the Issa are the largest branch), Afar (the main ethnic group in the Obock region), "Arabs" (primarily Yemeni), Ethiopians, and others. Somali Issa trace their ancestry to Shaykh Issa whom some believe to have had Arab (Yemeni) roots.

of Djiboutian civilians (Schraeder 1993). Qadira, a successful entrepreneur from Obock, attributed the Obockoise's broad acceptance of today's Yemeni refugees to their own experience of war and displacement in the 1990s and to their reliance on Yemen then, in particular, for life-saving food imports and as a place of refuge. Having fled Obock and lived as a refugee in Eritrea from 1991 to 1997, Qadira expressed empathy for the Yemeni refugees in town. But she also recalled having had to flee empty-handed and compared it to the sight of Yemenis arriving with luggage, cell phones, appliances, and money—and to the outpouring of donations the "Arab" refugees attracted initially. "They know [what to expect from] war; we did not," she told Peutz in January 2017—her statement echoing what Yemeni refugees in Djibouti had said or implied about the African refugees they had encountered in Yemen: *they understand what it means to be a refugee; we did not.*

In addition to supporting thousands of refugees, Djibouti suffers from high rates of poverty and unemployment. Nevertheless, and in stark contrast to South Korea, there was no demonstrable backlash against the Yemeni arrivals. On the one hand, if Djiboutians were hostile to the Yemenis, they did not voice this publicly. Under the country's authoritarian leadership, negative press, open dissent, and even demonstrations expressing dissatisfaction with government policies are uncommon, if not illegal (Metelits and Matti 2015). Indeed, the only demonstrations critical of the government's refugee policy were staged by the Yemeni refugees themselves. On the other hand, Djiboutians have also recognized the economic advantages that refugees bring. Since 2015, Yemeni-run restaurants and shops have transformed Djibouti's urban fabric (Lauret 2020). Yemenis were viewed less as job stealers ("economic migrants") than as job creators (migrating capital)—or, alternatively, as cheap, undocumented labor. Djibouti and its citizens also benefit from the humanitarian aid economy that sustains the camps. Several Yemeni refugees in Obock sensed that it was less their own experience and skills that were valued than it was the international donations that flowed in on their behalf. "We are human oil," a forty-year-old refugee from Taiz bemoaned in October 2017, understanding his presence in Djibouti as a source of economic rent. "We are like oil for the Djiboutian government," an Adeni man in his mid-fifties said a year later. "The government lives off military bases and now also off camps. Like we are a source of fortune [*masdar rizq*] for them. . . . In their view, we are not refugees, but cattle [*baha'im*]." Others talked about being treated like "the goose that lays a golden egg"—with their economic value being stripped of any social or human value. "They treat us like cattle here," three Yemeni refugees told Peutz separately in March 2018, illustrating how they felt both dehumanized and exploited: "like cattle" corralled within the camp so that the government could capture the humanitarian aid intended for them.

If Yemeni refugees in Djibouti were bewildered, alarmed, and ashamed by their new living conditions and status, many were also relieved to have achieved at least some measure of international protection and assistance. Several of the Yemenis living in Markazi maintained that, despite the camp's hardships, they had acquired more "rights" and "value" as UNHCR-recognized refugees than they had had as Yemeni citizens in Yemen, where they had suffered discrimination on account of their "weak" genealogy, socio-occupational class/caste, mixed race, or gender—for example, as divorced women (Peutz 2019). "At least, I have a leg to stand on in this camp; I have rights as all refugees [French: *réfugiés*] do," a Somali Yemeni widow from Taiz told Peutz in December 2016. These rights included, in their view, the right to work, education, health care, and dignity, as well as the "right" to the monthly food rations they received from the World Food Programme. "At least here, even if we are living in windstorms and heat and tents, we feel like we're human beings," said Ahmed, a truck driver from Mawza in October 2017, thereby countering the claims of dehumanization expressed by some of his neighbors at the same time. "People come from Europe, America, Ethiopia, and from all the [international] organizations to check whether my water is clean or not, to inspect our health, and so on," he explained. "Back in Yemen, no one would look after me because I am not from a tribe or the son of a shaykh or the son of a merchant. In Yemen, they look after those with power and influence. If you are poor, marginalized, you have no value." Frequently denigrated in Yemen—"you, servant! [*ya khadim*], they'd say"—Ahmed told Peutz the following January that he had long hoped to leave his home country, "but no country would have taken me as a refugee—the United Nations wouldn't have taken me. It would've said, 'There is no war in your country.'"

Indeed, several of the Yemenis living in Markazi had sought asylum in various countries prior to this war. "I've been trying to leave the Arab and Islamic world for seventeen years now," said Ghaith, a mid-thirty-year-old accountant from Aden, in March 2018. "There is no true life to be had there. There are no human rights, no order, no way to earn a living, no jobs. There is nothing there. The only thing we have is injustice, corruption, oppression, and misery." Between 2009 and 2013, Ghaith lived in Djibouti city while his repeated requests for asylum were rejected on insufficient grounds. In 2013, Ghaith returned to Yemen, looking for a more stable life. "I settled there until the war came," he said. "I then fled Yemen afraid of dying. My house had been struck, and my wife had died. I began to think again, after seventeen years, that this may be an opportunity for me to leave this country, to leave Arab and Islamic society, and go to a different place." For those who had attempted or just dreamed of escaping various forms of oppression and discrimination in Yemen, the war had presented "a window of opportunity": a way to "escape to a better place," Nora, a twice-married woman from Aden told Peutz in October 2017. Like others, Ghaith and Nora hoped that their UNHCR recognition and protection as refugees opened the possibility, however remote, to their third-country resettlement in the Global North. Now "child[ren] of the UN," as Ahmed put it, marginalized Yemenis had acquired an *ascendant* status. "I was [like] a refugee in Yemen, but without international recognition. My appearance was that of a refugee. Now I am a real refugee," he declared in January 2018.

Whereas in Djibouti previously marginalized Yemenis felt validated by their legal recognition as ("real") refugees, in Jeju, the new Yemeni arrivals felt demoralized by being publicly denounced as "fake refugees." Notably, these arrivals included Yemenis who had fled to and through Djibouti several years earlier, where they had been recognized as refugees and, in some cases, had resided in the Markazi camp. Nevertheless, on June 12, 2018, a petition posted on the website of South Korea's Blue House (presidential office) called for the government headed by liberal President

Moon Jae-in—himself the son of wartime refugees from North Korea—to refuse to accept the refugees in Jeju because "Muslims do not see women as human beings" and they will commit "sexual crimes." Due to its Islamophobic nature, the petition was deleted that same day (Ko 2018). However, a second petition posted on June 13 continued to circulate, gathering more than 714,000 signatures—well over the 200,000 needed to elicit an official response. Questioning why the "illegal refugee applicants" had traveled to distant South Korea instead of Europe, this petition called for the abolition of the 2013 Refugee Act (Sang-gi Pak 2018). The Blue House responded to the petition on August 1, explaining that the Yemenis had entered South Korea legally while also trying to assure its citizens that their own security was paramount (Republic of Korea Blue House 2018).

Meanwhile, hundreds of protesters had taken to the streets in Jeju and Seoul holding signs saying "Fake Refugees Out" and "Nation First" (Choe 2018a; Seo 2018). Others took to social media to circulate rumors that the Yemenis were "rapists" or "terrorists." Organized largely by Korea's Christian Right, this antiasylum movement portrayed the Yemenis as not only religiously and socially conservative but also sexually depraved. It also conflated them with all other (in their view) problematic minorities. Thus, for example, a flyer Heo found distributed at one of the churches in Jeju warned that "Muslims and homosexual refugees will come after hearing visa-free rumors!!" (Heo 2021). Observers attributed this virulent antirefugee sentiment to South Korea's high youth unemployment, economic precarity, plummeting marriage rates, rising misogyny, and deep xenophobia (Koo 2018). A survey conducted that summer revealed that the populations most opposed to granting asylum to the Yemeni refugees were Korean youth in their twenties and thirties, middle-income households, and women—the very groups expected to be most progressive and therefore most accepting of migrants and refugees (Park 2018). Yet they were also the Koreans most threatened by the idea of foreigners stealing "their" jobs and of "Muslims" importing or extending misogynistic practices.

One reason that Yemenis were suspected of being economic migrants in search of profit instead of ("genuine") refugees (*nanmin*) or humanitarian-status holders (Korean: *ndojŏkch'eryuja*)—the two forms of recognition afforded by South Korea's 2013 Refugee Act—is because so few of them accorded with the figure of the *p'inanmin* ("people escaping from a disaster") based largely on the impoverished North Korean "war refugees" and Vietnamese "boat people" escaping communism over land or by boat in the 1940s–1950s and 1975–92, respectively (N. H.-J. Kim 2021). In contrast, most of the Yemeni asylum seekers were male professionals under forty, who had arrived in stylish attire and with smartphones in hand. This profile—and the sight of young Arab men congregating in downtown Jeju—troubled the expectation that refugees are poor, vulnerable, and female or accompanied by families. At a "talk concert" in September 2018 to raise funds for an independent film on the Yemenis in Jeju, the Korean directors invited Zaki, a young man from Sanaa, to describe his first impressions of South Korea. In fluent English, Zaki parodied the lectures the Yemenis had received about jaywalking, proper recycling, and dental hygiene. While an employer had tried to teach him how to brush his teeth ("I was like, come on, for God's sake, I'm not Tarzan! We speak English. We've traveled!" Zaki laughed), his hotel owner had asked him why, if he was a refugee, he was able to dress well. "I was shocked," Zaki told the audience. "Being a refugee doesn't mean that I have to be poor. I was working in Malaysia for two years, so I bought these shoes with my own money." While it was evident that the Yemenis who had reached Jeju were generally more affluent or better connected than were the ones who settled in the refugee camp in Djibouti—the cost of the flights alone were out of reach for most of the Markazi refugees—not all the Yemenis in Jeju were well-off. Several men told us how they had secured loans from relatives or how their family had liquidated their assets (selling land or their mother's wedding jewelry) to pay for their tickets. Few families could afford to send more than one member abroad. Often, it was the young men who traveled to evade conscription by the Houthis, to flee threats from other armed groups, or to seek ways to provide for their family members at home. The flight of young men from Yemen was the price of escaping a war zone *and* an investment in these men's and their family's future.

But the paradigmatic figure of the vulnerable refugee loomed large, even though or because the local Jeju islanders had only recently begun excavating their own repressed memory of violence and displacement. April 2018, the very month that the Yemenis began to flock to Jeju, marked the seventieth anniversary of the Jeju April 3 (1948) Massacre.[11] Some local islanders drew direct connections between their relatives' past displacement and the displaced Yemenis today.[12] The director of "Jeju Dark Tours," an NGO that focuses on the history and commemoration of the April 3 Massacre, and one of the key persons to organize the Jeju People's Coalition for Refugee Rights told us how she viewed her work with the Yemeni refugees as a way of extending their NGO's peace activism into other countries. Similarly, at a Protestant Evangelical church service we attended during the Chuseok Thanksgiving holiday in September 2018, the pastor drew connections between the civil war in Syria and Yemen, child soldiers in Sierra Leone, and the 1948 killings in Jeju. Yet for all the islanders' empathy, gendered perceptions of the "real" refugee and of men's proper role in war lingered. For example, on the same day as the Chuseok service, a South Korean reporter asked Peutz why most of the Yemeni asylum seekers were male given that, during the Korean war, the men had stayed behind to defend their country against the occupiers.[13] Others could not understand why these Yemenis had had to arrive on *their* shores. "They [Koreans] thought, *How did these people come by air? How did a refugee enter via an airport? We know that refugees*

11. Shortly prior to the Korean War (1950–53), and during the US military occupation (1945–48), the Korean army brutally crushed a communist uprising on Jeju Island that began on April 3, 1948. The Jeju massacre ("April 3 Event") ended with thirty thousand deaths (roughly 10 percent of Jeju's population) and tens of thousands of islanders fleeing by boat to Shikoku Island in Japan (Morris-Suzuki 2011).

12. Jeju Island had also been the site in 1988 of the first of many boat landings of refugees from Vietnam. Prior to this event, Vietnamese "boat people" had been rescued at sea and transferred to South Korea (N. H.-J. Kim 2021, 13).

13. A UNHCR employee in Djibouti expressed similar gendered expectations, telling Peutz, "In Africa, women and children leave, and the men stay and fight. Here [among the Yemeni refugees], it's the opposite." He then explained how, in many cases, the Yemeni men traveled to Djibouti alone to see how the conditions were before bringing over their families or to find employment to provide for their families in Yemen (Obock, Jan. 2020).

*can cross the sea, can cross borders. Now, the distance between Yemen and Korea is great. Why didn't you apply for asylum in neighboring countries?"* Marwan panned in September 2018. "They don't know that we were already rejected by neighboring countries."

The Yemenis we met in Jeju were shocked to find themselves at the center of this national firestorm, one that had as much to do with the rise of conservative populism and fears of secular liberalization in Korea as it did about the Yemeni refugees—or any of South Korea's refugees, for that matter (Heo 2021). "We believed and expected that when we got to Korea, our case was going to be accepted," said Karim, an English major from Sanaa. "We were surprised when we came that the Koreans made us feel like we were lying to them. . . . It was as if they didn't believe that there was truly a war in Yemen. We felt that they were only focused on Syria—the entire world was. Yemen is called 'the forgotten war' because no one knows about it." Karim had fled to Malaysia in October 2015 after being conscripted by the Houthis. When Karim arrived in Jeju in May 2018, he requested asylum directly at the airport—in contrast to the majority of the Yemenis on his flight who entered the country as tourists and applied for asylum thereafter. Karim felt that he should be "honest and clear from the outset," he told us in September 2018: a decision he thought had "bothered" the immigration officers who then detained him in the terminal until his approval came through days later. "When we entered, we were surprised by the protests that we were fake refugees. I was shocked. Fake on what basis? We came through the airport and we entered using the country's system. . . . We entered *legally,*" he said. Like Marwan, Bassam, and others, Karim was astounded to discover that their reasons for leaving war-torn Yemen would be anything but clear. "Go stay in Yemen for a week and see if we're fake refugees or not!" Karim told us as if he were addressing the Korean public.

While some of the Yemenis we met were able to shrug off the hostile accusations, relieved and excited to have found "security" (*amn*) in a new land, others felt dejected. They found it unsettling to be accused of being "terrorists" when they had suffered from and sought to escape acts of terrorism in Yemen. They were taken aback by the media's unrelenting focus on their religion and their (male) sexuality.[14] And they were surprised to find themselves subject to evangelization. Within weeks of their arrival, Jeju's Evangelicals were regular visitors to the Olleh Hotel, where they distributed Arabic-language Bibles, sang praise songs, and invited the Yemenis to Sunday services for food and worship. Some Korean Evangelical missionary groups traveled to Jeju from the mainland to train for their longer-term missions in Muslim countries.[15] Indeed, Korean missionaries regularly visit the Yemeni refugees in Djibouti's Markazi camp, raising the possibility that Korean missionaries traveled between Jeju and Djibouti along the same routes that the Yemeni asylum seekers had. Hakim, a mid-thirty-year-old self-professed atheist from Sa'dah who had sought to escape the Houthi proselytization in Yemen, spoke to the painful irony of the situation: "We fled from *da'wa* [invitation to Islam] to arrive in a place where there is also *da'wa* [invitation to Christianity]," he told us in September 2018.

As if the accusations and proselytization were not distressful enough—layered as it was on top of the Yemenis' own experiences of displacement and alienation—these largely middle-class Yemenis were also struggling with what it meant for them to be labeled and to self-identify as a refugee. One of the first things Zaki said when introducing himself at the "talk concert" was, "And, yeah, I'm a refugee. It's something I'm not ashamed to say because it's my situation"—underscoring the stigma attached to the term. Several of the Yemeni asylum seekers we met in Djibouti and South Korea emphasized their (in their view) positive interactions with Somali, Eritrean, and Ethiopian refugees in Yemen, often glossing over the

14. We witnessed, for instance, Zaki, the young man featured during the "talk concert," being asked onstage by his Korean friends, "How do you solve your sexual desire?" Zaki deflected the question, saying that he had recently learned that about 20 percent of the Korean population were single men. "Tell me how 20 percent of the Korean population will deal with sex," he told the audience, "and I can tell you about five hundred Yemenis."

15. One Korean missionary assigned to the Yemeni refugees referred to their first three to six months in Korea as the "golden time" for proselytization to prevent them from "becom[ing] extremist Muslims" (Hwang and Ahn-Park 2018).

racialized discrimination Africans encounter there. Many claimed repeatedly that, in contrast to their own situation, the Somali refugees in Yemen had been well taken care of, that they had considered their Somali neighbors as their equals, and that, as Marwan, said, "we never thought of them as refugees [*laji'in*]"—again, a series of statements confirming the stigma attached to both "refugees" and Somalis in Yemen. In a country where Africans and Black Yemenis have long been marginalized, this association of "refugees" with Africans renders "the refugee" a double aberration: foreign and black.

But what many of the Yemeni asylum seekers meant by these claims is that they had grown of age in a country that had been welcoming of refugees in a way that few countries have been welcoming of them. As the only state on the Arabian Peninsula that is a signatory to the Refugee Convention and its Protocol, Yemen has long accepted refugees from several nearby countries. Indeed, in 2020, Yemen was host to the world's second-largest number of Somali refugees (after Kenya). "Yemen is one of the countries that has accepted the highest number of refugees. If they were Egyptians, we accepted them. If they were Djiboutian or Somalis, we accepted them. We accepted all nationalities. It was a country that was open to the world," said Farah, a former media and communications major from Ibb, in September 2018. "But when our crisis came, no one accepted us." As university students, Farah and her fiancé, Faris, had experienced Yemen's official hospitality toward refugees intimately. Before the war, Faris had been active in an initiative to assist Syrian refugees in Sanaa. In fact, it was the threats he received as a result of this volunteer work that triggered his own escape from Yemen. Initially, he fled to Saudi Arabia, where his parents were living. Unable to work there legally and fearing deportation back to Yemen, Faris moved to Malaysia in early 2018, where Farah had fled to nine months earlier. When they heard that South Korea was "open" for refugees, they traveled there at once, expecting the same kind of government assistance that Syrians and some of their Yemeni friends had received in Germany, such as language training, a monthly allowance to help them get settled, and subsidized opportunities to continue their studies. At the very least, they expected the same kind of "welcome" Syrians had received in Yemen. And they expected more, in fact, from South

Korea, precisely because it had benefited financially from the cheap oil and natural gas that Yemen had "given" the country until 2014—a claim voiced by several Yemenis in Jeju. A half hour into our discussion of the "privileges" they had expected to receive as refugees and the hardships they encountered instead, we asked Farah and Faris what it means to them to be a "refugee." Faris broke down in tears. "It is difficult," Farah said quietly. Fleeing a war zone to become a refugee had been traumatic enough; being met less with sincere assistance than with accusations of insincerity is not what Farah and Faris or the other Yemenis in Jeju had expected.

## Humanitarian Status and Human (Refugee) Rights

Even for the Yemenis who secured refugee status, what this status signified remained variable and unstable. In both contexts, Yemenis expecting to be granted certain "rights" as refugees were disappointed by the humanitarian overtures that fell short of what they knew refugees to be receiving in other countries. In addition, the arrival of the Yemeni refugees in both Djibouti and South Korea coincided roughly with broader shifts in their governments' refugee laws and policies. Although these shifts were framed as an expansion of refugee rights, they introduced humanitarian reason (Fassin 2012) and status distinctions that diminished the prospects of Yemenis achieving what they had hoped for in becoming "refugees." The Republic of Korea had only recently enacted its own refugee law in 2013 and remained hesitant to accept large numbers of refugees on a permanent basis. Instead, it granted the majority of the Yemeni asylum seekers who arrived in 2018 "humanitarian status" ("permission to stay on humanitarian grounds"), a status short of refugee recognition. The Republic of Djibouti decreed new refugee laws in December 2017 aiming to safeguard and strengthen all of its refugees' access to education, health care, employment, and eventual naturalization. Whereas these laws were part of a broader move toward refugee "integration," many Yemeni refugees interpreted it, too, as a diluted status: a form of humanitarian care that negated their want and "right" to be resettled. Thus, while accusations flew over who was and was not a "real refugee," Yemeni refugees in Djibouti and asylum seekers in South Korea were similarly questioning the validity of these laws: Was their new status determination legitimate?

Despite Djibouti's blanket, prima facie recognition of all Yemenis claiming asylum, many of the Yemenis living in the Markazi camp have become increasingly anxious about their refugee status. By late 2016, if not earlier, various Yemeni government officials and their Djiboutian counterparts had taken to calling the Yemenis living in Djibouti "displaced" (*nazihin*) rather than "refugees" (*laji'in*). For example, when, in early January 2017, the Yemeni ambassador to Djibouti visited the Markazi camp, he apparently had tried to reassure the Yemenis he addressed that they were *nazihin* still under Yemeni protection who would be able to return to Yemen soon. "Don't you know that Obock is a governorate of Yemen?" a young man jested to Peutz (who was present during this visit but had not heard the ambassador's speech directly). "The UNHCR says we are refugees [French, *réfugiés*], but they call us displaced [*nazihin*]—as if we've just moved from one city to the next," he explained. "But we crossed the sea!" Other refugees Peutz met were similarly incensed. Some demanded to know why Yemeni government officials were permitted to visit a camp of refugees under UNHCR protection who had fled Yemen and its government(s). They saw the food distributions over which the Yemeni ambassador and other Yemeni government visitors presided as nothing less than photo-ops used to portray them internationally as "displaced" citizens receiving and accepting help from their own government. Some were convinced that the Saudi, Yemeni, and Djibouti governments were colluding to recast them as de facto IDPs in order to preserve international support for the Saudi-led war (by concealing the fact that the war had produced "refugees" who might make their way to Europe and North America) and to keep the Yemenis from being resettled elsewhere (so that the Djibouti government could continue to profit from their presence). If the Hadi government had aimed to project a caring embrace of its population by referring to the Markazi residents as "the Yemenis displaced in Djibouti," the Yemeni refugees in Markazi felt stifled—and alarmed—by its extended grip. During the weeks and months and years that followed, the refugees still hoping for third-country resettlement kept insisting that they were *laji'in*, not *nazihin*. "I consider myself a refugee [*laji'*] because we moved from country to country, continent to continent, sea to sea. They [Djiboutian officials] considered us displaced, though," a young man from Taiz told Peutz in March 2017. "I consider myself a refugee here, not displaced. I am a refugee. I am a *real* refugee. I have no relatives here," Idris, a retired professional from Aden said in English in January 2020. The fact that this statement still had to be made, nearly five years after his arrival and UNHCR registration in Djibouti, indicates how unstable this status had become.

With officials casting doubt on whether the UNHCR-recognized refugees were "real" refugees or merely temporarily "displaced"—casting the net of "internal" displacement across the shores of the Red Sea—the Yemenis living in the Markazi camp drew their own distinctions between who was and was not a bona fide refugee. On several occasions, camp residents pulled Peutz aside to tell her the open "secret" that not all the refugees in the camp were truly Yemeni and that not all the Yemenis were "real" refugees. As if constrained by the same discriminatory mind-set they had sought to flee, these refugees distinguished between the camp residents who are "pure" Yemeni/Arab (*asli*), those persons who are biracial (*muwallad*), and those individuals they claim to be "imposters" for they are not Yemeni but Djiboutian citizens with Somali Yemeni roots. The camp residents also distinguished between those persons who have remained in the camp since 2015 (the "refugees") and the ones who move between Djibouti and their coastal villages in Yemen to engage in trade or tend to their families on both sides of the Red Sea (the "displaced"). "The camp here has a disease. The problem in this camp is that some people are here as refugees, while others are only refugees on paper [*laji'in bi-l-waraq*]. They have refugee cards, but they are not refugees. They keep going back and forth to Yemen when they wish," said Ahmed in January 2018. "There's a very small minority here that are true refugees [*laji'in fi'lan*]," a man from Taiz repeated in January 2020, expressing his concern that the comings and goings of their fellow camp residents will dilute their own claim for the necessity of third-country resettlement or that the "imposters" will be resettled in their place.

At stake for these UNHCR-recognized refugees is whether their hard-won status will open the door to their future third-country resettlement or will keep them contained in a desolate desert camp. The longer the refugees remain in Markazi, the less likely their resettlement has become. In

2017, Djibouti became one of the first countries worldwide to pilot the Comprehensive Refugee Response Framework. This framework was designed to enhance refugee self-reliance through improved access to education, health care, legal assistance, and employment (Hansen 2018). It also set the path for the adoption of the Global Compact on Refugees by the United Nations General Assembly in 2018. Called "a new deal for refugees," the compact aims to provide greater support for refugees and the host countries receiving them by helping, among other things, to integrate refugees within national systems.[16] In keeping with this vision, the government of Djibouti passed its "progressive" new refugee laws, paving the way for the inclusion of refugees in the national health and educational systems, and announced that the country's refugee camps would henceforth be considered villages (Wachiaya 2017). In theory, these laws extend to Djibouti's refugees many of the same services and rights provided its citizens. In practice, the refugees lost the parallel medical and educational services formerly provided in the camps by international NGOs—and government services have been lacking.

At the same time, Saudi Arabia's King Salman Humanitarian Aid and Relief Center (KSRelief) moved forward with the construction of three hundred prefabricated air-conditioned housing units, a new school building, and a new mosque within the perimeters of the gated Markazi camp. In October 2018, a delegation from KSRelief inaugurated what they called "the *Saudi* village" in the midst of the UN camp. Occurring as it had in the wake of the murder of the Saudi journalist Jamal Khashoggi, several refugees wondered if the Saudi government was using this "humanitarian" gesture as a way to polish its tarnished reputation. Others wondered if they should accept a new housing unit, fearing that if they were to move physically from their impermanent tents to these more durable containers, they would be moving jurisdictionally from the tent of UN international protection to the de facto prison of permanent displacement. "I know that if you go into these houses, you give away your right of being

---

16. See https://www.unhcr.org/a-new-deal-for-refugees.html and the Global Compact, section 3.4, available at https://www.unhcr.org/5c658aed4.pdf.

a refugee. If you get a house, that means you're displaced, not a refugee. That's what they say," Saleh, a Somali Yemeni refugee from Taiz, asserted in March 2018. UNHCR employees had tried to assure Saleh that he could choose to accept the house or remain in his tent. Like many others, Saleh (mis)understood it as a choice between accepting the label "displaced" or retaining his refugee status. "Some people, myself included, prefer to remain as refugees. I don't need a fucking house here. . . . I need to remain a refugee; I need to survive and get the fuck out of here. . . . If we move there, we become displaced citizens, not refugees. There is no way back from that," he said, in English.

While the refugees in Markazi were being moved into their new housing units inside the so-called Saudi village within the camp, the Yemenis in Jeju were awaiting the final release of the government's decisions regarding their applications for asylum. In September 2018, the Ministry of Justice had granted twenty-three Yemenis the permit for a one-year humanitarian stay: a purposefully small number of permits, according to a person active in the Jeju People's Coalition for Refugee Rights, through which the state aimed to assess public opinion before completing its reviews. The Ministry of Justice released its decisions regarding the status of the remaining 461 Yemeni asylum seekers in mid-October and mid-December (Choe 2018b). Of the 484 Yemenis in Jeju whose requests for asylum had been assessed in 2018, 412 were granted a one-year humanitarian stay, 56 were denied, 14 applications were canceled, and only 2 were granted refugee status. The difference between refugee and humanitarian status is politically and materially significant.[17] A "refugee" is granted an indefinite period of stay in South Korea (subject to review), freedom of movement, state health insurance, family unification, and the possibility for citizenship after five years of residence. A "humanitarian-status

---

17. Whereas a "refugee" is defined strictly on the basis of having a "well-founded fear of being persecuted," a "humanitarian-status holder" refers to "any alien to whom [the definition of refugee] does not apply but for whom there are reasonable grounds to believe that his/her life or personal freedom may be egregiously violated by torture or other inhumane treatment or punishment or other circumstances" (Republic of Korea 2013).

holder" is permitted a (renewable) one-year stay and the ability to move freely and work within South Korea, but without the ability to bring over family members or apply for citizenship. Moreover, as Arzoo Osanloo reminds us, "The underlying philosophies of the two approaches to the human—human rights and humanitarianism—are distinct, perhaps even contrasting" (2020, 267). Intrinsic to our very humanity, human rights "precede the state" yet "compel states to act (or desist from acting)" to protect individuals or groups long-term. Humanitarianism, by contrast, "appeals to the state's [and others'] discretionary powers to act in bringing [temporary] relief to situations where rights and laws do not otherwise compel it to do so" (267). International (and state) protection for refugees is a "human right"; humanitarian care is a benevolent "gift."

The response of South Korean human rights activists was rapid, addressing problematic conditions of national public opinion and a reluctant politics of human rights. According to Jiyoon Kim, a senior research fellow at the Asan Institute for Policy Studies, an independent think tank based in Seoul, "The decision [to grant temporary permits] was made to reconcile the negative public opinion with the identity of a liberal government and to show the global community that South Korea is not a xenophobic country" (Harris 2018). Neologisms such as "refugee phobia" and an increased focus on amplified hate speech in the public domain have since defined emerging activist tactics against antimigrant sentiment (H. Kim 2018). Furthermore, Jeju activists joined with public interest lawyers based in Seoul to vocalize their rebuke of the Ministry of Justice's latest round of decisions and its discrepancy with international standards for refugee policy. In December 2018, Advocates for Public Interest Law (APIL) lawyers submitted a lawsuit against the state for not providing specific reasons for each of the 22 Yemenis whose applications were denied that month (APIL 2021). APIL's lawsuit alludes to the lack of transparency in the procedures for refugee review, which makes it impossible for the refugees to effectively present their legal appeals to the court. Meanwhile, among the Yemenis, various hypotheses circulated as to how and why some had been granted denials and others further interviews. Many suspected Facebook to have been a significant resource for inquiry into their personal and political backgrounds in Yemen; some believed their decisions had been postponed because they had posted images of Saddam Hussein, Lenin, or Che Guevara online. In other instances, asylum seekers were able to turn to their Facebook feed for evidence that they had received death threats and were thus in need of Korean state protection "owning to well-founded fear of being persecuted" in Yemen.

Perhaps expectedly, many of the 412 Yemeni asylum seekers who received humanitarian status were not as invested in attaining refugee status as their activist advocates have been. For some, a one-year humanitarian stay was deemed a sufficient amount of time given their expectations at the end of 2018 that the war would end soon. For others, the distinction between refugee and humanitarian status seemed relatively insignificant given that those granted humanitarian status could extend their stay with annual renewals and even those who were denied status were permitted several appeals. Moreover, humanitarian status would finally allow the Yemenis to migrate onward to Seoul, the coveted final destination for many because of its greater job market and established Muslim community. Shortly after the October decisions, around 240 of the 339 Yemenis who had been granted humanitarian status moved to the mainland despite the advice of their Jeju-based supporters, who feared that life in the capital—along with competition from other migrants and the lack of welfare infrastructure there—would be even more challenging. Faris, Farah, and Marwan moved to Mokpo to work for the Hyundai plant where women painted ships and men worked the assembly line; Jalal moved to Chungcheonbuk-do after landing an opening in an air-conditioning factory; Karim moved to Pusan without a job offer, but nearer to friends. This exodus of Yemenis from Jeju resulted in the NGOs closing their Korean-language classes and paring down their support infrastructure. But there were also some signs of Yemenis' imprint on the island: Korea's first Yemeni restaurant, Warda, opened near the Jungang Catholic Diocese/Naomi Center in the fall of 2018.

In December 2018, we met up with five Yemeni asylum seekers at a pizzeria the day the final decisions had been released. Seated at the table were men representing the full range of possible outcomes: the two Yemenis to have been granted the coveted refugee status, two men who had just been informed that they received a humanitarian stay, and one whose application was denied. None, however, was satisfied with the outcome. The Yemenis who had been granted refugee status were disappointed to learn that they would not be granted subsidies for language training, educational advancement, or housing assistance—unlike their Yemeni friends in Europe who were receiving this help in addition to cash assistance even while awaiting their status determination. Instead of studying Korean to resume their careers, they would have to take on wage labor to cover their living expenses. The Yemeni whose application was denied was frustrated but determined to appeal. Surprisingly, given what we had heard from other Yemeni humanitarian-status holders, the two men who received a humanitarian stay expressed the most disappointment. To them, the liminality of this "humanitarian" status—neither full refugee status nor a denial—seemed more like a political calculation than a (mis)recognition of their situation. Hakim, the atheist from Saʿdah, told us he had refused to sign the document and was planning to appeal the decision. He then spent much of the evening trying to convince Rashid to appeal his humanitarian-status determination, too: "not just for yourself, but because someday someone else will come and they will need [refugee status]. This is about human rights." He then turned to us and said, in English, "You asked me why I am sad. . . . It wasn't ever my dream to be recognized as a refugee in Korea. Maybe one of my dreams was to visit Korea, but not to be a refugee in Korea, okay? I feel sad because they don't consider me human."

**Conclusion**

Global forced displacement is outpacing global population growth. As of early 2021, more than 100 million people worldwide—more than 1 percent of humanity—have been forced to flee from their homes. During the past decade, between 2010 and 2019, the number of people displaced across borders or within their country of origin owing to war, conflict, persecution, climate change, hunger, poverty, and other social and political disturbances has nearly doubled. In the same decade, the total number of people displaced internally owing to conflict and violence has tripled: from 15 million in 2010 to 45.7 million in 2019 (UNHCR 2020). Despite the high level of internal displacement within Yemen, relatively few Yemenis have been accepted as refugees in other countries. And Yemeni refugees or Yemenis in refugee-like situations remain largely invisible in the international media.

In this chapter, we have compared the reception of Yemeni refugees in Djibouti, which granted prima facie recognition to all refugees from Yemen, with the treatment of Yemeni asylum seekers in South Korea, which granted "humanitarian" but not refugee status to the majority of the Yemeni citizens who entered Jeju Island in the spring of 2018. Another way of putting it is that we examined both Djibouti and Korea as variations of portals through which Yemeni refugees sought to "exit West" (Hamid 2017). In more ways than we can elaborate here, these contexts are distinct. Djibouti was less of a desired destination than a contingent one, due to its geographical closeness, its preexisting networks based on historic ties and regular trade links, and its familiar geography as a Muslim, Arabophone, and Arab League nation. South Korea was a desired destination, but also a very uncertain one: the Yemenis had to forge their own paths and navigate unfamiliar terrain in an unknown language. Broadly speaking, if the Yemenis in South Korea were considered suspect for having traveled so far and without their families, the Yemenis in Djibouti were considered suspect (largely by one another) for traveling too easily between Yemen and Djibouti, where they had significant family connections already. In other words, if the Yemenis in South Korea did not seem like genuine refugees because they had not arrived by sea, the Yemenis in Djibouti struggled to prove themselves "real refugees"—their official recognition notwithstanding—because the distance they crossed, cultural as well as geographical, was so narrow.

Yet as different as these host societies appear, both Djibouti and South Korea are curiously linked through their connections to Yemen. Both countries have profited from resource extraction and war profiteering in and related to Yemen. Djiboutian citizens have long benefited from government-subsidized gas and other goods imported from Yemen. Until 2014—the year that South Korea revoked its visa waiver for citizens from Yemen—South Korea benefited from a 2005 Saleh-era contract allowing it to purchase Yemen's liquefied natural gas at below market rates. Djibouti relies on rents from the foreign bases used to support the coalition's military intervention in Yemen. And between 2016 and 2021, South Korea sold US$75 million worth of weapons to Saudi Arabia and the United Arab

Emirates, thus providing its support for the coalition's military intervention, too.[18] The two countries are connected, moreover, by the Yemenis
who fled to and through them. And, in both contexts, Yemenis seeking
to escape the brutal war found themselves misrecognized. Having felt
like "virtual refugees" in Yemen, having been called "fake refugees" in
South Korea, and having been discursively reduced to "displaced persons"
in Djibouti, refuge-seeking Yemenis—racialized as "Arab" in Djibouti, as
"Muslim" in South Korea—struggled to be recognized as genuine refugees
with a legitimate claim to asylum.

As we have seen, the term "refugee" (*laji'/réfugié/nanmin*) travels
alongside human bodies carrying both negative and positive connotations
(Masquelier 2006; Sajjad 2018). For the Yemenis who had been accustomed to associating *refugee* with the Somalis, Ethiopians, and Eritreans
displaced in Yemen and were now experiencing racism, alienation, and
debasement abroad, the label is stigmatizing. "You know, a *refugee* means
an ignored person, a neglected person, a weak person. It's a bad status, really. . . . A refugee struggles for existence everywhere. There's no difference
between him and the animals, anywhere," Idris, the retired professional
from Aden, told Peutz in English in January 2020. For others, especially
the Yemenis who felt deeply ostracized and out of place within Yemen,
the label acknowledges and exposes their abjection and pain. At the same
time, most of the Yemenis we met had associated being or becoming a refugee with the liberatory potential to unlock portals to the Global North.
The same Idris who disparaged his status had not only insisted that he
was a "real refugee," but had also told Peutz in earlier years how "alive" he
felt as a refugee in Djibouti after living as a Yemeni citizen in Aden. This
appreciation stems from the awareness that, with the ever-increasing securitization of migration globally and the restrictions placed on the movements of Yemenis, in particular, the refugee label "is no longer a right but a
highly prized status" (Zetter 2007, 189). In today's world, being recognized
internationally and by host states as a refugee may be, for many of the
world's denizens, the only relatively safe and achievable route to gaining
access to the Global North. For the Yemenis in Djibouti, achieving refugee

18. For more data on this arms trade, see https://comtrade.un.org/data/.

status was a means to escape the region. For the Yemenis in South Korea, achieving refugee status was a means to stay.

Nevertheless, the liberatory promise of becoming a "refugee" is distinctly tragic in nature.[19] In both Djibouti and South Korea, the Yemeni refugees' dreams of a dignified future are perpetually receding beyond the horizon. On the one hand, these Yemenis have struggled to conform to their hosts' preconceived expectations of "real refugees" based on historical antecedents in these countries. "Real refugees" were not supposed to carry possessions, to plan, to visit their relatives, to travel commercially, to decline work, to pursue careers, or even to aspire to live "the good life." On the other hand, even when these Yemenis have been recognized as refugees or as persons in need of state protection, they must fight to claim and maintain these protections as *rights*. As *laji'in* (refugees) discursively downgraded to *nazihin* (displaced) in Djibouti and as potential *nanmin* (refugees) gifted a temporary humanitarian stay but not legal rights in South Korea—in this sense, similar to the *p'inanmin* (displaced) of the Cold War period (N. H.-J. Kim 2021)—Yemenis seeking refuge abroad have been willfully misrecognized and sorely ignored. For academics working on Yemen, to think *with* the word "refugee"—and to think with forcibly displaced Yemenis, moreover, who are themselves thinking with the word—is to bring into view the multiple forms of loss, injury, forced migration, family separation, racialization, alienation, and other challenges faced by Yemenis today. It is also to bring into view these Yemenis' expectations of and demands upon "the world" and their fundamental right to life, mobility, and protection. Fortunately, there is a growing cohort of scholars writing on Yemeni refugees today whose work may help to draw more attention and political goodwill to the millions of Yemenis displaced by the war.[20] In the meantime, Yemeni refugees will continue to work to secure their status and to search for portals to a better life. In August 2021, as the US military sought feverishly

19. We thank Ross Porter for this formulation and for his insightful comments on the chapter as a whole.

20. See, inter alia, al-Hadheri and Pernot (2022); al-Majali (2022); al-Maqtari (2022); Hall (2021, 2023); H. Kim (2018); N. Kim (2018); Lauret (2020, 2023); Muharram (2025); and Pernot (2023).

to evacuate US nationals and Afghan allies from Kabul, Idris sent Peutz images of documents attesting that his grandfather had been an Afghan refugee in Mecca. As a son of a son of an Afghan refugee, he wondered if the United States would be interested in helping him now.

## Acknowledgments

Research for this chapter was supported by New York University Abu Dhabi and the American Academy in Berlin (for Peutz) and the Korea Foundation, the Academy of Korean Studies, and the Northeast Asia Council of the Association for Asian Studies (for Heo). Peutz is grateful to ONARS and UNHCR in Djibouti, and Peutz and Heo are both grateful to Jeju Dark Tours, the Naomi Center, and Global Inner Peace in Jeju, South Korea, for their generous time and assistance during our fieldwork trips. We thank Mark Swislocki and the Global Asia Initiative at NYU Abu Dhabi for supporting our collaborative work and Laila Hashem, Jennifer Hough, Junho Lee, Sara Thabet, and Jisu Yeom for their invaluable research assistance at different stages of this chapter's preparation. We also thank Ross Porter and our anonymous reviewers for helping to see this work through to publication. We are especially grateful to our Yemeni interlocutors in Djibouti and in South Korea for sharing their experiences and insights with us.

## References

APIL. 2021. "Kongikpŏpsent'ŏ Ŏp'il [APIL Advocates for Public Interest Law]." https://apil.or.kr/.

Belan, Branko. 2018. "500 Yemeni Refugees Seek Shelter on Jeju Island." *10 Magazine*, June 20, 2018. https://10mag.com/500-yemeni-refugees-seek-shelter-on-jeju-island/.

Betts, Alexander. 2013. "Yemen: Contrasting Responses to Somalis and Ethiopians." In *Survival Migration: Failed Governance and the Crisis of Displacement*, edited by Alexander Betts, 160–72. Ithaca, NY: Cornell Univ. Press.

Cho, Su-jin. 2018. "'Chagungmini mŏnjŏda' Chejusŏ Yemen nanmin pandae chiphoe kaech'oe ['Our People Come First'—Rally Protesting Yemeni Refugees Held in Jeju]." *Nyusisŭ* [*Newsis*], June 30, 2018. https://newsis.com/view/?id=NISX20180630_0000350812&cID=10813&pID=10800.

Choe, Sang-Hun. 2018a. "Migrants Expected Warm Welcome on Korean Resort Island. They Were Wrong." *New York Times*, Sept. 12, 2018. https://www.ny times.com/2018/09/12/world/asia/south-korea-jeju-yemen-refugees.html.

———. 2018b. "South Korea Denies Refugee Status to Hundreds of Fleeing Yemenis." *New York Times*, Oct. 17, 2018. https://www.nytimes.com/2018/10/17 /world/asia/south-korea-yemeni-refugees.html.

Crisp, Jeff. 1984. "The Politics of Repatriation: Ethiopian Refugees in Djibouti, 1977–83." *Review of African Political Economy* 11, no. 30: 73–82.

de Regt, Marina. 2014. "Close Ties: Gender, Labour and Migration between Yemen and the Horn of Africa." In *Why Yemen Matters: A Society in Transition*, edited by Helen Lackner, 287–303. London: Saqi Books.

Fassin, Didier. 2012. *Humanitarian Reason: A Moral History of the Present*. Oakland: Univ. of California Press.

Gluck, Carol, and Anna Lowenhaupt Tsing. 2009. *Words in Motion: Toward a Global Lexicon*. Durham, NC: Duke Univ. Press.

Al-Hadheri, Samaher, and Morgann Barbara Pernot. 2022. "The Evolution of Yemeni Migration to Djibouti." Sana'a Center for Strategic Studies, Apr. 14, 2022. https://sanaacenter.org/publications/main-publications/17445.

Hall, Bogumila. 2021. "Yemeni Freedom and Mobility Dreams." *Middle East Research and Information Project (MERIP)*, Nov. 8, 2021. https://merip.org/2021 /08/yemeni-freedom-and-mobility-dreams/.

———. 2023. "Death and Solidarity in the 'Graveyard' at the Belarus-Poland Border." *Open Democracy*, Feb. 2, 2023. https://www.opendemocracy.net/en /author/bogumila-hall/.

Hamid, Mohsin. 2017. *Exit West*. New York: Riverhead Books.

Hansen, Randall. 2018. "The Comprehensive Refugee Response Framework: A Commentary." *Journal of Refugee Studies* 31: 131–51.

Harris, Bryan. 2018. "South Korea Grants Temporary Permits to Yemeni Refugees." *Financial Times*, Oct. 17, 2018. https://www.ft.com/content/45b3dad8 -d1b5-11e8-a9f2-7574db66bcd5.

Heo, Angie. 2021. "The Christian Right and Refugee Rights: The Border Politics of Anti-communism and Anti-discrimination in South Korea." *Religion and Society* 12, no. 1: 86–101.

HRW. 2021. "Yemen: Houthis Attacking Displaced Person's Camps." Mar. 23, 2021. https://www.hrw.org/news/2021/03/23/yemen-houthis-attacking-displaced -peoples-camps.

Hwang, Yuntae, and Yeara Ahn-Park. 2018. "500 Yemenis in Jeju-Do Seek Refugee Status: Welcome Them or Be Cautious?" *Kukmin Daily*, June 27, 2018. http://www.kukmindaily.co.kr/article/view.asp?arcid=0012475427.

IFRC [International Federation of Red Cross and Red Crescent Societies]. 2015. "Emergency Plan of Action (EPoA). Djibouti: Yemeni Refugees." Apr. 29, 2015. https://reliefweb.int/sites/reliefweb.int/files/resources/MDRDJ002.pdf.

IRB Canada [Immigration and Refugee Board of Canada]. 1991. *The Horn of Africa: Somalis in Djibouti, Ethiopia and Kenya*. Feb. 1, 1991. https://www.ref world.org/docid/3ae6a80f30.html.

Jelagat, Faith. 2020. "World Bank Ranks Djibouti Most Expensive Country in Africa." *Africa Sustainability Matters*, June 15, 2020. https://africasustain abilitymatters.com/world-bank-ranks-djibouti-most-expensive-country-in -africa/.

Kermeliotis, Teo. 2019. "'We Have Nothing': A Life in Limbo for Malaysia's Yemeni Refugees." *Al Jazeera*, Mar. 24, 2019. https://www.aljazeera.com/news /2019/3/24/we-have-nothing-a-life-in-limbo-for-malaysias-yemeni-refugees.

Kim, Do Own (Donna), Nathaniel Ming Curran, and Hyun Tae (Calvin) Kim. 2020. "Digital Feminism and Affective Splintering: South Korean Twitter Discourse on 500 Yemeni Refugees." *International Journal of Communication* 14: 4117–35. https://ijoc.org/index.php/ijoc/article/view/14322.

Kim, Hyŏn-mi. 2018. "Nanmin p'obiawa Han'guk chŏngch'ijŏk chŏngdongŭi sigansŏng [The Temporality of Refugee Phobia and Korean Political Affect]." *Hwanghaemunhwa [Hwanghae Review]* 101: 210–28.

Kim, Nami. 2018. "'Yŏsŏngin'gwŏn'ŭi' irŭmŭro maennŭn wihŏmhan yŏndae. Yemen nanminsuyongbandae ch'ŏngwŏn'gwa Isŭllamop'obia [Dangerous Solidarity in the Name of 'Women's Rights.' Yemeni Anti-refugee Petitions and Islamophobia]." *Che3sidaegŭrisŭdogyoyŏn'guso [Christian Institute for the 3rd Era]* 134: 2–5.

Kim, Nora Hui-Jung. 2021. "Cold War Refugees: South Korea's Entry into the International Refugee Regime, 1950–1992." *Journal of Refugee Studies* 35, no. 1: 435–53.

Ko, Dong-hwan. 2018. "Yemeni Refugees' Fate Tested on Jeju Island." *Korea Times*, June 17, 2018. https://www.koreatimes.co.kr/www/nation/2018/06/113_250 806.html.

Koo, Se-Woong. 2018. "South Korea's Enduring Racism." *New York Times*, July 1, 2018. https://www.nytimes.com/2018/07/01/opinion/south-korea-racism .html.

Lauret, Alexander. 2020. "Du réfugié Yéménite à l'entrepreneur: Quand l'exil de guerre devient opportunité économique à Djibouti." *Politique Africaine* 159: 145–68.

Lauret, Alexandre. 2023. *La Guerre et l'Exil: Yémen, 2015–2020*. Paris: Les Belles Lettres.

Lee, Yu-ji. 2018. "Nanmin nollane 'Cheju musajŭng ipkukpurhŏ' 24kaegugŭro 2pae hwaktae ['Ban on Visa-Free Entry to Jeju' Doubles to 24 Countries over Refugee Controversy]." *Mŏnit'udei* [*Money Today*], July 31, 2018. https://news.mt.co.kr/mtview.php?MRHT_T=&no=2018073114218230215.

Al-Majali, Solenn. 2022. "A Precarious Refuge: Yemeni Asylum-Seekers in Jordan." Sana'a Center for Strategic Studies, Feb. 14, 2022. https://sanaacenter.org/publications/main-publications/16557.

Al-Maqtari, Bushra. 2022 [2018]. *What Have You Left Behind? Voices from a Forgotten War*. Translated by Sawad Hussein. London: Fitzcarraldo Editions.

Masquelier, Adeline. 2006. "Why Katrina's Victims Aren't Refugees: Musings on a 'Dirty' Word." *American Anthropologist* 108, no. 4: 735–43.

Metelits, Claire, and Stephanie Matti. 2015. "Authoritarianism and Geostrategic Politics in Djibouti." In *Democratic Contestations on the Margins: Regimes in Small African Countries*, edited by Claire Metelits and Stephanie Matti. Lanham, MD: Lexington Books.

Morris-Suzuki, Tessa. 2011. "Guarding the Borders of Japan: Occupation, Korean War and Frontier Controls." *Asia-Pacific Journal/Japan Focus* 9, no. 3: 1–21. Article ID: 3490. https://apjjf.org/2011/9/8/Tessa-Morris-Suzuki/3490/article.html.

Muharram, Mohammed. 2025. "An Exiled Yemeni Scholar in Western Academia: Perils and Promises." In *Exiled Scholars in Western Academia: Refugees or Intellectuals?*, edited by Alfred Babo and Sayed Hassan Akhlaq, 223–45. London: Palgrave Macmillan.

Nuryap İnşaat. n.d. "Nuryap and Nevka Companies Completed the Obock Camp Project in Djibuti." Accessed Aug. 31, 2021. https://www.nuryapinsaat.com/en/news/nuryap-and-nevka-companies-completed-the-obock-camp-project-in-djibuti/.

Nyers, Peter. 2006. *Rethinking Refugees: Beyond States of Emergency*. New York: Routledge.

Organization of African Union [OAU]. 1969. "Convention Concerning the Specific Aspects of Refugee Problems in Africa ('OAU Convention')." Sept. 10, 1969. 1001 UNTS 45. https://www.refworld.org/docid/3ae6b36018.html.

Osanloo, Arzoo. 2020. *Forgiveness Work: Mercy, Law, and Victims' Rights in Iran.* Princeton, NJ: Princeton Univ. Press.

Pak, Sang-gi. 2018. "Tappyŏnwallyo: Chejudo pulbŏp nanmin sinch'ŏng munjee ttarŭn Nanminbŏp, musajŭng ipkuk, nanminsinch'ŏnghŏga p'yeji/kaehŏn ch'ŏngwŏnhamnida [Answer Completed: I Am Petitioning for the Abolution/Amendment of the Refugee Act, Visa-Free Entry and Asylum Application]." Taehanmin'guk Ch'ŏngwadae [Republic of Korea Blue House]. https://www1.president.go.kr/petitions/269548.

Pak, Sŏng-u. 2018. "Chejuŏmin 'Yemenindŭl yaegido haji malla' ŏmin'gwa nanminŭn wae tŭngdollyŏnna ['Don't Even Talk about Yemenis'—Why Jeju Fishermen Turned Their Backs on the Refugees]." *Chosŏn Ilbo*, Sept. 22, 2018. https://www.chosun.com/site/data/html_dir/2018/09/21/2018092102292.html.

Park, Nathan. 2018. "South Korea Is Going Crazy over a Handful of Refugees." *Foreign Policy*, Aug. 6, 2018. https://foreignpolicy.com/2018/08/06/south-korea-is-going-crazy-over-a-handful-of-refugees/.

Pernot, Morgann Barbara. 2022. "Au long des parcours migratoires, jouer avec les statuts juridiques, recomposer les identités." *Enfances Familles Générations* 41. https://journals.openedition.org/efg/14589#quotation.

Peutz, Nathalie. 2019. "'The Fault of Our Grandfathers': Yemen's Third Generation Migrants Seeking Refuge from Displacement." *International Journal of Middle East Studies* 51, no. 3: 1–20.

Republic of Djibouti. 2017. "Décret fixant les modalités d'exercice des droits fontamentaux des réfugiés et demandeurs d'asile en République de Djibouti." 2017-410/PR/MI, Dec. 7, 2017. https://www.refworld.org/docid/5a2eb7114.html.

Republic of Korea. 2013. "Law No. 11298 of 2012, Refugee Act [Republic of Korea]." https://www.refworld.org/docid/4fd5cd5a2.html.

Republic of Korea Blue House [Taehanmin'gukch'ŏngwadae]. 2018. "[Ch'ŏngwadae Live] Ch'ŏngwŏndappyŏn 'Nanminbŏp kwallyŏn' ch'ŏngwŏn [(Blue House Live) Response to the Petition Related to the 'Refugee Act']." *YouTube.* https://www.youtube.com/watch?v=r-6S79tXn-8&feature=youtu.be.

Sajjad, Tazreena. 2018. "What's In a Name: 'Refugees,' 'Migrants' and the Politics of Labelling." *Race & Class* 60, no. 2: 40–62.

Schraeder, Peter J. 1993. "Ethnic Politics in Djibouti: From 'Eye of the Hurricane' to 'Boiling Cauldron.'" *African Affairs* 92, no. 367: 203–21.

Seo, Bo. 2018. "In South Korea, Opposition to Yemeni Refugees Is a Cry for Help." CNN Opinion, Sept. 13, 2018. https://edition.cnn.com/2018/09/13/opinions/south-korea-jeju-yemenis-intl/index.html.

Thiollet, Hélène. 2014. "From Migration Hub to Asylum Crisis: The Changing Dynamics of Contemporary Migration in Yemen." In *Why Yemen Matters: A Society in Transition*, edited by Helen Lackner, 267–86. London: Saqi Books.

UNHCR. 2010. "South Korea: Refugee Granted Citizenship for First Time." Mar. 23, 2010. https://www.unhcr.org/news/briefing/2010/3/4ba89d939/south-korea -refugee-granted-citizenship-first-time.html.

———. 2012. "Submission by the United Nations High Commissioner for Refugees for the Office of the High Commissioner for Human Rights." Djibouti: Compilation Report—Universal Periodic Review, Oct. 2012. https://www .refworld.org/docid/5072836f2.html.

———. 2015a. "Djibouti Fact Sheet." Sept. 2015. https://data2.unhcr.org/en /documents/download/32302.

———. 2015b. "UNHCR Fact Sheet Djibouti." Dec. 2015. https://reliefweb.int /sites/reliefweb.int/files/resources/UNHCRDjiboutiFactSheetDecember 2015f.pdf.

———. 2015c. "Yemen Operation Update #7." May 29, 2015. https://data2.unhcr .org/en/documents/details/32066.

———. 2015d. "Yemen Situation Regional Refugee and Migrant Response Plan, January–December 2016." Dec. 2015. https://reliefweb.int/sites/reliefweb.int /files/resources/RegionalRMRPYemencrisis2016.pdf.

———. 2019. "UNHCR Fact Sheet Djibouti." Jan. 2019. https://reporting.unhcr .org/sites/default/files/UNHCR%20Djibouti%20Fact%20Sheet%20-%20 January%202019.pdf.

———. 2020. "Global Trends: Forced Displacement in 2019." June 18, 2020. https://www.unhcr.org/5ee200e37.pdf.

———. 2021. "UNHCR Operational Update Yemen." Feb. 26, 2021. https:// reporting.unhcr.org/sites/default/files/UNHCR%20Yemen%20Operational %20Update%20-%2026%20February%202021.pdf.

Wachiaya, Catherine. 2017. "UN Refugee Chief Praises Djibouti New Refugee Laws," *Relief Web*, Dec. 15, 2017. https://www.unhcr.org/news/latest/2017/12 /5a3416654/un-refugee-chief-praises-djibouti-new-refugee-laws.html.

Wakalat Khabr al-Yamaniyya. 2015. "The Speech of the Leader 'Ali 'Abdullah Saleh during His Meeting with a Delegation of the People of Taiz." *YouTube*, Mar. 9, 2015. https://www.youtube.com/watch?v=YQ2TGktCOYA.

Yoon, Myeong-Sook, Israel Fisseha, and So-Won Suk. 2020. "A Refugee Protection within a Less-Restrictive Immigration Policy and Refugee Protection in South Korea: A Policy Review of 2013's Refugee Act." *Asia-Pacific Journal of Convergent Research Interchange* 6, no. 2: 1–16. http://dx.doi.org/10.21742/apjcri.2020.02.01.

Zetter, Roger. 2007. "More Labels, Fewer Refugees: Remaking the Refugee Label in an Era of Globalization." *Journal of Refugee Studies* 20, no. 2: 172–92.

# 7

# Friendship

*Ethical Engagements and Dilemmas*
*in Times of War and Conflict*

Marina de Regt

On a gray winter day at the end of January 2020 an email pops up in my inbox. The sender is called Qasem Harba,[1] and the subject is "I hope you remember." I am at the university, busy preparing my classes but in the mood for distraction. Curious what this email is about I open the message, and read:

> Dear Marina,
> This is me Qasem, the young brother of Selma whom you used to visit in al-Hudayda, Yemen. I am in India doing my Ph.D. I am very happppppy to send this email to you. I was trying to write a paper about forced Yemeni migration and I was shocked to see your papers in front of me. This is incredible. I searched many years for you and now I found you. Please reply to my email. By the way, Selma is missing you so much and always remembers you.
> Yours,<br>Qasem

Attached are four pictures, one of a younger version of myself, grinding wheat on a stone; the next one of a *sandaqa*, a typical living unit in the squatter areas in al-Hudayda in the 1990s; and one of a well made of tires.

---

1. All names of persons used in this chapter are fictive.

I know these pictures very well; they had been taken with my own camera, and I have copies of them myself. The fourth picture shows an elderly white woman with gray hair, whom I immediately recognize: it is Thera de Haas, one of my former colleagues in the al-Hudayda Urban Primary Health Care Project, a Dutch-Yemeni development project that ran from 1984 until 1999 (see de Regt 2007). Next to her stands Selma, dressed in a black balto and headscarf. I did not need a picture of Selma to remember who she was. We worked closely together in al-Hudayda; she was one of the health extension agents (*murshidat sahhiyat*) trained and employed by the project. Selma was in her early twenties, the eldest daughter in a family of eight children, and a very dedicated health worker. We carried out a small-scale study on nutrition habits of infants and young children and enjoyed each other's company. I visited her family regularly; they lived in a squatter area that came into being during the Gulf Crisis. We often had lunch together, and I smoked *mada'a* (waterpipe) with her father, a very skinny but strong man with typical Tihama features, who was always sitting on a *qa'ada*, a hemp-strung couch, and liked to joke with me. Selma's mother was a very warm and friendly woman, who still spoke the Tihami dialect despite having lived for a long time in Saudi Arabia. I often had difficulties understanding her, but we liked each other a lot. Selma's sisters and brothers were very friendly as well, and always asked me why I did not visit them more often: "Where have you been? Why are we not seeing you?" were the standard questions I would hear when I would pass by. My visits to Yemen and al-Hudayda diminished, and it may have been 2009 when I last saw Selma, on a short trip from Sanaa to al-Hudayda. Or maybe it is even longer ago. I did not have her phone number, and we lost contact. I had, however, often wondered how she and her family were doing.

Qasem's message therefore was a very pleasant distraction from my work, and I replied enthusiastically, asking him about his family and Selma in particular. I expressed my concern about the situation in Yemen and asked for their phone number. Qasem replied the following day, and we decided to call each other. We spoke for almost an hour. He told me about the terrible situation in al-Hudayda, where his brothers and he himself had been threatened by Houthi militias as they had been active during the youth protests in the spring of 2011 and continued to speak out against injustice, and people around them spread rumors that they were anti-Houthi, even after the Houthis occupied al-Hudayda in September 2014. The family house had been demolished by the Houthis, and the family had been forced to leave al-Hudayda. Selma was doing relatively all right but she suffered from health problems, had stopped working, divorced and married again, and was hoping to have a child. Qasem was worried about his family and was regularly in touch with them. A few days after our first phone call I talked to Selma's sister Badriya and very briefly with Selma herself. Yet while Qasem and Badriya sometimes reached out to me asking how I am doing, I notice that I am having difficulties staying in touch with Yemeni friends and regularly ask myself why. Is it because I do not know how to respond to their stories about the situation in Yemen? Am I feeling guilty because I am having such an easy and secure life? Do I avoid contact because I feel powerless? Or are there other issues at stake? And how does this avoidance relate to my intentions to be an engaged scholar?

My renewed contact with Selma and her family, thanks to her brother who accidentally came across my name, is an excellent example of the way in which friends, former colleagues, and interlocutors engage with anthropologists, as Nathalie Peutz describes it in a short paper about her engagement with her interlocutors in Socotra (2014). "Engagement" and "engaged scholarship" are terms that have become very pertinent, and numerous articles and books have been published discussing the ways in which scientists, and social scientists in particular, can engage with their fields of study (for a good overview, see Low and Merry 2010). Following Low and Merry, Peutz makes a plea for a critical interrogation of the concept of "engagement" and argues that we should see engagement more "as a dialogic practice than as something the anthropologist (and anthropology) does (or does not)" (Peutz 2014, 1). In this chapter I would like to follow up on Peutz's call to critically analyze and empirically unpack the concepts of engagement and engaged scholarship and discuss their applicability to the field of Yemeni studies. In the past decade I have been struggling with the question of how to relate to Yemen. Just like anyone else who knows Yemen and feels connected to the country for whatever reason, the political situation and the subsequent war have affected me emotionally. In addition to the question of how I can continue my research without being able to do fieldwork in the country, the question of how to relate to my friends and former colleagues there looms large in my mind. My failure to keep in touch with them is not only due to their challenges of getting a good phone or internet connection but also to the fact that I find it hard to cope with their stories about the situation in which they have found themselves.

In this chapter, I will discuss a particular relationship between engagement and friendship and argue that the current situation in Yemen calls for an ethical commitment by scholars whereby "radical listening" (Rouse 2015) takes center stage. The conventional notion of engaged scholarship is based on the idea that scholars are relatively autonomous and self-determining moral individuals who decide how to give voice to their interlocutors and, in so doing, support their cause. However, although anthropologists may be attuned to how ethnographic realities are negotiated in the fieldwork encounter, in the name of critical distance we still see a reluctance among anthropologists to allow their research subjects to act upon them (or, at least, allow this "acting upon" to enter into their accounts) in a manner that is existentially compromising. Those individuals that practice this kind of engagement use their (ethnographic) knowledge to give insight into the Yemeni war, for example, but they rarely make reference to the moral demands that are made upon them by their interlocutors. This type of engagement, therefore, differs profoundly from what I see as an ethical engagement, in which the anthropologist must continuously ask him- or herself what they *ought* to do, usually without a clear answer in sight, and in the process become subject to their interlocutors. I argue that those who dare to enter this world of engagement will inevitably be confronted with ethical dilemmas, doubts, fears, conflicts, dangers, and irreconcilability. Yet it is in my view of utmost importance that engaged anthropologists open themselves up to this domain if they are to produce knowledge in a way that takes seriously the needs and demands of their research subjects. In what follows, I show how the conceptual language of friendship brings to the fore a very different ethnographic world of engagement, a world in which anthropologists become the subjects of their interlocutors (as "friends") in a much more asymmetrical manner than is typically acknowledged.

## Stepping into the Field, and Never Leaving It

My own relation with Yemen dates back to 1991, when I took up a job in a Dutch-Yemeni development project in Radaʿ. I had specialized in the Middle East and North Africa and in feminist anthropology with a special focus on development. I had done research among female carpet workers in Rabat, Morocco, and the chance to go to Yemen and work in development was a dream come true. After having worked for one and a half years in Radaʿ, I moved to al-Hudayda to become a project anthropologist in a bilateral project of the Yemeni and Dutch government, the al-Hudayda Urban Primary Health Care Project. I loved living and working in Yemen and made many friends. In 1998, I returned to the Netherlands to do a PhD where I could reflect on and write about my experiences in Yemen, focusing in particular on the female primary health-care workers (*murshidat sahhiyat*) in the project. From my master's research onward, I had aspired to do research that was socially relevant. Thus, doing a PhD after several years of applied development work was, in my eyes, justified. I was not doing academic work without any applied social significance, as my work was to be based on years of development work. In that sense, my own trajectory was very much in line with discussions that have taken place over the past couple of decades around engagement and engaged anthropology, in which applied anthropology is seen as one of the main ways of being an engaged scholar (see, for example, Van Willigen 2002; Pink 2005; Rylko-Bauer, Singer, and Van Willigen 2006; and Nolan 2017). Yet during the course of my PhD I became increasingly critical of development aid, which was mainly the result of my reading of critical anthropological studies of development and reflecting upon my experiences in development projects in Yemen. I was able to look from a certain distance at the projects I had worked on and saw how the training and employment of Yemeni female health-care workers formed part of the agendas of foreign donor organizations and the Yemeni government (de Regt 2007). This experience can be seen as the first unsettling moment of my "engagement" with Yemen.

My PhD and later postdoctoral research enabled me to visit my friends in Yemen regularly, and when I was in the Netherlands I continued to stay in touch with a number of former colleagues and friends. Mobile phones had made their way into the country in the late 1990s, and calling became much easier. Yet calling was still something that I had to initiate, and very few friends called me.[2] The only friend who regularly kept in touch with me was Noura. I had met Noura in September 1993, when I had just moved to al-Hudayda. I liked her a lot and visited her very regularly in the years that I lived in the city. I really considered her my best friend, sharing together both our joys and sorrows. We would see each other almost weekly; we talked about things that were happening in our own lives, problems at work, gossip about people we knew in common, about things that were happening in the lives of our family and friends. Noura's mother died when I was still living in al-Hudayda, and my own mother died a few years after my return to the Netherlands. Noura always asked about my brothers, niece, and nephews, and I shared stories about my (aging) father. I would always bring a small album with pictures to Yemen, and we would also take pictures together. In 2003 I took Noura with me to Ethiopia, where I was doing fieldwork, in the hope that she would be able to trace back some of her relatives, but that was to no avail. It was a memorable trip for both of us. However, our friendship soon entered deep water when I started to support her financially, and eventually it came to an end.

### Noura: The End of a Friendship

> Anthropological field research typically includes everyday practices
> of sharing, support, and personal interaction. Such relationships,
> which include friendship and even forms of kinship, can be thought
> of as a form of engagement. (Low and Merry 2010, 207)

While the study of friendship has received ample attention by anthropologists in the past two decades—as a social relationship that can be as significant as kinship relationships (see, for example, Bell and Coleman 1999;

2. Calling internationally was and still is expensive, which was one of the reasons, although another reason might have been the geographical and time difference between us.

and Desai and Killick 2010)—relatively few have written about their own friendships with people in the field. As I discussed in an earlier article, "Anthropologists emphasize the importance of close relationships in the field to ensure the collection of high quality data" (de Regt 2019, 106), but they rarely reflect on these relationships in their work. Key informants who have turned into friends are often thanked in the acknowledgments of books, but the nature of their friendships remains somewhat vague. In the mentioned article, I focused in particular on reciprocity and the role of money in friendships, especially with people who are economically less well-off. I described and analyzed my changing friendship with Noura, to whom I began sending money when she developed chronic health problems and needed regular medication.

As a result of the deteriorating political and economic situation in Yemen, Noura's demands for money increased; she retired in 2012, but she did not receive her pension for quite some time. In addition, her health problems worsened when she developed diabetes and kidney problems alongside her heart problems. She phoned me every three weeks asking for money to buy her medication. I increasingly started to dislike the way in which our friendship was developing, from what I had considered to be a "real friendship" to a relationship in which I saw myself more as a money provider. Noura's health issues and financial needs had become the basis of our phone conversations. She would frequently cry on the phone, desperately asking me for help, which I often found heartbreaking but sometimes also annoying. Sometimes I did not pick up the phone and only listened to her voice messages a few days later, as I was dreading facing her demands. I regularly mentioned that I did not want to continue as the amounts were increasing, to which she always replied that the situation in Yemen was extremely bad. Yemeni friends in the Netherlands would tell me that I had to stop supporting her on a regular basis, as they themselves sent money only to close relatives. "You are doing a great thing by sending money to her, Marina, but you don't have to do it systematically. She needs to find other resources. You are not responsible for her," they would say. Yet I did feel responsible and also guilty of living in a stable and wealthy country while she was living in a war zone and faced extreme difficulties making ends meet. And so I continued sending money.

I concluded the article in 2019 with a plea to continue supporting friends in the field who are struggling to keep their heads above water and called for more openness and discussion about the material and immaterial gains of "anthropological" friendships. However, in that same year my financial support to Noura came to an end, which also meant the end of our friendship. One of the main reasons was the fact that she refused the support I arranged via a local nongovernmental organization in al-Hudayda. Via a Yemeni friend in the Netherlands, I had reached out to an NGO that supported people in need of assistance and explained Noura's health condition to one of the female employees. She contacted Noura and offered to visit her, but Noura responded angrily and rejected her support. She answered that her health situation was none of their business and that my financial support to her was something between me and her. Last but not least, Noura had become very angry at me when I had told her for the umpteenth time that I was not willing to send money anymore. She apologized later, but I felt very bad about it as I began to question her intentions. Maybe those people who had told me time and again that she was just making use of me were right? That she was always so nice to me simply because she needed my money? Since then I have been in touch with Noura a few times, but always rejected her requests for money, which were the only reason for her calls. She asked me why I let her down, and I told her that I wanted to be friends but without having to transfer money. After that exchange, she no longer responded to my messages.

The end of my friendship with Noura was painful and can be seen as the second unsettling moment in my engagement with Yemen. I often wondered how she was doing, but I did not dare to call her anymore, afraid to hear about her health and living conditions. Reading about the situation in Yemen affects me emotionally, but hearing about the difficulties friends go through is even worse. Yet there are differences. I had two other friends whom I supported financially, both also "women without men" (Jansen 1987). They were divorced; one had two married daughters, and the other was childless and living with her sister's family. The greatest difference between them and Noura is that they only occasionally asked me for financial help and had other reasons to stay in contact besides requests for money. One of these friends is Fayza.

**Fayza: Mutual Interests?**

When I met Fayza in al-Hudayda in the early 1990s, she was a very lively and talkative young woman in her twenties. Her mother was of Yemeni Eritrean descent, and her father was Yemeni. She had three older sisters and two brothers and was the youngest of the family. Her mother was a domestic worker, cleaning houses of foreign development workers, a job that Fayza took over when her mother quit. She also cleaned my house once a week, and doing so was the initial basis for our friendship. When I left al-Hudayda, and Yemen, in 1998 and the other two women for whom she worked also left Yemen, Fayza lost her employment and spent her days at home. Her parents were divorced, her father had moved back to his parental village in the mountains, and her mother died shortly after I had left al-Hudayda. Fayza then decided to move in with one of her sisters in Sanaa.

I kept in touch with Fayza after I left Yemen and always visited her when I returned. She was very outspoken, and we always had a lot of things to talk about. She was not interested in getting married, which was quite unusual for a woman in her thirties, and wanted to work. One of her sisters lived in the United States and invested money in a public telephone shop in the city, which she managed. You could find her almost always sitting behind the counter. When mobile phones became common, she installed a few computers and an internet connection in the shop. However, the shop never became profitable and closed after a number of years. During my last visit to Yemen, in March 2013, Fayza was sitting idle at home.

When the war erupted in 2015, I tried to get in touch with Fayza, but her phone number was not working anymore. It took around one and a half years before we reconnected. She was extremely happy to hear from me and we talked for a long time. Since then, we often send each other voice messages through WhatsApp. Fayza likes to talk about the situation in Yemen, in contrast with many other friends who reply only briefly to my questions about the political and economic situation. She enjoys giving detailed descriptions of what she experiences and hears around her. In the past few years her voice messages became a rich source of information for me, and I started using them when approached by the media. Radio stations are often interested in airing direct observations from local people living in Yemen, and Fayza is always willing to send me a voice message, not minding that they are broadcast: "I want the world to know what is going on here" is her usual response.

In one of the voice messages, Fayza told me that she had found out that some of her married friends were having extramarital relationships in order to make ends meet. She was surprised about it herself and asked me if I would be interested in hearing their full stories. We agreed that she would ask these women whether they were willing to be interviewed. I would pay Fayza for her work as an interviewer, and the interviewees would also get a small financial reward. In this way it would be a so-called win-win situation, with all of us benefiting: Fayza and the women financially and me because I wanted to tell their stories. I left the choice of whom to interview to Fayza and emphasized that the women should be telling their stories voluntarily and consenting in the use of their stories for academic purposes. Fayza interviewed around ten women, some of them Yemeni, others Ethiopian or of mixed Yemeni Ethiopian background. She enjoyed interviewing and proved to be very good at it, encouraging women to talk openly about their lives.

Fayza's voice messages were often very pessimistic about her life and the situation in Yemen. The work she was doing for me was not full-time, and I also did not want to give her money regularly after my negative experiences with Noura. She was desperately looking for ways to leave Yemen and asked me a few times if I could help her to migrate to Europe. She would do anything to change her life. I told her how difficult it was to come to Europe because of all the visa regulations, which she understood. Our voice exchanges were, however, not always about the situation in Yemen. She was also very interested in my life and always inquired about my father, who was aging and suffering from various mental and physical health issues.

The interviews that Fayza collected I saved on my password-protected computer but did not listen to them. Instead, I had the recordings transcribed by a number of Yemeni women living in the Netherlands. I often wonder why I did not listen to them myself. Lack of time was one of the most obvious reasons, but it was not the only one. I had difficulties being engaged with Yemen because of the war and dreaded listening to the stories. While, rationally, I felt a strong responsibility toward engaging with Yemen, emotionally I have found myself detaching from what is going on in the country. The stories of my friends depress me, and I often do not know what to say because the situation is so horrendous. Yet I am also aware that they are in need of friends who listen to them, with whom they can share their joys and sorrows, who can help when needed, and to feel that they are not forgotten. This knowledge brings me to my friendship with ʿAʾisha.

**ʿAʾisha: The Pain of Not Being Able to Help**

ʿAʾisha lived in Radaʿ and was a former colleague from the Radaʿ Integrated Development Project, a large rural development project funded by the Dutch government, where I worked between 1991 and 1993. She was trained as a health extension agent, and we had worked together closely. ʿAʾisha came from a lower social-status group, and her family background was looked down upon in Radaʿ, a tribal area southeast of Sanaa. We stayed in touch when I moved to al-Hudayda and made sure to see each other regularly in Radaʿ, Sanaa, or al-Hudayda. ʿAʾisha married Muhammad against the wish of his *qabili* (tribal) family, which became a source of conflict and led to divorce a few years later.[3] Whereas in patrilineal Yemen children usually stay with their father after a divorce, ʿAʾisha succeeded in keeping the custody of her two daughters and brought them up single-handedly, despite continuous pressure from Muhammad and his family. She married again, this time as the second wife of a man whose first wife and children lived in Sanaa, but this marriage also failed. I always tried to visit ʿAʾisha when I was in Yemen, but it became increasingly difficult to go to Radaʿ. Foreigners were required to obtain travel permits, and certain areas such as Radaʿ District were considered risky and dangerous. The last time I went to Radaʿ was in December 2009 when I dressed up as a Yemeni woman, wearing a black balto and a face veil, but despite doing so was stopped at a checkpoint and taken to ʿAʾisha's house by security guards.

In recent years ʿAʾisha developed health issues and occasionally contacted me asking for financial assistance. I sometimes sent her money but

3. *Qabili* families do not accept marriages with women who are of lower social-status groups.

not on a regular basis because I was afraid that she would become financially dependent on me, like Noura. ʿAʾisha was always very grateful: "I don't know what to say, you are always there for me when I need help and I don't want to be a burden for you, I am so sorry," followed by a crying emoticon. ʿAʾisha regularly sent me emoticons, smileys with kisses, and gifs to wish me a blessed Friday, and she told me how much she loved me. She was feeling lonely; her two daughters had married, and she was living alone and struggling with her health. I knew that her short messages were meant to trigger a response from me, but I found it very hard to call her and often just replied with equally brief messages.

In April 2021 ʿAʾisha wrote to me saying that COVID-19 was spreading rapidly in Radaʿ and that many people were dying. She was afraid of catching the virus, and I told her to stay inside as much as possible. A week later she sent me a picture of herself, something she had never done before. She looked beautiful, older than the last time I had seen her, but in good shape despite all her health issues. She asked me to send her a picture of myself as well and told me that she loved me a lot. She didn't reply to the picture I sent her, which surprised me as she normally replied quickly. A few days later she wrote to me saying she had been hospitalized with COVID and sent me pictures of herself in a hospital bed. "I am very ill, please help me, Marina, I am going to die, Corona is very expensive, please help me," followed by, "Marina, if I die, will you then forgive me for all the trouble that I caused you?"

ʿAʾisha's messages were heartbreaking, and I quickly got in touch with a number of Dutch friends who also knew her. We transferred 500 euros to ʿAʾisha's daughter in a desperate attempt to help her. When I asked the next day how ʿAʾisha was doing, her daughter informed me that her mother was out of the hospital and taking oxygen at home. These messages were also accompanied by pictures of ʿAʾisha wearing an oxygen mask along with voice messages in which she cried out for help. She was still very ill, and the oxygen was very expensive. "One tank is 50,000 Yemeni riyal,"[4] ʿAʾisha's daughter wrote to me. I did not dare to ask her how long she could

---

4. Fifty thousand Yemeni riyal was about 160 euros in May 2021.

use a tank for, afraid that I would have to transfer money again. Yet it was also a way to cope with my feeling of powerlessness in the face of structural inequalities, the immense gap between my own life and the lives of 'A'isha and her loved ones. I preferred to stay at a distance. I did not want to be too closely involved in the fight for 'A'isha's life and tried to avoid any feelings of moral responsibility. Two days later I received a message that 'A'isha had died. The oxygen had not been enough, and she had lost the fight against COVID.

'A'isha's death hit me hard. She was one of the few friends I was regularly in touch with, and I had known her for almost thirty years. I loved her dearly. I often felt guilty for not having called her when I knew that she was in need of contact and help. Just like my other friends, she did not want anything other than for someone to listen to her, to know that she was not forgotten. In the last few weeks before her death she often sent short messages telling me that she loved me a lot, and I wondered if she had felt the same way as the end of her life approached. Her initiative to exchange pictures was also a way of getting closer, and her request for me to forgive her was probably inspired by her knowledge that death was near. Being a practicing Muslim, she believed she would face the Day of Judgment when she died and wanted to come clear with what she considered her sins. But while 'A'isha asked me for forgiveness for all the times she shared her problems with me, which were sometimes accompanied by requests for money, I in turn ask for forgiveness for all the times that I did not reply to her messages. I fell (and still fall) short in my responses to my Yemeni friends. I am not able to deal with the realities they live in, and I struggle to accept the fact that the Yemen I knew is no more. The death of 'A'isha confronts me with the limits of what I can do, both for my Yemeni friends and for Yemen at large, and is therefore extremely painful.

## Toward an Ethical Engagement in Friendship and Fieldwork

Anthropological debates about engagement mainly focus on the role of the anthropologist in the lives of the people they study and the positive implications this engagement may have. Engaged anthropologists such as Low and Merry (2010, 204) are personally "committed to an anthropological practice that respects the dignity and rights of all humans and has a beneficent effect on the promotion of social justice." The various ways they describe putting anthropological knowledge to use for society, and in so doing bringing about what they regard as positive social change, are all very applaudable, and very few anthropologists will deny their importance. But what about situations in which anthropologists prefer not to be engaged and even try to detach themselves from situations that are too difficult to handle emotionally? And what about when friends, colleagues, and interlocutors in the field become the ones that are acting and the anthropologist is the person who is acted upon (Peutz 2014)? Qasem's email, Noura's phone calls, Fayza's wish to conduct interviews, and 'A'isha's WhatsApp messages are all examples of Yemeni friends engaging with me instead of me engaging with them. I am not the one taking the initiative; I am merely responding to them.

The common notion of engaged scholarship is premised on the idea that researchers enjoy an excessive degree of moral autonomy in deciding who is to be given voice in their fieldwork and, in so doing, supported in their cause. In this type of engagement, anthropologists promote a form of critical distance that mitigates the risk of their "research subjects" making claims or demands upon them that might become existentially compromising. Those scholars who practice this kind of engagement use their (ethnographic) knowledge to give insight into the Yemeni war, for example, but rarely make reference to their own subject positions and the moral dilemmas they face in relation to their Yemeni interlocutors. This type of engagement differs profoundly from what I will define as an ethical engagement, in which anthropologists must continually ask themselves what they ought to do having been rendered a subject to be acted upon by their interlocutors, or "friends." Although in recent decades we have seen a pronounced turn to the study of ethics in anthropology, the discussions focus primarily on the ethical struggles among the anthropologists' interlocutors, rarely giving serious attention to the moral demands made upon anthropologists themselves in the fieldwork process and the myriad of ethical quandaries such demands produce. My notion of ethical engagement is very different from that of scholars such as Nancy Scheper-Hughes (1995) whose parallel notion rests on a rather unproblematized notion of right and wrong. In her call for a militant anthropology, in which anthropologists are asked to show solidarity with those individuals they study, use their pens to report human rights abuses, and take part in (political) struggles against oppression and other forms of social inequality, she assumes that anthropologists know what the right thing is in order to help their interlocutors. Her plea for political engagement and activism has been a source of inspiration for many and contributed to ongoing debates about the role of anthropology in today's world (see, for example, Sluka 2000, 12). However, I argue that ethical engagement implies continuous reflection on what is right and wrong and that it is not always clear-cut what we ought to do.

This lack of clarity becomes particularly evident in the examples I gave of the moral dilemmas I was confronted by in my friendships with three Yemeni women, leading me to a number of fundamental questions about moral engagement. What if we turned the situation upside down and considered the anthropologist as a moral actor who is compelled to make significant ethical decisions in deeply disturbing circumstances? What possibilities come into view when scholars are not able to engage themselves in the lifeworlds of their research participants from a relatively safe distance, or with a clear vision of "the good" or "the right," but instead are drawn into their world and faced with "moral danger," such as the danger of having to decide about life and death, in the most literal sense of the words? Moreover, what kind of ethnographic worlds begin to appear when we shift our language of engagement from that of the self-reflexive participant observer to that of "friend"? The language of friendship, and all it entails, sheds a very different light on the world of ethical turmoil within which the anthropologist is directly involved.[5]

Anthropologists emphasize the importance of close and long-term relationships in the field as the condition for collecting high-quality data with ethnographic depth. However, they often pay relatively little attention to their friendships with informants and other people in the field. They may refer to key informants as friends, yet in their ethnographic writing they rarely appear *as* friends—and all that friendship implies in terms of relationality—or not explicitly so (see de Regt 2019, 106). Building up

5. I would like to thank Ross Porter for bringing these reflections to my attention.

relationships of trust and confidence is, however, one of the key aspects of anthropological fieldwork. Friends can be crucial sources of information in times of war and conflict, as they can provide us with inside perspectives on the lived realities on the ground to which researchers have little access. This realization has also been endorsed by other researchers of Yemen (see Brandt 2017; Augustin 2018). But maintaining these friendships can be challenging for a variety of reasons, which go far beyond problems of long-distance communication via internet and telephone. One of the most important reasons, in my view, is the difficulty of "balancing reciprocity" across both spatial and economic distances in times of war and conflict (see Mains 2012; de Regt 2019). In the case of my friendship with Noura, it felt as if our relationship was based solely on my money transfers, and I missed sharing thoughts, experiences, and emotions with her, which for me I considered key to a good friendship. I talked repeatedly about this feeling with her, and she always made clear that it was not the money that counted for her, but the fact that it meant that there was someone in this world who cared about her. I realized that while Noura had been able to "return my gifts" during my visits to Yemen, it had now become impossible because of the war. She could no longer host me, cook for me, make me feel comfortable, and listen to my stories. Our friendship, and the reciprocity friendship demands, had been disrupted by the war.[6]

Maybe the reason so few anthropologists have written about their friendships with people they meet during their fieldwork is because friendships go beyond the kind of relations expected of research and, indeed, may complicate research findings. Some scholars are explicit about the need to distance oneself in order to be able to analyze data. Sluka and Robben (2012) speak of the necessity of "detachment" after fieldwork: following intense participation in the lives of their research participants, anthropologists need to go home and distance themselves so that they can reflect on their experiences and analyze their data with a degree of clarity.

6. Another form of reciprocity is the support of anthropologists for the political cause of their interlocutors, such as in the case of Palestine. Anthropologists have, for example, been targeted because of their open support of a free Palestine (which is a very current issue at the moment of finalizing this chapter).

Detachment is thus the counterconstitutive dimension of participant observation. Contrastingly, friendship relations beyond the field complicate such detachment, as Daniel Mains (2020) describes in his discussion of friendship, fieldwork, and the (de)construction of knowledge. While Mains values the friendships that he built up during his research in Ethiopia, for instance, he also came to the conclusion that these friendships complicated his research findings: "Friendship generates knowledge, but with time the accumulation of depth, complexity, and detail destroy the possibility of fitting lives into neat categories of analysis" (2020). But is it not the messiness wrought by moral demands placed upon the fieldworker—and consequent ambiguities surrounding friend versus informant/interlocutor knowledge—that we should also be seeking to understand? Are the ways in which we relate to our interlocutors and, perhaps more crucially, the ways in which they relate to us not of utmost importance in this endeavor?

In the past few decades, it has become more commonplace to reflect upon the role of emotions and affect during and after fieldwork, and numerous works have been dedicated to this topic (for example, Kleinman and Copp 1993; Davies and Spencer 2010; Beatty 2010; Trigger, Forsey, and Meurk 2012). Renato Rosaldo's classic article "Grief and a Headhunter's Rage" (1989) was an eye-opener for many because of the way in which he showed how his own grief about the death of his wife made him understand Ilongot society better. For the Ilongot, headhunting is a practice born of anger for the loss of a loved one. "He (an Ilongot) says that rage, born of grief, impels him to kill his fellow human beings. He claims that he needs a place . . . 'to carry his anger.' The act of . . . tossing away the victim's head enables him . . . (to) throw away the anger of his bereavement" (Rosaldo 1989, 58). While Rosaldo first had difficulties understanding this anger, the sudden loss of his wife, who fell off a cliff during fieldwork, triggered similar feelings of rage in him. He was angry at her because she abandoned him, that she fell and died, and this emotion allowed him to better understand the rage of the Ilongot when someone they cared for had died.

Ann-Christin Zuntz (2018) experienced similar feelings of anger when one of her best friends in Jordan died during labor. She was angry at the health system but realized that there was no one to blame; her friend's death could not have been prevented. When she went on to write up her dissertation, she decided not to include the story. "At the time, I felt reluctant about including into a doctoral thesis something as private and painful as a friend's passing. I also worried about reducing her in my writing to a 'dead refugee,' to cut down the complexity of her life and ties with others to legal and humanitarian labels." But when she eventually decided to write about it, in a short online article, she discovered how important her social relations in the field were in coping with the loss of her friend. Just like Rosaldo, she realized that only when "the ethnographic mission collapses" (Rosaldo 2014)—as it does in times of intense grief—these "scaffolders" ("those who create the silent infrastructure of fieldwork, but seldom get a mention in articles, monographs and conference presentations") become visible again" (Zuntz 2018, n.p.).

**Conclusion**

For me, writing about my friends and reflecting on the ways in which our friendship has changed because of the war are a way to come to terms with the situation in Yemen. Yet it is also more than that. I have felt compelled to write about the expectations that my friends have of me because I believe that these expectations bring into question what it means to be an anthropologist in times of extreme suffering and force us to reflect on what kind of knowledge we can or should produce about Yemen. My own analysis of fieldwork and friendship in the field has been strongly influenced by the war, having forced me to rethink my own engagement with the country, which in turn has been inspired by the ways in which Yemenis engage with me.

Over the past decade, and in particular since the eruption of the present war, many academics working on Yemen have used their (ethnographic) knowledge to give insight into the situation by way of short articles, presentations, and interviews for a general public. Those individuals who consider themselves engaged scholars also work together with governmental and nongovernmental organizations, research institutes, and think tanks and formulate recommendations about how to end the war. Yet they rarely make reference to the moral demands explicitly placed upon them by their Yemeni interlocutors. It is, in my view, of utmost importance that scholars overcome their reluctance to address such demands as if they were distinct from the field of scholarly inquiry. This is particularly so in such times of suffering when moral turmoil, also extending to the scholar, is the "reality" of the ethnographic encounter (see Nordstrom and Robben 1996). In addition, these are not just ethical questions for individual anthropologists, but also a wider problem of war, violence, and foreign intervention. The contemporary political economy of oil and weapons has led to extremely difficult situations such as the ones that I have described in this chapter.

I have suggested that introducing the intimate language of friendship into one's analysis means taking a risk, a risk that anthropologists are usually keen to avoid because of the myriad moral dilemmas they are forced to confront as a result. When we do dare to include friendships in our work, we become subjects in an ethical world over which we have far less moral agency than if we continue to insist on rigid distinctions between self and other, observer and observed. It means that we are no longer simply writing up the lifeworlds of other people (of our "interlocutors"/ research participants/informants/and so on) but that we have to write ourselves into these worlds and not as those persons who stay at a distance but as subjects ourselves. To do so may be deeply disturbing, for it reveals our vulnerability, but I believe that this vulnerability is crucial in the forging of an ethical anthropology (see Behar 1996; Page 2017). I have described four unsettling moments in my own engagement with Yemen—moments in which I felt very vulnerable as I was confronted with moral dilemmas: first, my disappointment with development work, which I initially saw as the ideal application for an engaged anthropology; second, the end of my financial support and subsequent friendship with Noura, having previously viewed financial support for friends in times of crisis as an important form of engagement; third, my reluctance to listen to the interviews Fayza recorded for me, despite having seen these as an important means to remain engaged with Yemen; and fourth, my limited response to 'A'isha's WhatsApp messages and her ultimate death, which filled me with grief and regret for not having been able to rescue her.

Through these four unsettling moments I have sought to show that there is no clear-cut methodological solution to such moments of moral danger—when we do not necessarily know what the right thing is that we should do, yet we want to be "engaged" nevertheless. By introducing the language of friendship, we automatically enter a field of intense risk in which we ourselves are made "subjects" in a way that quickly dispels myths of the heroic, moral, fieldworker. We must, therefore, learn to write about ourselves and our engagements with the situation in Yemen in terms of the personal demands that are placed upon us by our friends and interlocutors. What does an anthropology look like that includes all such dilemmas, pain, torment, and the irreconcilability of the world? An ethical anthropology is, in my view, an anthropology that is humanizing to the extent that it does not shy away from the danger of becoming subject to one's subjects, relinquishing prior fidelity to long-entrenched conventions about critical distance and moral agency.[7]

The conceptual language I propose for this volume is one that both grows out of and takes seriously worlds of friendship. Whether it be conventional or postmodern forms of ethnographic writing, enduring fidelities to the notion of critical distance presumes a relatively autonomous and self-determining fieldworker who is able to make clear-cut moral choices about how best to award agency or voice to their subjects. This presumption often means that the anthropologist refuses to let their interlocutors or research subjects act upon them in a way that could be existentially compromising or that would appear to muddy their ethnographic elaborations. From the vantage point of this world of ethnographic knowledge production in the Yemeni case, the anthropologist may make public statements condemning the war, but it is a commitment that takes a degree of comfort in grand statements and denouncements, in contrast to the relative discomfort and indeed danger that comes from engaged listening and thus receptiveness to the demands that our subjects place on us as individuals. This is a world that is at once ethically engaged but also potentially alienating. What is required to disrupt this world, I propose, is a new kind of ethnographic sensitivity that centers around "radical listening" to the demands and expectations of our subjects. When we as anthropologists open ourselves up to this world, we must be prepared for confrontations

7. Again, I would like to thank Ross Porter for sharing his reflections on this issue and allowing me to include them in this chapter.

with moral danger, doubt, conflict, irreconcilability, and ultimately to become subjects ourselves.

## Acknowledgments

I am highly indebted to Ross Porter for the excellent comments he made on an earlier version of this paper. I would also like to thank Alexandra Greene and the members of the Identity, Diversity, and Inclusion discussion group for their useful feedback on the paper.

## References

Augustin, Anne-Linda Amira. 2018. "Rumours, Fears and Solidarity in Fieldwork in Times of Political Turmoil on the Verge of War in Southern Yemen." *Contemporary Social Science* 13, nos. 3–4: 444–56.

Beatty, Andrew. 2010. "How Did It Feel for You? Emotion, Narrative, and the Limits of Ethnography." *American Anthropologist* 112, no. 3: 430–43.

Behar, Ruth. 1996. *The Vulnerable Observer: Anthropology that Breaks Your Heart*. Boston: Beacon Press.

Bell, Sandra, and Simon Coleman, eds. 1999. *The Anthropology of Friendship*. Oxford: Berg.

Brandt, Marieke. 2017. "Delocalization of Fieldwork and (Re)construction of Place: Doing Ethnography in Wartime Yemen." *Journal of Middle East Studies* 49, no. 3: 506–10.

Davies, James, and Dimitrina Spencer, eds. 2010. *Emotions in the Field: The Psychology and Anthropology of Fieldwork Experience*. Stanford, CA: Stanford Univ. Press.

de Regt, Marina. 2007. *Pioneers or Pawns? Women Health Workers and the Politics of Development in Yemen*. Syracuse, NY: Syracuse Univ. Press.

———. 2015. "Noura and Me: Friendship as Method in Times of Crisis." *Urban Anthropology and Studies of Cultural Systems and World Economic Development* 44, no. 1: 43–70.

———. 2019. "In Friendship One Does Not Count Such Things: Friendship and Money in War-Torn Yemen." *Etnofoor* 31, no. 1: 99–112.

Desai, Amit, and Evan Killick, eds. 2010. *The Ways of Friendship: Anthropological Perspectives*. New York: Berghahn Books.

Gay y Blasco, Paloma, and Liria Hernández. 2020. *Writing Friendship: A Reciprocal Ethnography*. New York: Palgrave Macmillan.

Hochschild, Arlie Russell. 2003 [1983]. *The Managed Heart: Commercialization of Human Feeling.* Berkeley: Univ. of California Press.

Jansen, Willy. 1987. *Women without Men: Gender and Marginality in an Algerian Town.* Leiden: Brill.

Kleinman, Sherryl, and Martha A. Copp. 1993. *Emotions and Fieldwork.* Newbury Park, CA: Sage.

Low, Setha M., and Sally Engle Merry. 2010. "Engaged Anthropology: Diversity and Dilemmas." *Current Anthropology* 51, no. 2: 203–14.

Mains, Daniel. 2012. "Friends and Money: Balancing Affection and Reciprocity among Young Men in Urban Ethiopia." *American Ethnologist* 40, no. 2: 335–46.

———. 2020. "Friendship, Fieldwork and the (De)construction of Knowledge." In *Field Stories: Experience, Affect, and the Lessons of Anthropology in the Twenty-First Century*, edited by William H. Leggett and Ida Fadzillah Leggett, 76–94. Lanham, MD: Lexington Books.

Nolan, Riall W. 2017. *Using Anthropology in the World: A Guide to Becoming an Anthropologist Practitioner.* New York: Routledge.

Nordstrom, Carolyn, and Antonius C. G. M. Robben, eds. 1996. *Fieldwork under Fire: Contemporary Studies of Violence and Culture.* Berkeley: Univ. of California Press.

Paerregaard, Karsten. 2003. "The Resonance of Fieldwork: Ethnographers, Informants and the Creation of Anthropological Knowledge." *Social Anthropology* 10, no. 3: 319–34.

Page, Tiffany. 2017. "Vulnerable Writing as a Feminist Methodological Practice." *Feminist Review* 115: 13–29.

Peutz, Nathalie. 2014. "Engaging the Anthropologist." Paper presented at the workshop "Engaged Anthropology," Princeton Univ., Apr. 4, 2014.

———. 2019. "Comment: The Importance of Listening." *American Ethnologist* 46, no. 3: 276–77.

Pink, Sarah. 2006. *Applications of Anthropology: Professional Anthropology in the Twenty-First Century.* New York and London: Berghahn.

Rosaldo, Renato. 1989. *Culture and Truth: The Remaking of Social Analysis.* Boston: Beacon Press.

———. 2014. *The Day of Shelly's Death: The Poetry and Ethnography of Grief.* Durham, NC: Duke Univ. Press.

Rouse, Carolyn. 2015. *Listening Is a Radical Act: World Anthropologies and the Decentering of Western Thought.* Cape Town: Makhulu Moving Images. https://www.imdb.com/title/tt4644220/.

Rylko-Bauer, Barbara, Meryll Singer, and John Van Willigen. 2006. "Reclaiming Applied Anthropology: Its Past, Present, and Future." *American Anthropologist* 18, no. 1: 178–90.

Scheper-Hughes, Nancy. 1995. "The Primacy of the Ethical: Propositions for a Militant Anthropology." *Current Anthropology* 36, no. 3: 409–40.

Sluka, Jeffrey A. 2000. *Death Squad: The Anthropology of State Terror.* Philadelphia: Univ. of Pennsylvania Press.

Sluka, Jeffrey, and Anthonius Robben. 2012. *Ethnographic Fieldwork: An Anthropological Reader.* Hoboken, NJ: Wiley-Blackwell.

Trigger, David, Martin Forsey, and Carla Meurk. 2012. "Revelatory Moments in Fieldwork." *Qualitative Research* 12, no. 5: 513–27.

Van Willigen, John. 2002. *Applied Anthropology: An Introduction.* Westport, CT: Bergin & Garvey.

Zuntz, Ann-Christin. 2018. "In Praise of the Scaffolding." *Allegra Lab*, July 2018. https://allegralaboratory.net/in-praise-of-the-scaffolding/.

CONTRIBUTORS

INDEX

# Contributors

Steven C. Caton is professor emeritus at Harvard University where he mentored graduate students doing research in the Middle East as well as on Muslims in the United States, Canada, and France from 1998 until the present. He has done long-term field research in Yemen since 1979 and in the Gulf since 2014. In connection to his Yemen research his main works are *"Peaks of Yemen I Summon"* (1990), *Yemen Chronicle* (2005), and *Yemen* (editor, 2013). He is currently working on a book involving the history and contemporary uses of water in Yemen.

Susanne Dahlgren is the director of the Finnish Institute in the Middle East located in Beirut, Lebanon. Before going to Beirut, she taught anthropology at Tampere University and acted as a visiting research associate professor in the National University of Singapore. She is the author of *Contesting Realities: Public Sphere and Morality in Southern Yemen* (2010) and coeditor (with Monika Lindbekk) of *Gender and Judging in Muslim Courts: Emerging Scholarship and Debates* (2020). Her writing focuses on law, society, social movements, and family from the late colonial era to present-day contestations. Currently, she is preparing a book manuscript on the historical state, seen from the perspective of administration and everyday state practice in three mutually different locations in Yemen, and another on the history of family court practice in Aden.

Marina de Regt is associate professor at the Department of Social and Cultural Anthropology of Vrije Universiteit Amsterdam, the Netherlands. She specializes in gender, labor, and migration in Yemen and Ethiopia. She is the author of *Pioneers or Pawns? Women Health Workers and the Politics of Development in Yemen* (2007), coeditor with Bina Fernandez of *Migrant Domestic Workers in the Middle East: The Home and the World* (2014), and coauthor of *Adolescent Girls Migration in the Global South: Transitions into Adulthood* (with Katarzyna Grabska and Nicoletta Del Franco) (2019).

Kamilia al-Eriani teaches criminology at the School of Social and Political Sciences, University of Melbourne. Her work and research interests include state cultural politics, forms of modern violence, and modes of ethical politics in Yemen. Her work explores the effects of multiple powers, modern-secular and traditional, circulating within discursive political and cultural fields; the subjectivities they produce; and human relations established or dissolved within structures and fields of powers.

Angie Heo is associate professor of anthropology of religion at the University of Chicago Divinity School. She is the author of *The Political Lives of Saints: Christian-Muslim Mediation in Egypt* (2018) and coeditor with Jeanne Kormina of the special issue "Religion and Borders in (Post-) Cold War Peripheries" in the *Journal of Religion* (2019). While writing this article in the spring of 2021, she was a Connaught Global Challenge Fellow at the University of Toronto.

Professor emerita of anthropology at the London School of Economics, Martha Mundy writes on law and the state, kinship and family, and agrarian systems. Before joining the LSE in 1996, she taught at Yarmouk University Jordan, UCLA, the American University of Beirut, and Lyon 2 Lumière University. Monographs include *Domestic Government: Kinship, Community and Polity in North Yemen* (1995) and (with Saumarez Smith) *Governing Property, Making the Modern State: Law, Administration and Production in Ottoman Syria* (2007). Since 2012 she has worked on the agrarian history of South Lebanon and contemporary problems of agriculture in Yemen.

Luca Nevola is Middle East regional specialist at the Armed Conflict Location & Event Data Project (ACLED). He holds a PhD in cultural anthropology from the University of Milano–Bicocca and conducted fieldwork research in highland Yemen between 2009 and 2013. He wrote extensively on Yemen's minority groups and tribes, focusing on racial discrimination, genealogical essentialism, and religious repression. His current research explores the relationship between political elites and violence. Among numerous articles and chapters on Yemen, he is the author of *Houthis in the Making: Nostalgia, Populism, and the Politicization of Hashemite Descent* (2020).

Nathalie Peutz is associate professor of anthropology in the Program of Arab Crossroads Studies at New York University Abu Dhabi. She is the author of

*Islands of Heritage: Environment and Conservation in Yemen* (2018) and coeditor with Nicholas De Genova of *The Deportation Regime: Sovereignty, Space and the Freedom of Movement* (2010). While writing this article in the spring of 2021, she was a fellow at the American Academy in Berlin.

Ross Porter is a lecturer in anthropology at the Institute of Arab and Islamic Studies at the University of Exeter. His research focuses on issues surrounding time, ethics, and freedom, with an ethnographic focus on revolutionary politics and personhood in contemporary Yemen. He is currently working on a book manuscript based on his fieldwork in a revolutionary camp in Sanaa.

# Index

al-'Abbadi, Ahmad 'Uwaidi, 90–91
'Abd al-Wahhab, 'Abd al-Raqib, 55
abjection, 12, 171, 202
Abou-Zeid, Ahmed, 110
Abrams, Phillip, 11
Abu Ghraib prison, 26, 27
Abu-Lughod, Lila, 110, 111
actor-network theory (ANT), 144
Aden, Port of, 20, 23, 158–60; British Eastern Aden Protectorate and, 163; state administration and, 143, 148–50, 153–57; unification and, 150–52
Aden University, 80; Yemeni Centre for Cultural Research and, 81
Adorno, Theodor, 17n2
Advocates for Public Interest Law (APIL), 198
Afghanistan, 25, 204
*African Political Systems* (Fortes and Evans-Pritchard), 111
Africans, 169, 192
Agamben, Giorgio, 25–27
agency, 45; critical distance and, 230; critique of the state and, 10; everyday states and, 162; friendship and, 229; languages of stateness and, 11; religion and, 62n20; the state and, 141–42, 144–45, 147, 163
Agrama, Hussein Ali, 54

agriculture, 76–80, 82–85, 95–96, 98; 1979 agricultural census and, 81; sociology of, 85–87. *See also* land
Ahmad (pseudonym), 116–18
Ahmad, Imam, 124
al-Ahmar, 'Abdullah, 151
'Ain Shams University, 89, 91
'A'isha (pseudonym), 221–23, 229
*akhuwwa* (brotherhood), 132–34
alcohol, 142, 155–57, 159–60, 162–63
Alexandria, University of, 89
al-'Alimi, Rashad, 77n3, 90–91
al-Qai'da, 55, 146
alterity, 69; modes of critique, 1; *sacra* and, 128; transformative concepts and, 13
alter-politics, 5, 9
Amber, Salwa, 152, 161
American Institute of Yemeni Studies, 81
*amn wa istiqrar* (security and stability), 44, 70–71
al-'Amri, Hassan, 55
analysis of data, 226–27
ancestry, 112
Ansar Allah (Houthis), 2, 7, 24, 35, 70, 212–13; refugees and, 168, 188, 190–91; security and, 55–59; *sharaf* and, 108, 132–33; *Tribal Charter of Sharaf* and, 10

241

anthropological theory, 4
anti-modes of critique, 1; alter-modes of critique and, 13
anti-state, 10–11
Appadurai, Arjun, 4
apparatus (of the state), 140, 142–46, 150–51, 160–61
apparatuses of everyday life, 124, 133
Arabian Gulf, 23
Arabian Peninsula, 18, 21, 23, 36; Arab Spring and, 34; borders and, 31–33, 37; financial power of, 78; maritime barriers to, 30
Arabs, 184, 202
Arab Spring, 23, 34–35, 37
ARAMCO oil company, 23
al-'Arashi, Qadi 'Abd al-Karim, 88
Arendt, Hannah, 28
aristocracy, 112
Asad, Talal, 51
Asan Institute for Policy Studies, 198
Asia, refugee circuits and, 169
*asl* (origin), 107, 127, 130
asylum, 168–71, 176–80, 182–83, 186–90, 192–94, 201–2; Djibouti and, 173; Facebook and, 199; Jeju Island and, 197; Korean missionaries and, 191; South Korea and, 180–81
Atchrati, Ahmad, 69
authoritarianism, 6
autocracy, 20, 34
al-'Awdi, Hamud, 90, 91, 93
*'ayb* (shame), 68; women and, 124; young women and, 114. *See also* shame

Bahrain, 34, 180
Bahrain Royal Charity Organization, 175
Bani Matar tribal area, 107, 113, 118

barriers, 30–32
Bédoucha, Geneviève, 83
*Behind the Veil in Arabia* (Wikan), 129
being-with-others, 131
beneficence (*ihsan*), 9, 47, 62–65, 68–71
Benjamin, Walter, 26
Berger, Peter, 109
Bergson, Henri, 36
al-Bidh, 'Ali Salim, 152
biopower, 25–27, 31
Blumi, Isa, 20
boat people, 188
bodily *hexis*, 129–30
borders, 29–33; imperialism and, 36–37; third-space and, 32
Boron, Atilio A., 20n5
boundaries, 30–32, 37
Bourdieu, Pierre, 122–24
Boyer, Pascal, 119
Britain, 23; Protectorate era and, 148–49, 160
British Eastern Aden Protectorate, 163
Bujra, Abdullah, 81
Buzan, Wæver, and de Wilde, 42

capitalism, 19; agrarian change and, 82–83; resistance to, 33
Carapico, Sheila, 83
categorization, 12
Caton, Steven, 8, 129
censuses, 81; 1979 agricultural census, 81; 1983 agricultural census, 86, 96
center, politics of, 7
Central Planning Organisation, 81
certainty, 6, 8, 44–45, 56; Ansar Allah and, 58–59; illusory sense of, 66; self-elation and, 60; tyranny of, 70; violent interventions and, 70
challenge, 122–23

change, 46; as becoming, 37; as being
    change, 35–37
Change Square, 22
charity, 6, 8, 41, 44, 47n6, 64. *See also*
    Yaman Jadid
Chaudhry, Kiren, 84, 148n13, 151; public
    spending and, 161
Christian Right, 187
civilian population, 24
civil service, 141–43, 147–50, 153–57,
    159–62
civil war, revolutionary morality and,
    131
class, 78, 82, 95–96; formation of, 85;
    grammar of, 9; honor and, 109; land
    and, 85, 87; Nasserite Egypt and, 85
Cold War, 52; displacement and, 203;
    postcolonialism and, 53
colonialism, 23; necropolitics and, 27;
    Republican Revolution and, 49; state
    administration and, 148–49
commoditization, 162
*Commoners, Climbers, and Notables: A*
    *Sampler of Studies on Social Ranking*
    *in the Middle East* (Serjeant), 112
communism, 54, 55
community, 63, 68–71; equilibrium and,
    61; insecurity and, 44, 48; security
    and, 45, 47, 51, 59
Comprehensive Refugee Response
    Framework, 173, 196
concepts, 8; alter-modes of critique and,
    13; facts and, 98; friendship and, 230;
    gatekeeping and, 4; honor (*sharaf*)
    and, 106–10; honor's mismatched
    forms of, 10; Islam as key, 94; knowl-
    edge production and, 80; of *namus*,
    111–12; *qabila* and, 86; refugees
    and, 12; social life of, 3–5; stateness
    and, 11

Confederation of Yemeni Development
    Associations, 84
conflict, 4
Connolly, William, 62
Constellation, 17
contestation, 1, 4, 6
contingency, 45, 52–53, 55–56, 60, 65
Convention Governing the Specific As-
    pects of Refugee Problems in Africa
    (OAU), 172
Convention Relating to the Status of
    Refugees (1951 Convention and 1967
    Protocol), 172, 175, 177; Arabian
    Peninsula and, 192
corruption (*fasad*), 24, 142, 147, 157–58,
    161–64
cosmologies, 121, 131
Council of Tribal and Popular Cohesion,
    132
critical distance, 214, 224, 230
critical engagement, 4–6, 11–12;
    as critical politics, 1–2. *See also*
    engagement
critique, 10; anti- and alter- forms of, 13
"Critique of Violence" (Benjamin), 26
cultural heritage, 27; war and, 24, 37

da Col, Giovanni, 109
Dahlgren, Susanne, 11
daughters, 113–14, 118, 124–26
de Haas, Thera, 212
democracy, 153; being change and, 35;
    imperialism and, 21; imperialist
    intervention and, 20
de Regt, Marina, 12–13
*Destroying Yemen* (Blumi), 20
desubjectivity, 53–54
desubjugation, 5
detachment, 226–27

development, 94–95; agrarian studies
and, 83–84; Dutch-Yemeni development, 215, 221; engaged anthropology and, 229; international forms
of, 77, 94–95; research privatization
and, 98
Dhofar Province, Oman, 32
difference, 13; boundaries and, 31; political engagement and, 1; study of, 3–4
al-Din, Imam Yahya Hamid, 49–50;
imamate of, 50–53
displacement, 170–71, 182–84, 189, 191;
population growth and, 200; refugees
distinguished from, 194–97, 202–3
distortion (*tahrif*), 56–57
divorce, 221
Djibouti, Republic of, 12, 168–72,
181–85, 188, 201–3; Malaysia and,
177; "real" refugee status and, 186;
refugees and, 173–77, 193–96;
refugees to Yemen from, 192; South
Korea and, 176, 179, 191
Doctors Without Borders, 24
Dresch, Paul, 65, 110; segmentary
lineage theory and, 111–13; *Tribes,
Government, and History in Yemen,*
105
Dumont, Louis, 111
duration, 36, 37
Durkheim, Émile, 10, 89
Dutch-Yemeni development, 212, 221

economic history, three-stage model of,
82
economic migration, 171, 184–85, 187;
"real" refugees and, 182
economic reforms of 1986, 151
egalitarianism, 6, 9, 82, 86

Egypt, 151, 159–60; honor and, 110;
Jeju Island and, 178; as model for
higher education, 89; refugees and,
172; refugees to Yemen from, 192;
September 1962 revolution and, 85;
USSR and, 53
emic identities, 12, 113, 171
emotion, 129–31; fieldwork and, 227–28;
*sharaf* and, 133
empire, 20, 36–37; sovereignty of, 27. *See
also* imperialism
*Empire* (Hardt and Negri), 18–21
endless war, 38
engagement, 213–16, 218, 220, 223–25,
228–30; critical forms of, 4–6, 11–12;
as critical politics, 1–2
engineered structures, 77–78
English-language publishing world,
94–95
equilibrium, 59, 61, 69
equivocation, 107, 122, 131
al-Eriani, Kamilia, 8–9
Eritrea, 173; refugees and, 184, 191
ethics, 68–71; engagement and, 214,
229–30; friendship and, 224–25; God
as an articulation of, 61; Islam and,
41, 48–50; new legal system and, 52;
self-cultivation and, 45, 65; self-
reform and, 43–44; *sharaf* and, 134.
*See also* morality
Ethiopia, 173, 183, 191
ethnocide, 24
ethnographic particularism, 113
ethnography, 2–5, 11–12; borders and,
32; critique and, 1, 6; friendship
and, 12–13; grammar of class and, 9;
immanence-transcendence tension
and, 8; imperialism and, 37; revolutionary praxis and, 3

Europe, 17–18, 23; refugees and, 200; weapons sales and, 21

European Renaissance, 19

European Union, 77

Evans-Pritchard, Edward, 22; *The Nuer*, 111

everyday life, 6, 11–12, 116; apparatuses of, 124, 133; charity and, 41; ethics and, 131; ethos of insecurity and, 10; field research and, 216; insecurity and, 43–44, 46, 66–67; language of stateness and, 162; *sharaf* and, 106–7, 120–21, 125; the state and, 141–42, 144, 146; uncertainty and, 61

extramarital relationships, 220

Facebook, 43, 198–99

facts, 80, 95, 98; *qabila* and, 86; securitization and, 98

faith, 57, 59–61, 63, 69–71; (in)security and, 48; self-reform and, 43, 45; uncertainty and, 9

faithful identity, 57, 59

"fake" refugees, 171, 181–82, 186–87, 190

al-Faqih, Wahiba Ghalib, 91

father of the nation narrative, 146–47, 155

Fayza (pseudonym), 219–20, 229

fear, 42–46, 52–53, 59–63, 65–66, 69; piety and, 48

federation, 34

Ferguson, James, 145

Filkins, Dexter, 25

*fiqh*, 55–56, 58

floating signifiers, 115–16, 129, 131, 133

flow, 162

food production, 24

Foucault, Michel, 25–27

France, 94

Free Yemeni Movement, 85

French Center for Yemeni Studies, 81

friendship, 6, 12–13, 222–25, 227–30; engagement and, 213–16; with Harba family, 211–13; money and, 217–20

gatekeeping concepts, 4, 9

Gellner, Ernest, 22

gender, 57, 149; refugees and, 172, 185, 189

genealogy, 9, 86; ethnography and, 3; otherness and, 133; shared identity and, 128; weakness and, 12, 185; Wolof hierarchical system and, 130

Gerholm, Thomas, 82

Germany, 192

Ghanim, Fadl Abu, 90

al-Ghashmi, Ahmad, 88

al-Ghazali, Abu Hamid, 9, 60–64; Islamic revivalism and, 50; perseverance and, 65–66; therapy of the soul and, 48

*ghira* (protective outrage), 128, 130–31, 133. *See also* rage

Gilsenan, Michael, 163

Global Compact on Refugees, 196

Global Inner Peace, 180

globalization, 19, 21; resistance to, 33

Global North, 186, 202

Global South, 33; postcolonialism and, 53

God, knowledge of, 61, 63, 68

governmentality, local forms of, 4

Great Dam (Marib), 24

Greece, 26

Griaule, Marcel, 106n13

"Grief and a Headhunter's Rage" (Rosaldo), 227

Guelleh, Ismail Omar, 173

Gulf Council Initiative, 34, 42n2
Gupta, Akhil, 145

Hadhramawt region, 20; bombardment of, 23
Hadi, 'Abd Rabbuh Mansur, 96; government of, 42, 44; refugees and, 168
Hage, Ghassan, 1, 6
Hallaq, Wael, 50n8
al-Hamdi, Ibrahim, 84; major shaykhs and, 85, 87; National Democratic Front and, 88; rural development and, 95
Hammad, 'Abd al-Salam Nur al-Din, 90
Hansen, Thomas Blom, 142
*haqq* (claim, property), 121–22, 124
*haram* (forbidden), 121–23, 123
Hardt, Michael, 18–21; empire and, 37; revolution and, 33
Hasan, Ra'ufa, 77
hell (seal of evil), 60, 64–66
Heo, Angie, 12, 187
Herzfeld, Michael, 113, 128
hierarchy, 112, 130, 133; alcohol and, 158; shares system and, 162
Himyarite Kingdom, 25
Hobbes, Thomas, 22, 44–45, 49, 52–53, 61
home, political imagination and, 12
*Homo sacer*, 26
honor (*sharaf*), 6, 10, 105–7, 111–13; anthropology and, 108–11; '*ayb* and, 68; challenge and riposte and, 122–23; *haqq* and, 121–22; '*ird* and, 116–17; offense and, 124, 126; power and, 4; as prestige, 118; Qays case study and, 113–15; segmentary proclivity and, 127–28; warfare and, 22. *See also sharaf*

"Honour and Shame among the Bedouins of Egypt" (Abou-Zeid), 110
*Honour and Shame: The Values of Mediterranean Society* (Peristiany), 109–10
hope, 43–45, 48, 52–53, 59–63, 66; ethical truth and, 69; perseverance and, 64
Horn of Africa, 33
hospitality, 109, 123
households, 9, 78, 85, 86; agrarian change and, 76; studies of, 93; subsistence agriculture and, 83
al-Houthi, 'Abd al-Malik, 56; moral decency and, 57
Houthis (Ansar Allah), 2, 7, 24, 35, 70, 212–13; refugees and, 168, 188, 190–91; security and, 55–59; *sharaf* and, 108, 132–33; *Tribal Charter of Sharaf* and, 10
al-Hudayda, Yemen, 211–13, 215–16, 218, 219, 221
al-Hudayda Urban Primary Health Care Project, 212, 215
humanitarianism, 179–80, 184–85, 196–200, 203; competitive forms of, 12; economic migrants and, 187; human rights and, 193; "real" refugees and, 182; refugee status and, 201
human rights, 24, 171, 173, 185–86, 196–98, 202–3; humanitarian status and, 193, 200; Kuala Lumpur flights and, 178; South Korea and, 177; UNHCR and, 175
Hummad, Nuriya 'Ali, 91, 93
Humphrey, Caroline, 144
*h'urma* (honor), 122–23. *See also* honor

*Il faut défendre la société* (Foucault), 25
Ilongot society, 227

imamate, 149, 151, 159; overthrow of, 80

al-Iman University, 92

immanence, 8, 19

imperialism, 8, 17–21, 23–24, 36–37; Ansar Allah and, 57; borders and, 29, 33; US-led, 78; warfare and, 23–24, 26–27

individualism, 68; languages of stateness and, 11

Indonesia, 163

information technologies, 19

infrastructure, 37; testing weapon precision on, 24

*inqilab* (coup), 150, 151n16

(in)security, 41–44, 43–45, 65, 68–70; economic and social forms of, 46; everyday ethos of, 6, 10; Islamic tradition and, 48; uncertainty and, 59. *See also* security

"L'interférence entre les concepts de classe et de catégorie sociale dans la société Yéménite" (Sha'lan), 82

internally displaced persons (IDPs), 170, 183, 194–95, 200

International Monetary Fund, 19, 81

International Organization for Migration, 174

international relations (IR), 54

interventionism, 2

Iran, 54; intervention and, 20; military assistance and, 24; revolution and, 35; war preparedness and, 21

Iraq, 25; Abu Ghraib and, 26; refugees and, 182

'ird (honor of women), 107, 110, 116–17, 122; insulting one's, 120; offense and, 126; *sharaf* as, 128

Irvine, Judith, 129, 130

al-Iryani, Qadi 'Abd al-Rahman, 51; ouster of, 84

al-Islah Party, 55, 92

Islam, 62, 68–69; agrarian change and, 78; charity and, 41, 47n6; honor and, 114; identity and, 55; (in)security and, 44; as key concept for research, 94; legal subjectivity and, 56; refugees from, 186, 191; security and, 48–51, 57–59; virtue and, 66; *wajh Allah* (the face of Allah) in, 69

Islamic Front, 9

Islamism, 53–54, 55; National Democratic Front and, 89; North Yemen and, 49

Islamophobia, 181, 187, 202

Jabali tribesmen, 31–32

Jeju April 3 Massacre (1948), 189

Jeju Island, South Korea, 169, 171, 176–80, 186–90, 197–99, 201; refugees and, 12, 181–82, 191–93

Jeju Migrants Center, 180

Jeju Office of Immigration, 181

Jeju Peace and Human Rights Institute, 180

Jeju People's Coalition for Refugee Rights, 180, 189, 197

Jordan, 87

*al-Jumhuriyya Bayn al-Saltana wa-l-Qabila fi al-Yaman al-Shamali* (al-Saqqaf), 82

Kabyle society, 122

*karama* (dignity), 107, 114–15, 117; *haqq* and, 122; insulting one's, 120

Khalidi, Lamya, 24

Khashoggi, Jamal, 26, 196

*al-khatima* (the faithful's end), 64–66

Kim, Jiyoon, 198

King Salman Humanitarian Aid and
Relief Center (KSRelief), 175, 196
*Kitab al-Khawf wa-l-Raja'* (*The Book of
Fear and Hope*) (al-Ghazali), 60
knowledge production, 2, 9, 11; agrarian
change and, 76; ethical engagement
and, 214; friendship and, 227; in-
stitutions central to, 80–81; policy-
oriented agendas and, 146; radical
listening and, 230; Yemen Arab
Republic and, 89–93
Kopp, Horst, 83
Korean War, 189
Kuala Lumpur, Malaysia, 178
Kuthreh (pseudonym), 118–19, 121, 127
Kuwait Fund, 77

labor, 98; agrarian studies and, 93, 96;
departure of, 83, 85; three-stage
model of economic history and, 82
Lahum, Sinan Abu, 151
land, 6, 9–10, 87–89; agrarian change
and, 76, 78; ownership and, 85–87,
98; al-Saqqaf and, 85–86. *See also*
agriculture
landholding, 82, 88, 93, 96, 98
landlordism, 85, 87–88
land reform, 80, 85, 89
land registration, 77, 86
languages of stateness, 11, 142–43, 155,
159, 162, 163
Latour, Bruno, 144
leadership, 35
Leftists, 54–55
legal systems, 22–23, 26, 49–52, 55–56
*Leviathan* (Hobbes), 22, 52–53
Levinas, Emmanuel, 69
Lévi-Strauss, Claude, 115
lexical approaches, 107, 131

liberalism, 2
liberationist movements, 7
local development associations (LDAs),
29, 84
local government, 6
localism, gatekeeping concepts and, 4
Low, Setha M., 213, 223

al-Mahra, Yemen, 152, 154
Mains, Daniel, 227
Malaysia, 169, 172; refugees and, 176,
190, 192; Yemeni diaspora and,
177–79
*mana*-terms, 115–16, 119
al-Maqalih, 'Abd al-'Aziz, 90
Markazi refugee camp, 174–76, 180,
182–83, 185–86, 188, 194–97; Korean
missionaries and, 191
*Market, Mosque and Mafraj: Social
Inequality in a Yemeni Town* (Gerholm), 82
Marxism, 19
masculinity, 110–11; male agency, 9, 83,
86; *qaba'il* and, 108; *rajula* and, 107,
121–22
materiality, 59, 142, 162–63; contingency
and, 55; Hobbes and, 52, 61; the state
and, 144–45, 147; wealth and, 66
Mbembe, Achille, 25, 27
Mediterranean region, 110, 111, 131
Meeker, Michael M., 111
Melanesian marriage arrangements, 162
Merry, Sally Engle, 213, 223
Messick, Brinkley, 50, 55
Mexico, 33
Middle East studies, 146
migration, 28–31; economic forms of,
171–72, 184–85, 187; securitization
of, 202, Yemeni literature of, 28n10

militant anthropology, 224
Ministry for Public Health (Yemen), 154
Ministry of Economy (Yemen), 98
Ministry of Finance (Yemen), 157, 158
Ministry of Justice (South Korea), 180, 197, 198
Mitchell, Timothy, 140–44
modernism, 52, 70
modernity, 19; Republican Revolution and, 49; secular power and, 51; weak state and, 54
Mohammad (pseudonym for Yaman Jadid founder), 46–48, 62–65
Moon Jae-in, 187
morality, 8; contradictory desires and, 61; moral engagement and, 224–25, 228, 229–31; moral order and, 44, 49–50, 56–58; moral oughts and, 5; sharaf and, 130–34. See also ethics
mountains, 30
al-Mu'ayyid, Huriya 'Abbas, 77, 87n24
Muhammad, the Prophet, 124
multiplicity, 44–45, 48–49, 53–56, 59–62, 70; subjectivity and, 67; temporality and, 64
multitude, the, 19; democracy of, 8, 21; revolution and, 33, 35
Mundy, Martha, 4, 9–10, 21; coalition war causing starvation and, 27; imperialist warfare and, 24
Muslim Brotherhood, 87, 89–90, 92
Mutawakkilite Kingdom, 49–50, 150–51

najat (salvation), 60–61, 65
namus (sexual honor), 111–12
Naomi Migrant Pastoral Center, 180, 199
Nasser, Gamal Abdel, 52, 54, 55
Nasserite model, 85
National Democratic Front, 55, 88–89

National Dialogue Conference, 34
nationalism, 53
National Liberation Front, 9
National Refugee Law (Djibouti), 173
nature, state of, 22, 52–54; divine sovereignty and, 60
necropolitics, 25, 27
Negri, Antonio, 18–21; empire and, 37; revolution and, 33
neoliberalism, 47n6, 76, 94
networks, 141, 144–45; navigating state administration and, 154; the state and, 161–62
Nevola, Luca, 4, 10
New York Declaration for Refugees and Migrants, 173
9/11, 49, 54; religion and, 55
niqab (face covering), 113–14
nongovernmental organizations (NGOs), 94, 95, 215; health care and, 218; Jeju Island and, 199; loss of services from, 196; refugees and, 176, 180, 185, 189
nonhuman, the, 143–45, 162–63; corruption and, 163; materiality of state and, 11
nonstate relations, 5
non-Yemeni researchers, 94–95
North Korea, 188
North Yemen, 80, 141–44, 147–50, 158–59, 161–62; republican formation and, 51–56; security and, 42, 49–51, 55–56; unification and, 150–53. See also Yemen Arab Republic
Norwegian Refugee Council, 174
Noura (pseudonym), 216–18, 226, 229
Nuer, The (Evans-Pritchard), 111
Nu'man, 'Abdullah Ahmad, 86; 1983 agricultural census and, 96
Nu'man, Ahmad, 51

objectification, 131

Obock, Djibouti, 171, 174–75, 184, 194

occupation, 33; necropolitics and, 27

Occupy Wall Street movement, 34, 35

offense, 122, 124, 126

Office National d'Assistance aux Réfugiés et Sinistrés (ONARS), 172

Ogotemmeli (Dogon elder), 115

oil pipelines, 20

Olleh Hotel (Jeju), 179, 180, 191

Oman, 30, 169; border with, 31–33

open-door policy, 83–85, 173–74

orientalism, 23

*Origins of Totalitarianism, The* (Arendt), 28

Osanloo, Arzoo, 198

otherness, 31; biopower as, 26; engagement and, 229; honor and, 109; internal/external axis of honor and, 114; recognition of the face of, 69; *sharaf* and, 131, 133

'Othman, 'Abdo 'Ali, 77, 89, 93

Ottomans, 23, 49; economic history and, 82

outsiders, 141, 143–46, 148


Palestine, 182

participant observation, 227

patrimonial system, 163

people as tribes ideology, 9, 87

People's Democratic Republic of Yemen (PDRY), 11, 78–79, 81, 88–90; agrarian change and, 85; cooperative organization in, 84; the state and, 141–43, 147–49, 154; state administration and, 152. *See also* South Yemen

Peristiany, J. G., 109

perseverance, 48, 62–66

personhood, 10

perversion (*inhiraf*), 56–57

Peters, Emrys, 22

Peutz, Nathalie, 12, 176, 182–86, 202, 213; Afghan refugees and, 204; displacement and, 194; male asylum seekers and, 189

piety, 43, 45, 48, 56–58, 62, 67; (in)security and, 65–66

Pitt-Rivers, Julian, 109

political language, 2, 8

political science, 94

*Politics of Stratification: A Study of Political Change in a South Arabian Town* (Bujra), 81–82

Porter, Ross, 35, 37

postcolonialism, 53

postmodernism, 19

power, 4; biopower and, 25–27; conception of time and, 70; modern state and, 41–42, 49–56, 58–59; network distribution of, 145; refugee engagements with, 12; Sanaa and, 161; state and, 140–41, 147–48, 151–52; truth and, 5; weakness of, 44–45. *See also* security; states

Presidential Council, 152, 161

prestige, 118

progress, 44–46, 49, 52–54; al-Ghazali's techniques of the self and, 60; liberal Islamic notions of, 51

property, 10, 86. *See also haqq*

Protestant Evangelical church, 180, 189, 191

public health services, 24


*qabila* (tribe), 86; Serjeant and, 112; *sharaf* and, 133–34; tribal bonds and, 134. *See also* tribesmen

Qatar, 18, 180; Red Crescent in, 175
Qays (pseudonym), 113–15

race, 29, 31; *racisme* and, 25–27; refugees and, 182, 192, 195, 203
Rada', Yemen, 215
Rada' Integrated Development Project, 221
Radcliffe-Brown, A. R., 11
radical listening, 214, 230
rage, 119, 128–29, 227. *See also ghira*
rationality, 48, 58–59
realpolitik, evasion of, 7
"real" refugees, 171, 181–82, 186, 189, 193, 201–3; UNHCR and, 195
reciprocity, 4, 123–24, 217, 226
*Recognizing Islam* (Gilsenan), 163
Red Crescent, 175
Red Cross, 179
Refugee Act of 2013 (South Korea), 177n8, 187, 188, 193
refugees, 27–29, 168–72, 191–93, 193–95, 201–4; borders and, 30; competitive humanitarianism and, 12; displaced persons distinguished from, 194–97; Djibouti and, 172–76, 186–90; Global North-South borders and, 33; humanitarian status and, 193, 196–200; imperialism and, 36–37; power and, 4; as "real" vs. "fake," 181–85; South Korea and, 177–81; status of, 6
relationality, 225–26
religion, 55; agency and, 62n20; Hobbes and, 52; Leviathan and, 53; secularism and, 51, 54; security and, 49. *See also* Islam
republicanism, 51–56; ideology of people as tribes and, 87; overthrow of

imamate and, 80; state administration and, 150–51
Republican Revolution (1962), 49, 150–51; refugees and, 29
Republic of Yemen (RoY), 141, 142; birth of, 42; democracy in, 153; tribal militias and, 22
research capacity, 81–85, 94–96, 98; centers for knowledge production and, 80; Mundy's experiences and, 76–78; Sanaa University and, 89–93
resistance, 33; desubjugation and, 5
revolution, 33–37; corruption and, 161; imperialism and, 36–37
Revolution of 2011, 7–8; class formation and, 95–97; Yaman Jadid and, 46
Rida, Rashid, 51
Robben, Anthonius, 226
Robbins, Jerome, 134
Rogers, Joshua, 159
Romans, 26
Rosaldo, Renato, 227, 228
Rub' al-Khali desert, 30
ruins, world turned into, 42–43
rural life, 6, 7; economic exploitation and, 9–10. *See also* agriculture
rural studies, 93; non-Yemeni researchers and, 94–95
Russian Revolution, 35

Sabaean Kingdom, 25
*sacra*, 105, 110, 123–25, 128, 131, 133
*sadaqa* (voluntary gesture of beneficence), 65–67. *See also* beneficence
Salafis, 56
Salalah, Oman, 32
Saleh, 'Ali 'Abdullah, 7; agrarian change and, 98; corruption and, 155; diploma of, 97; Islamism and, 49;

Saleh, 'Ali 'Abdullah (*con't*)
    Mundy's research and, 77; Muslim
    Brotherhood and, 90; National
    Democratic Front and, 88–89; Na-
    tional Liberation Front's defeat by, 9;
    patronage system and, 146; refugees
    and, 29, 168; Saudi backing and, 88;
    statistical knowledge and, 96; unity
    agreement and, 152; universities
    and, 92
Sanaa, Yemen, 142–43, 154–56, 159–62;
    corruption and, 157–58; the North-
    ern state and, 147–50; siege of, 87–88;
    unity and, 152–53
Sanaa University, 77, 80, 89–93; Yemeni
    Centre of Studies and Research and, 81
Sanhan tribal area, 107
al-Saqqaf, 'Abd al-'Aziz, 161
al-Saqqaf, 'Abu Bakr, 9, 82–83, 85–86
Saudi Arabia (KSA), 23–26; Ahmad case
    study and, 117; borders with, 31; co-
    alition led by, 2, 7; ideology of people
    as tribes and, 87; imperialism and,
    17–18, 20–21, 34–35, 37; Khashoggi
    as *Homo sacer* and, 26; King Salman
    Humanitarian Aid and Relief Center,
    175, 196; migration to, 171; National
    Democratic Front and, 88–89; refu-
    gee funding by, 196–97; refugees and,
    168–69, 192; regional geopolitics and,
    180; security and, 53–55, 57, 70; se-
    curity interests and, 42; South Korea
    and, 201; tribal institutions and, 86;
    Yemeni "lawlessness" and, 8; Yemeni
    working class in, 83
*sayyid* (descendent of Prophet Muham-
    mad), 116n17, 151n17
Scheper-Hughes, Nancy, 224
Schneider, Jane, 111
seal of evil (*su' al-khatima*), 60, 64–66

secularism, 49–53; rationality and,
    58–59; security and, 44–45, 54–56, 70
security (*amn*), 6, 41–45, 49–51; borders
    and, 32–33; al-Ghazali and, 60–62,
    66; Hobbes and, 44–45, 49, 52–53, 61;
    (in)security and, 43–45, 59, 68–70;
    insecurity and, 41–44; migration and,
    202; moral order and, 56, 58; private
    means of violence and, 86; production
    of facts and, 98; refugees and, 190;
    rural studies and, 94; tribal institution
    and, 90; uncertainty and, 8–9; United
    States and, 53–55; Yaman Jadid and,
    46–48, 61–65; Yemen Arab Republic
    and, 83. *See also* states
segmentary lineage theory, 9, 111–13,
    127–28; functionalist model of, 22;
    *sharaf* and, 118
self, 68–69; engagement and, 229; faith
    and, 71; al-Ghazali's techniques of
    the, 60; governance of, 61; perfor-
    mance of, 59; property and, 121;
    self-authentication, comprehension,
    realization and, 68; self-critique and,
    43–44; self-cultivation and, 44–45,
    61, 63, 65, 70–71; self-depletion and,
    123; self-ego and, 68; self-elation
    and, 60, 64; self-reflection and, 62;
    self-reform and, 43–45, 70; temporal
    experience of, 56
*Sentiment of Honour in Kabyle Society,
    The* (Bourdieu), 122
Serjeant, Robert B., 112
sexual crimes, 187
*sha'b* (people), 86
Sha'lan, Tha'ira, 82
shame (*'ayb*), 109–10; binary of honor
    and, 112–13; breaking the *sharaf* and,
    119; declaration of innocence and,
    132. *See also 'ayb*

*sharaf* (honor), 105–7, 110–13, 127–28, 131–34; case studies of, 119–22; emotional structure and, 129–31; *haram* and, 123; women and, 123–27; young girl case study of, 113–17. *See also* honor

*Al-Shara'ih al-Ijtima'iyya al-Taqlidiyya fi al-Mujtama' al-Yamani* (al-Sharjabi), 82

shares, system of, 155, 161, 162–63

*shari'a*, 22, 49–51, 55

*sharif* (honorable man), 106, 120–21, 124–25, 127

al-Sharjabi, Qa'id, 82, 91

al-Sharqi, 'Ali, 120

al-Shawkani, Muhammad, 50, 51–52; *shari'a* and, 55

shaykhs, 85, 87–89

Sheba, temple of Queen of, 24

Shryock, Andrew, 109

Sierra Leone, 189

Sluka, Jeffrey, 226

Smith, William Robertson, 111n9

social differentiation, 81

Socialist Party, 92

social justice, 224–25

social life, emic ideations of, 12

social media, 43; human rights and, 178

social sciences, 34

society, 3; state relations and, 140–41, 144, 146, 153, 162

sociology, 89–93, 95; of agrarian change, 85–87; agriculture and, 85–86; demystifying the state idea in, 11; knowledge production and, 9, 76–77, 80; network webs and, 144; *Verstehen* in, 34

Socotra Island, Yemen, 20, 94, 213

Somalia, 173; displacement and, 195; refugees and, 168, 182, 192; sociocultural ties with, 183

soul, 43, 45, 59–63, 68–69; multiple subjectivities and, 48, 67; soft war of, 57; uncertainty and, 53

South Korea, 12, 168–71, 176–80, 186–90, 197–201; refugees and, 181–82, 184, 191–93, 202–4

South Yemen, 141–44, 148, 154, 156, 158, 160–62; communism and, 54; independence movement of, 7; looter narrative and, 147; overthrow of imamate and, 80; PDRY and, 81; share system and, 163; unification and, 150–53. *See also* People's Democratic Republic of Yemen (PDRY)

sovereignty, 19; Agamben on, 25–27; being change and, 35; borders and, 31–33; divine grace and, 60; Leviathan and, 52–53; modern forms of, 49; self-ego and, 68; Tanzimat program and, 50; totalizing notion of security and, 70

spatiality, 145

stability (*istiqrar*), 42, 45, 70–71

state-as-ruler metaphor, 146; father-of-the-nation and, 147

stateness, languages of, 11, 142–43, 155, 159, 162, 163

states, 6, 145–47; actor-network theory and, 144; Althusserian understanding of, 142n3; biopower and, 25–27; civil service and, 153–57; conception of time and, 70; corruption and, 157–59, 161–64; critique of, 10–11; hegemonic class and, 9; languages of stateness and, 142–43; North and, 147–50; power and, 4; security and, 41–42, 49–56, 58–59; society and, 140–41; unity and, 150–53; weakness of, 42, 44–45, 54; whiskey trade and, 155–57, 159–60, 162–63. *See also* security

statistical knowledge, 80; state statistical surveys and, 86
Stepputat, Finn, 142
Strathern, Marilyn, 141, 162
structural change, 35, 36, 37
subjectivity, 48–51, 59–61, 66–68; de-subjectivity and, 53–54; engagement and, 230–31; Islamic law and, 56–57; temporal forms of, 44–45, 70
Sudan, 172, 178–79
Sunni Shafiʻi, 50
Supreme Military Council, 87–88
surveillance, 58–59
symbolic power, 129
Syria, 168, 170, 182, 189, 190; refugees to Yemen from, 192

Tamim, Khalid ʻAbdullah, 91
Tanzimat state program, 49–50
temporality, 36, 44–45, 51, 53–56, 59–62, 70; multiplicity of, 48, 64. See also duration; time
territorial limits, 30–31
terrorism, 7, 32, 54; refugees and, 187, 190
therapy of the soul, 48; fear and hope as, 61–63, 66, 69
thingness (of state), 141, 143, 162
think tanks, 95
Tihama coastal plain, 77; class power and, 87; landlordism and, 85
Tihama Development Authority, 78
time, 43–45, 60–61; multiplicity of experiences and, 64; secular power and, 51; security and, 52–53, 70; temporality and, 54. See also temporality
totalitarianism, 33
tourism, 20, 94n43, 113, 176–80, 190
transcendence, 8; imperialism and, 19–20, 21

transnationalism, 19
Tribal Charter of Sharaf, The (Ansar Allah), 10, 107, 131–33
Tribes, Government, and History in Yemen (Dresch), 105, 112
tribesmen (qabaʼil), 146; boundaries and, 30–32; honor and, 105–8; imperial intervention and, 8; militias and, 22–23; people as tribes ideology, 9; security and, 54–55; segmentarist visions of, 9; tribal customary law and, 119, 124; tribal institutions and, 86–87, 90. See also qabila
tributary economy, 82–83
truth, 5
Tutwiler, Richard, 82, 83

uncertainty, 8–9, 57–58, 59, 61, 65, 70–71; Hobbes and, 53; piety and, 48; security and, 44–46
ungovernable, the, 6–8
unification, 7, 11, 49, 53, 86; the state and, 141–43, 147–50, 152–56, 160–61
United Arab Emirates (UAE), 8; Empire and, 37; federation and, 34; imperialism and, 17–18, 20–21, 23–24, 35; South Korea and, 201–2
United Kingdom, 29
United Nations, 28, 170, 186; Global Compact on Refugees, 196
United Nations Development Pro-gramme, 81
United Nations High Commissioner for Refugees (UNHCR), 172, 174, 183, 185; displacement and, 194, 195, 197; Malaysia and, 177; recognition by, 186
United Nations Refugee Convention, 169
United States (US), 42, 53–55, 57, 70; Abu Ghraib and, 26; ARAMCO oil

and, 23; doctoral training in, 89; imperialism and, 17–18, 78; Mexican border with, 31; Monroe Doctrine of, 20; refugees and, 29, 203–4; weapons sales and, 21, 24, 25

universalism, 3–4, 45, 52–53, 54n14

university research, 76–77, 80, 84, 92–94; Sanaa University and, 89–92

unknowability, 9, 65

urban studies, 93

USSR (Union of Soviet Socialist Republics), 53, 54

Varisco, Daniel, 83

Vietnam, 188

virtual citizens, 6

virtual refugees, 12

virtue, 45, 48, 59–60, 62–65, 67–69; *amn wa iman* as security and, 43; honor and, 109; Islamic virtue and, 66

visa-waiver policies, 177, 179

voluntarism, 8–9

vulnerability, 12, 127, 133, 229; uncertainty and, 70–71; unknowability and, 65

Wadi Mawr, 77

Wadi Rima', 78

Wahhabism, 23, 57

warfare, 21–26; honor and, 114–15; imperialism and, 27, 36–37; Yemeni studies and, 38

war zone engagement, 214, 217, 219–20, 224, 226, 228–30; Houthi militias and, 212–13

water resources, 20, 24

weakness, genealogy and, 12, 185; defense of property and, 122; refugee status and, 202

wealth, 47, 48, 64–67; corruption and, 161

Western societies, 95; development aid and, 94, 98; ethnographic concepts and, 3; *ghira* and, 130; honor and, 108–9, 110, 131; Yemeni studies and, 146

whiskey trade, 142, 155–57, 159–60, 162–63; corruption and, 163

Wikan, Unni, 108, 110; *Behind the Veil in Arabia*, 129

Williams, Bernard, 132n21

Willis, John, 49

Wolof society, 129–30

women, 149, 158–59; embodied emotion and, 129–31; extramarital relationships and, 220; honor and, 110; *'ird* and, 116–17; Qays case study and, 113–15; *sharaf* and, 123–27; as sharifa, 126; surveillance of, 58

World Bank, 19, 77, 81

World Food Programme, 185

worldliness, 43, 49, 62, 64–68

X, image of, 16–17

Yaman Jadid (New Yemen), 41, 43–44, 46–48, 59, 61–65, 69–71; ethical subjectivity and, 67–68; Islamic legal subjectivity and, 56

Yemen, Kingdom of, 22

Yemen Arab Republic (YAR), 11, 78–81, 86–87, 150; fiscal policies of, 161; formation of, 53; knowledge production and, 89–93; Mundy research in, 77; open-door policy and, 83, 84–85; PDRY and, 89–90; researchers and, 94; the state and, 141, 147–48; state unity and, 151–52. *See also* North Yemen

Yemeni Centre for Cultural Research, 81

Yemeni Centre of Studies and Research, 81
Yemeni studies, 38; engagement and,
213; the state and, 145–46
Yemen Youth Revolution (2011), 7–8;
rural distress and, 95–97; Yaman
Jadid and, 46. *See also* revolution

*zakat* (almsgiving), 65n24, 67
Zaydism, 50–51, 78; Ansar Allah and, 56

al-Zaynabiyat forces, 58
Ziadé, Nassib G., 152n19
al-Zindani, ʿAbd al-Majid, 92
zones of theory, 27, 38; borders as, 29;
Dresch and, 111; imperialism and, 18;
revolution and, 33; war as, 21; Yemen
as, 146
al-Zubayri, Mohammad, 51; land and,
85; *qabila* and, 86
Zuntz, Ann-Christin, 227

www.ingramcontent.com/pod-product-compliance
Lightning Source LLC
Chambersburg PA
CBHW061351040925
32068CB00005B/17